# Mandated Reporting of Child Abuse and Neglect

# Mandated Reporting of Child Abuse and Neglect

*A Practical Guide for Social Workers*

**KENNETH J. LAU, LCSW-R**
**KATHRYN KRASE, MSW, JD**
**RICHARD H. MORSE, MSW**

SPRINGER PUBLISHING COMPANY
New York

Springer Publishing Company, LLC
11 West 42nd Street
New York, NY 10036–8002
www.springerpub.com

*Acquisitions Editor: Jennifer Perillo*
*Production Manager: Cindy Fullerton*
*Cover Design: Mimi Flow*
*Composition: Aptara Inc.*

09  10  11  12  13/  5  4  3  2  1

---

**Library of Congress Cataloging-in-Publication Data**

Lau, Kenneth J.
  Mandated reporting of child abuse and neglect : a practical guide for social workers / Kenneth J. Lau, Kathryn Krase, Richard Morse.
      p.   cm.
    Includes index.
    ISBN 978-0-8261-1098-5 (alk. paper)
   1. Child abuse—United States.   2. Child abuse—Reporting—United States. 3. Child abuse—Law and legislation—United States.   4. Child welfare workers—United States—Handbooks, manuals, etc.   I. Krase, Kathryn. II. Morse, Richard, 1945–   III. Title.

HV6626.52.L38   2009
362.76′630973–dc22                                                    2008043752

---

Printed in Canada by Transcontinental Printing.

*This book is dedicated to all of the social workers, caseworkers, nurses, therapists, foster parents, police officers, attorneys, doctors, and volunteers who work hard every day to keep America's children from harm: though your work is often unrecognized, you are the heroes of the generations to come.*

# Contents

**Kenneth J. Lau, LCSW-R,** is a licensed certified social worker who has been employed at Children FIRST, Fordham University, as program director for the past 17 years. In addition, he has been employed part-time at Westchester Jewish Community Center, Treatment Center for Trauma and Abuse as the coordinator of sex offender services for over 20 years. In June 2008, he was the recipient of the Rohmer Award at WJCS, which recognizes excellence in "outstanding professional accomplishments." He is also on the training faculty for the New York State Children's Justice Task Force Forensic Best Practice Training. Mr. Lau has been training caseworkers, mental health workers, law enforcement personnel, and attorneys throughout New York State on issues related to child sexual abuse for over 25 years. He teaches classes at Fordham related to interpersonal trauma and the identification and reporting child abuse course that is required for mandated reporters to be licensed in New York State. Mr. Lau has been accepted as an expert in the area of child sexual abuse and offending behavior in both family and criminal court in New York State.

Mr. Lau coordinated the sex abuse investigations in Nassau County for over 6 years. In that capacity, he worked closely with child protective services, law enforcement, the district attorney's office and other members of the Nassau County multidisciplinary team. He serves as a consultant to other educators, caseworkers, law enforcement personnel, and mental health care providers on the investigation and treatment of victims of sexual abuse and their families.

In May 2005 he was elected president of the New York State Association for the Treatment of Sexual Abusers. Mr. Lau is the proud parent of two grown children who are practicing professionals working with children and families.

**Kathryn Krase, MSW, JD,** earned her master's in social work and juris doctor as the first joint-degree law and social work student at Fordham University in 2000/2001. She is currently completing her doctorate in social work in child and family policy at Fordham. Ms. Krase served as the program director for the Parent Education and Custody Effectiveness (PEACE) Program in New York City Family Court while also a lawyer for children with the New York Society for the Prevention of Cruelty to Children in Manhattan Family Court. She was a borough coordinator for Court Appointed Special Advocates (CASA) in Bronx Family Court. She has served as the clinical social work supervisor for the Family Defense Clinic of New York University School of Law. She also was assistant director of Fordham's Interdisciplinary Center for Family and Child Advocacy, where she served as the chair of the Mandated Reporter Committee of the Interdisciplinary Task Force. Ms. Krase currently teaches Social Justice, Social Work and the Law, Research, and Social Policy to graduate social work students. She trains mandated reporters of various roles on their responsibilities. She has a strong interest in promoting innovative learning strategies in social work education and supports interdisciplinary practice movements in the child welfare system. Ms. Krase is most thrilled to be the mother of Jack Anthony Cahill.

**Richard H. Morse, MSW,** retired at the end of 2006 after working for the Suffolk County Department of Social Services in New York for over 38 years. In this span, he worked in several parts of the department, but most of his career was spent in child protective services, where he worked as a field investigator nights and weekends on an emergency services team. He served as the supervisor of the department's first specialized abuse unit—one of the first uses of the multidisciplinary approach to child abuse investigations in New York State. Mr. Morse earned his master's in social work from Adelphi University in 1977. Later, he became the director of investigations for Child Protective Services. As part of his responsibilities in that position, and also as an adjunct faculty member for Suffolk County Community College, Mr. Morse has provided instruction for hundreds of groups of mandated reporters. Mr. Morse currently serves as an adjunct assistant professor in psychology at Suffolk County Community College and occasionally serves in various voluntary capacities in the child welfare community. Mr. Morse is the father of two grown children and resides in South Jamesport on the north fork of Long Island, where he enjoys sailing in its local bays.

# Foreword

More than 100 years ago, the case of Mary Ellen galvanized the then fledgling charity organization movement into action to protect children from abuse. Mary Ellen was a 9-year-old child who had been severely abused by caretakers who falsely maintained that they were related to her and woefully mistreated and physically abused her. With no agency in place to represent her, an advocate and early caseworker, Etta Wheeler, turned to the New York Society for the Prevention of Cruelty to Animals (NYSPCA) for assistance after learning of Mary Ellen's situation. The court case brought by the NYSPCA was not only successful in protecting Mary Ellen from further abuse but also resulted in criminal prosecution and prison time for her "stepmother."

Thus began what was to become the child protection movement in the United States and the beginning of the controversy that still exists today about the proper role of the state in protecting children from abuse. Since the mid-1970s, however, we have held as a society that we must assume responsibility for the well-being of children when their parents or caretakers are unable, unfit, or unwilling to do so. This stance reflects the philosophy that the larger society must invest in its children and protect and nurture them so that they grow up to be productive, stable, and—to the extent possible—fulfilled citizens.

A major mechanism for the protection of children by the public sector is the establishment of the child protective system, which is driven by a need to respond to reported accounts of suspected child abuse and maltreatment. For more than 30 years now, social workers and other professionals who work with children have been mandated reporters of suspected child abuse and neglect. While controversy continues to swirl in child and family professional circles about definitional issues, reporting, and the role of the child protective system, this book adroitly sidesteps being drawn into that debate in the interest of assisting the mandated reporter with practical concerns. To that extent, this book provides a much needed reference guide for the practitioner who is a mandated reporter of child abuse and neglect.

Written by three experienced social workers (one author holds a joint law-social work degree), it provides a useful, practical road map for the professional who is faced with suspicions of child abuse and neglect and unsure about what to do. After a brief review of the history of the development of the reporting system, it offers an informative discussion distinguishing the professional social worker from the caseworker and elaborating the many arenas in which social workers may find themselves faced with a dilemma about whether to report, and how to do this. The authors then offer a descriptive summary of the definitions of abuse and neglect.

The book then tackles the difference between risk factors for and signs of abuse and neglect, elaborating the latter in a manner that should be helpful to the practitioner. It then guides the reader through situations in which a report will be required, how to make a report, and what to expect from the system following the report—all very useful information from those who have been in the field and in the thick of these issues for year

The last three chapters are particularly important, raising the ethical issues in mandating reporting, the legal protections, and consequences of reporting and the role of law enforcement in child abuse investigations. The appendix provides an extremely useful summary of all of the state statutes, supping information about who is mandated to report, what is mandated to be reported, and immunity as well as the legal consequences for failure to report—in each state.

Overall, this is an extremely useful and timely resource for all social work practitioners and offers a practical common sense and informative manual for those confronted with the thorny complex, but compelling, need to determine their role and responsibilities when confronted with suspicions of child maltreatment.

—Virginia C. Strand, DSW
Professor, Fordham University Graduate School of Social Service

# Preface

Mandated reporting of child abuse, neglect, and maltreatment is a daunting responsibility shared by many professionals who work with children and families. Social workers are just one of the professional groups required by law to register their concerns of potential child abuse or neglect to government officials. Many are not aware of this obligation, and many more are unsure of how to fulfill their responsibility without crossing ethical and legal boundaries. This book will address how the intricacies of social work practice are impacted by the role of social worker as mandated reporter.

Child abuse, neglect, and maltreatment affect not only the child who is abused but also the adult that child later becomes. Child abuse is quite often a significant factor in the development of numerous social ills: domestic violence, antisocial behavior, incarceration, prostitution, and sexual assault as well as drug and alcohol abuse. In addition, the foster care system is constantly challenged to find a sufficient number of available qualified parent substitutes to care for the many victims of abuse and neglect. As a society, ignoring this problem is like paying the minimum on a credit card and somehow expecting the balance to disappear. Failing to intervene in a case of child abuse or neglect guarantees social workers that their schedules will be full next week, next month, next year—and well into the next generation.

The role of mandated reporter was originally created through legislative action in response to a perceived epidemic of child abuse and neglect. It resulted in the changing of numerous governmental systems across the county. Chapter 1 explores the evolution of mandated reporting, from the first federal initiatives to the state and local policies that ultimately resulted from them.

Chapter 2 explores the many different roles that social workers play in their work with children and families. Whether serving as a psychotherapist, a case manager, or as part of an interdisciplinary team in a school, child welfare agency, health service provider, or other setting, the role of the social worker as mandated reporter is unique. These differing roles, and many others, will be explored.

Many mandated reporters are concerned that they are not well enough informed to appropriately respond to indicators of child maltreatment. Unfortunately, mandated reporter training in many states is insufficient in both time and substance. As a result, there are high rates of both underreporting and overreporting of child abuse and neglect. In many recent high-profile cases, the failure of professionals to fulfill their legal responsibilities resulted in the continuation of sexual and physical abuse—and, tragically, some incidents of child fatalities. Chapters 3 to 5 attempt to redress these deficits by defining key terms and outlining important physical, behavioral, and social risk factors and signs that may indicate the occurrence of child abuse of neglect.

Mandated reporters are often unaware of the process involved in fulfilling their legal obligations. Chapters 6 and 7 provide guidance on the procedure of reporting, including when to make a report, what information to include, and what to expect during the reporting process. Because laws and procedures vary by community, these chapters examine national trends as well as important regional, state, and local differences.

The report is often only the beginning of an investigative process that may ultimately involve child protective services and, in some cases, local law enforcement. Chapters 8 and 11 offer an inside look on what happens to a case after a report is made.

Research and anecdotal evidence support the contention that social workers are often confused by their ethical obligations with regard to mandated reporting—for example, negotiating client confidentiality and the obligation to breach client trust to fulfill their legal duty. Chapter 9 discusses these and other ethical dilemmas raised by mandated reporting.

Chapter 10 discusses the legal thresholds a mandated reporter must meet and outlines the possible criminal and civil liabilities that may be faced by those who fail to meet their responsibilities. On the other hand, many potential reporters may fear the legal consequences if a report turns out to be unsubstantiated. Fortunately, special legal protections are extended to mandated reporters who make reports in good faith. This is also discussed in chapter 10.

An important theme throughout this book is the importance of collaboration and cooperation among all professionals who serve children and families. In the 30 years or so since the passage of the Child Abuse Prevention and Treatment Act, we have seen the child protective service system, which was somewhat isolated from the fields of law enforcement, medicine, and education in the beginning, evolve to the point where it is now required to interface on a steady basis with police and probation departments, the medical community, the educational community, mental health services, community agencies, and the judicial system. Accompanying that growth has been the ever-increasing likelihood that professional social workers will be employed by probation, schools, community programs, hospitals, mental health clinics, courts, and employment services. In addition, during this time, we have seen more and more professional social workers take employment in public social services agencies in fields such as foster care, day care, rehabilitation services, and child protective services itself.

The embedded nature of the professional social worker's relationship to this network of agencies and institutions is so difficult to separate from the core mission of the profession that it may seem almost unnecessary to have the law require, or mandate, that social workers—along with doctors, dentists, nurses, teachers, day care workers, and a whole array of professionals who see children on a day-to-day basis—report their suspicions of child abuse or neglect. Most social workers operate within an ethical framework that is already entirely compatible with the concept of reporting all reasonable suspicions of abuse and neglect. Still, many remain confused about what is required of them and are unsure of the ramifications of complying with the reporting. This book has been written to serve those social workers.

As social work professionals, we are a special part of the community involved in raising each child. Ideally, all children should be able to grow and develop into adulthood without the possibility of being physically or sexually abused, neglected, or maltreated. In the absence of that reality, the community needs to be sure that the entity responsible for fortifying each child's right to live free from harm—child protective services—is armed with the information, resources, and support necessary to meet the needs of children. Mandated reporting is a big part of that support.

We hope that all social workers—whether those planning to enter the field, those already practicing, those familiar with mandated reporting, or those who are entirely new to their responsibilities—will find this a useful, clear and comprehensive resource.

# Acknowledgments

The authors of this book spent many hours reviewing literature, writing, and coordinating their efforts to produce a book that would be a helpful guide for social workers when faced with the responsibility to identify and report cases of child abuse and neglect. This accomplishment could not have been met without the support of Children FIRST at Fordham University and one of the school's finest social work students, Jamie Edwards.

# 1 Introduction to Mandated Reporting

The system of mandated reporting was created in response to a growing recognition of the devastation that child abuse and neglect causes in American families. Child abuse affects millions of children and families in the United States and around the world. Approximately 3.3 million reports of child abuse or neglect were made in the United States in 2005 (U.S. Department of Health and Human Services, 2007). These reports represent over 6 million children (8% of all children in the United States), as some reports include more than one child (U.S. Department of Health and Human Services, 2007). Policy makers have struggled to find a way to address child abuse and neglect while attending to the needs of children and their families. Mandated reporting is an attempt at such a policy.

## HISTORY OF THE RESPONSE TO CHILD ABUSE AND NEGLECT

Prior to 1873, child rearing was generally left to parents with little or no governmental interference. Parents who could not afford to take care of their children could voluntarily place their children with philanthropic and religious organizations. Orphans or impoverished children were often placed in orphanages or with other families in an early form of foster care.

In 1873, the case of "Mary Ellen" led to the creation of the first child welfare agency in the world, the New York Society for the Prevention of Cruelty to Children (NYSPCC). Mary Ellen was a child who was abused by her caretaker. A "friendly visitor" (early social worker) who found the child in need sought the advice of legal counsel to protect her from further harm and punish her caretaker. The law at the time provided no specific protection for children from abuse at the hands of their caretakers. The lawyer, Elbridge Gerry, creatively used an obscure section of the law to prosecute Mary Ellen's caretaker (NYSPCC, 2000). As a result of this intervention, Gerry and others formed NYSPCC, which took on the role of investigating and prosecuting child abuse cases in New York City. Other societies for the prevention of cruelty to children (SPCCs) were formed around the world in response. These societies were private entities that were funded by the wealthy.

Many SPCCs are still in existence today, including the NYSPCC. However, the role of the SPCC has changed dramatically since its introduction over 130 years ago. As government run child protective services (CPS) came into being and expanded in the mid to late twentieth century, SPCCs adapted to provide other services to families and children.

The replacement of SPCCs by government-sponsored CPS was due in large part to a monumental study in emergency medicine. In the 1950s, a group of doctors led by C. Henry Kempe studied broken bones in children. With the increasing using of x-ray technology, doctors were better able to identify broken bones; in many cases, they were able to see older injuries as well as recent broken bones when they examined an x-ray. Past injuries identified in x-rays were often unexplained by the child and parents, suggesting that child abuse was the only other cause. Shocked by the possibility that parents could be harming their children in such a way, these doctors conducted further research. In 1962, Kempe and colleagues published a seminal report in the *Journal of the American Medical Association* introducing *battered child syndrome*, which was defined as "a clinical condition in young children who have received serious physical abuse, generally from a parent or foster parent" (Kempe, Silverman, Steele, Droegemueller, & Silver, 1962, p. 17).

Due to the increasing recognition of child abuse as a serious problem, the government took on the role of investigation and prosecution of these cases, replacing the traditionally private provision of these services through SPCCs. From the 1960s on, state governments developed their own systems for responding to child abuse, often guided by suggestions from the federal government.

Starting with the Child Abuse Prevention and Treatment Act (CAPTA) of 1974, which will be described in detail later in this chapter, the federal government continued to influence the role of CPS in individual states. CAPTA has been reauthorized regularly over the past 30 years, with the most recent reauthorization occurring in 2003. At each reauthorization, amendments are made in an effort to improve the system and reflect current concerns in the system.

## THE HISTORY OF U.S. CHILD WELFARE POLICIES

Many early policy proposals were offered in an effort to prevent child abuse and protect abused children from further harm (Hutchison, 1993). Mandating physicians to report child abuse and neglect was a consistent recommendation in the early phases of policy development (Hutchison). It was believed that if professionals who have contact with children and families, namely medical personnel, were required to report suspected child abuse, the government could step in and protect children at risk before they were irreversibly harmed.

By 1967, all 50 states and the District of Columbia passed legislation that required doctors and other medical personnel to report suspected child maltreatment (Hutchison, 1993).

This first wave of mandated reporting legislation was limited in scope, especially when compared with current laws. The original legislation only applied to doctors and other medical personnel. This legislation was also limited in the types of behaviors that were reportable. The law required medical personnel to report "serious physical injuries" and/or "non-accidental injuries" (Besharov, 1986). Other forms of maltreatment, including emotional abuse and neglect, were not reportable.

### Federal Involvement in Child Welfare and Mandated Reporting

The first laws addressing child abuse and neglect and instituting systems of mandated reporting were designed at the state level. With each state authoring its own legislation, there was a lot of variability in the language of the laws across the country. The federal government eventually stepped in to encourage uniformity. Prompted by a decade's worth of research and caucusing of professionals, the federal government passed CAPTA (Public Law 93–247).

CAPTA created the National Center for Child Abuse and Neglect (NCCAN) (Hutchison, 1993). NCCAN was charged with developing model legislation in the area of child welfare for states to adopt. Such model legislation included defining child abuse, suggesting organizational structure for agencies that receive reports of suspected abuse and neglect, and suggesting a longer list of professionals who should be mandated to report suspected child abuse and neglect (Hutchison, 1993).

In the mid-1970s, NCCAN sponsored an advisory committee to develop this model legislation. This committee consisted primarily of lawyers, judges, doctors, academics, and representatives from policy think tanks (Sussman & Cohen, 1975). Unfortunately, the advisory committee lacked participation from public welfare workers who would ultimately run the system at the state level. Also missing from the advisory committee were professionals (other than doctors) who would be required to report suspected child abuse as a result of the legislation, such as social workers and educational personnel.

Due to the separations in the role of state and federal governments as outlined in the U.S. Constitution, the federal government cannot force states to adopt its suggestions in certain areas of law. Child welfare is one such area in which the federal government cannot impose its suggestions on the states. In order to encourage states to follow federal suit, incentive systems were designed. States that conformed to the model legislation proffered by the federal NCCAN were rewarded with federal money to support state child protection services (Hutchison, 1993). Largely as a result of the financial incentive, by 1980 most states passed all model legislation promulgated by the NCCAN. Adoption of NCCAN model legislation resulted in increased uniformity across states at the time. (Subsequent changes in state law since then have resulted again in variability across states, although much less so than before the federal efforts.)

NCCAN model legislation resulted in a broadened definition of child abuse, by including not only physical and emotional abuse but also including neglect and sexual abuse as well in the list of reportable cases (Hutchison, 1993).

NCCAN was also largely responsible for an expansion of the role of mandated reporter. NCCAN model legislation recommended that law enforcement, educational, social service, and mental health personnel are added to the list of mandated reporters from state to state.

As the role of mandated reporter expanded to increasingly more professionals and the definition of reportable conditions diversified, the number of reported cases of suspected child abuse and/or maltreatment skyrocketed. The number of annual reports in the United States increased 225% between 1976 and 1987 (Hutchison, 1993) and increased approximately 300% to 500% since 1986 (U.S. Department of Health and Human Services, 2007). This increase in reports is not necessarily due to an increase in the incidence of child maltreatment. The growth in reports may also be explained by the expanding list of mandated reporters, the expansion in the list of reportable conditions, and increased public awareness of child abuse through the media (Hutchison).

## State Central Registers of Child Maltreatment

In addition to suggesting which cases should be reportable and who should be mandated to make reports, the NCCAN advisory committee also made suggestions for how states should structure their systems. The advisory committee recommended the institution of a central register for reports of maltreatment in each state (Sussman & Cohen, 1975). As originally designed, each state central register would keep track of reports of suspected abuse and catalog the determination of each report so that they could be referenced in the future and aggregated for statistical purposes.

At the time of the drafting of the model legislation, mandated reporters in most states made reports to their local child protective service agency, usually run by the county government. The model legislation proffered by NCCAN required that the local child protective service report to the state central register after receiving a report from a local reporter. A main reason for creating a central register was to centralize data management in an effort to lessen the fiscal impact on the local county CPS and improve tracking of families involved in child welfare (Sussman & Cohen, 1975).

In some states, including New York, the central register accepts all reports and transmits the information to the local child protective service agency, usually at the county level, to start an investigation. Using a central register to receive reports streamlines the reporting process so that reporters do not need access to multiple phone numbers to report maltreatment across county lines.

## Government Responsibility for Investigating Child Abuse and Neglect

Beyond determining which agencies of the government would receive reports of child abuse and neglect, the NCCAN also had to decide which agency would investigate the allegations. The character and function of the agency charged with these responsibilities was a great concern to the NCCAN advisory committee (Sussman & Cohen, 1975). Law enforcement, juvenile courts, and departments of social service were the three state-level agencies that the advisory committee considered making responsible for receiving and responding to reports of child maltreatment.

There were many reasons to support law enforcement spearheading child abuse reporting and investigation. Many forms of child maltreatment were already under the purview of law enforcement, such as sexual abuse and severe physical abuse (Sussman & Cohen, 1975). The police departments were already staffed around the clock, every day of the year, so the infrastructure was already available (Sussman & Cohen). Additionally, American citizens were already accustomed to calling the police for help, so another system would not have to be learned (Sussman & Cohen). There was concern, however, that the police lacked the ability to provide therapeutic resources to afflicted families (Sussman & Cohen).

The juvenile courts at the time were deemed inappropriate because the role of investigator was not one with which the court personnel felt comfortable. Since the courts ultimately decided the validity of allegations, they should not also be responsible for the investigation (Sussman & Cohen, 1975). As well, the juvenile courts of this era were responding to numerous U.S. Supreme Court decisions that were drastically changing their methods of practice. Such cases were making these courts reflect the more rigid standards of practice found in criminal court. For instance, the Court's decision in *In re Gault* (1967) provided those accused of juvenile delinquency many rights previously denied to them, including the right to counsel and the right against self-incrimination.

The NCCAN ultimately determined that state departments of social services were the most appropriate venue for receiving and investigating reports of child maltreatment. It was assumed that these departments would be best able to develop specialized offices for CPS (Sussman & Cohen, 1975). These departments were expected to provide social service or treatment to families who needed such intervention (Sussman & Cohen). The department of social services was also seen as a nonpunitive option: The hope was that reporters and families would see the department of social services as offering help, not just punishing wrongdoing (Sussman & Cohen). However, there was concern that since departments of social service were often viewed as "poor people's agencies," child maltreatment might, as a result, be perceived as a problem exclusively of the poor (Sussman & Cohen).

By the time model legislation had been devised by the federal government in the 1970s, more than half of the states already had a model under which reports of suspected child abuse were received by the state department of social services (Sussman & Cohen, 1975). Currently, in most states, CPS continues to be housed in such a department on the state level.

## COSTS OF CHILD ABUSE

The immediate injuries to child abuse victims are obvious, such as cuts and bruises, but the long-term consequences are more difficult to observe and measure. Child abuse and neglect continue to be major social problems, not just because of their prevalence but also because of the effects on America's children and families. Child abuse and neglect lead to physical health, mental health, behavioral, and societal consequences for victims in their childhood and adulthood. Abused and neglected children may suffer from impaired brain development and general poor physical health as a result of the maltreatment (Dallum, 2001; U.S. Department of Health and Human Services, 2007). Children who are the victims of child abuse or neglect are more likely to have mental or emotional health problems as well as cognitive and social difficulties (Child Welfare Information Gateway, 2006).

A history of child abuse victimization increases a child's likelihood of delinquent behavior (Smith & Thornberry, 1995). Such a history also increases a child's likelihood of adult criminal behavior by 28% and violent crime involvement by 30% (Maxfield & Widom, 1996). Additionally, maltreated children are more likely to become abusers themselves (Wang & Holton, 2007).

Child abuse and neglect also imposes a financial cost. Financing the large bureaucracy of the child welfare system in all 50 states costs the U.S. federal, state, and local governments over $23 billion per year (Scarcella, Bess, Zielewski, & Geen, 2006). As well, services developed in response to the social needs of children and families affected by child abuse and neglect, including mental health services, cost more than $70 billion per year in the United States (Wang & Holton, 2007). Other costs of child abuse and neglect that are more difficult to measure include lost productivity in work and school.

## REPORTS OF CHILD ABUSE AND NEGLECT

In each state, there is a public entity under the control of the state government, CPS, which receives all reports of child abuse or neglect in that state. Although the federal government financially supports CPS departments across the country, the federal government does not administer them.

When CPS receives a report, they must first determine whether the report should be taken and investigated. There are two major reasons that a report is not taken and investigated. The first is a lack of necessary information to investigate the report. For instance, CPS cannot investigate a report when the reporter does not know where the child and/or caretaker can be found.

The other major reason that a report is not taken and investigated is that the report does not meet the definitions of abuse or neglect. For instance, CPS will not take a report if the allegations made do not add up to child abuse or neglect. Frustratingly, many reports by mandated reporters are refused because of this reason. This is why it is so important for mandated reporters to be educated so that they know what constitutes abuse and neglect, a topic that will be discussed in later chapters.

If the report *is* taken by CPS, the allegations must be investigated. After investigation, CPS makes a decision if they have enough evidence to substantiate the allegations. Of the total reports attempted in the United States in 2005, only 62% reached the investigation stage (U.S. Department of Health and Human Services, 2007). Of those reports that were investigated, only one-third were eventually substantiated (U.S. Department of Health and Human Services). That means that only approximately 20% of reports made to CPS are sufficiently supported through the investigation.

## Services as a Result of a Substantiated Report to Child Protective Services

When a case is substantiated, CPS must make a decision as to whether they will offer the family services, including foster care, or not. Not all children who are found to be abused or neglected are removed from their families. In fact, one of the original goals of CPS was to identify families in need of support in an effort to keep them together. Although over 300,000 children ended up in foster care as a result of a child abuse or neglect report in 2005, many more families remained together after a report of abuse or neglect was substantiated (U.S. Department of Health and Human Services, 2007). Many of the families that remain intact are offered and receive preventive services. Preventive services are specifically designed to address the family's issues while keeping the family intact.

Foster care is a major service provided to families in distress. In theory, by removing children from their homes, foster care allows parents to resolve their difficulties so that they are prepared to resume caring for their child. Federal law encourages states to keep families intact wherever possible. Foster care should be viewed as a service reserved for cases where there is imminent danger to the child if he or she remains in the care of the parents.

## The Role of Mandated Reporters

Professionals, mostly mandated reporters, make more than half of the reports that CPS receives in a given year in the United States. In 2005, teachers and school officials made over 15% of all reports to CPS, the largest single report source (U.S. Department of Health and Human Services, 2007). Law enforcement, namely the police, made about 15% of reports (U.S. Department of Health and Human Services). Social services workers, including social workers, made 10% of all reports received by CPS in 2005 (U.S. Department of Health and Human Services).

Nonprofessionals (such as family members, neighbors, and anonymous tipsters) also make reports to CPS. Of nonprofessional sources, anonymous reporters make the most reports, 9% of total reports. Although reports are received by professionals and nonprofessionals alike, reports by professional reporters are substantiated at a higher rate than those of nonprofessional reporters.

## CRITICISMS OF MANDATED REPORTING

Although it is clear that child abuse cases are increasingly reported and adjudicated at least partly due to mandated reporting, the system of mandated reporting continues to receive criticism. Underreporting, overreporting, and discrimination are three criticisms of the current state of the mandated reporting system.

Research shows that more than half of mandated reporters fail to report cases where they suspect child abuse and maltreatment (Delaronde, King, Bendel, & Reece, 2000). There are many reasons mandated reporters cite for not reporting. Mandated reporters often lack certainty of what cases are reportable (Zellman & Antler, 1990). This is particularly true when the case involves nonphysical forms of abuse. Most professionals understand that certain physical acts against a child are reportable, such as physical and sexual abuse (Alvarez, Kenny, Donohue, & Carpin, 2004); on the other hand, neglect is often cited as the most complicated to identify and therefore most difficult to determine when to report. However, neglect constitutes most of the reportable cases (Alvarez et al.). Even less clear are the cases of emotional abuse (Alvarez et al.).

Mandated reporters also cite confusion about or concern for the process of reporting suspected child abuse or neglect (Kesner & Robinson, 2002; Reiniger, Robison, & McHugh, 1995). Some mandated reporters believe they have insufficient evidence to make a report (Delaronde et al., 2000). Others argue that reporting may produce more harm than good. Some mandated reporters suggest that they, the reporters, can better handle the case than CPS (Delaronde et al.). Mandated reporters with a therapeutic relationship with the family often cite ethical conflict as a deterrent to reporting (Delaronde et al.). Mandated reporters have also expressed concern with their internal agency procedure/protocol as to when a case may be reportable (Alvarez et al., 2004).

No matter what the reason for not reporting suspected maltreatment, it is clear that many children are left at risk because many mandated reporters do not report their suspicions, even though they are legally obligated to do so.

Underreporting is not the only problem with the current state of mandated reporting. Overreporting of suspicions is also a problem. More than half of all reports of child abuse and maltreatment are ultimately unsubstantiated (U.S. Department of Health and Human Services, 2007). This overreporting overwhelms services that are supposed to target at-risk children and families (Ainsworth, 2002; Besharov, 1986) by requiring investigations that are unnecessary. Also as a result of overreporting, many children and families suffer from unwarranted intrusion and disruption.

In most states, mandated reporters are not required to receive training on their responsibilities. As a result, mandated reporters may be fulfilling their legal obligation to report without understanding if their suspicions rise to a level that requires a report.

Beyond underreporting and overreporting, racially disproportionate reporting is another troubling issue. The National Incidence Studies, performed by the U.S. Department of Health and Human Services, consistently show that child maltreatment does not discriminate by race (Sedlak & Broadhurst, 1996). However, nonwhite children are disproportionately reported for child maltreatment, especially by mandated reporters. Disproportionate reporting may be due in part to disproportionate rates of poverty among nonwhite Americans, but bias may also contribute to this phenomenon.

The drafters of the model legislation were cognizant of the potential for systematic bias against poor and disenfranchised families:

> [A]s a result of the often vague definitions of neglect and the consequent discretion granted reporters, it is probable that cultural, racial and economic distinctions between the report and the reported will influence and unfairly bias the reporting of certain groups of children. (Sussman & Cohen, 1975)

The drafters realized that since poor and disenfranchised families are more likely to come in contact with mandated reporters than wealthier families, they might be more likely to be reported. Additionally, professionals who are mandated reporters may be less likely to report wealthier families, even when they have reasonable suspicion. The mandated reporter may feel that a wealthier family does not need to be involved in CPS; instead, they may work with the family to improve their functioning without alerting CPS. Other mandated reporters may choose not to report wealthier families because they are concerned that they will lose potential clients if they report their suspicions.

Another concern for discrimination in the reporting of child abuse involves racially disproportionate reporting. Nonwhite children are reported at a higher rate than they are found in the general population. One reason for this disproportionate reporting may be that nonwhite children are more likely than white children to be poor and live in single-family homes—two major risk factors for child abuse and neglect. Another reason for this disproportionate reporting may be racial bias, whether intentional or not.

Efforts to prevent discrimination in the reporting and investigation of child abuse and maltreatment are needed. Improving training for mandated reporters is one way to address this concern. Although intended to protect children and families, mandated reporting of child maltreatment may also contribute to institutional classism and racism.

Sedlak, A., & Broadhurst, D. D. (1996). *Executive summary of the Third National Incidence Study of Child Abuse and Neglect.* U.S. Department of Health and Human Services, Administration on Children, Youth and Families. Washington, DC: U.S. Government Printing Office.

Smith, C. & Thornberry, T. (1995). The relationship between childhood maltreatment and adolescent involvement in delinquency. *Criminology, 33*(4), 451–477.

Sussman, A., & Cohen, S. (1975). *Reporting child abuse and neglect: Guidelines for legislation.* Cambridge, MA: Ballinger Publishing Company.

U.S. Department of Health and Human Services, Administration on Children, Youth and Families. (2007). *Child maltreatment 2005.* Washington, DC: U.S. Government Printing Office.

Wang, C. T., & Holton, J. (2007). *Total estimated cost of child abuse and neglect in the United States.* Prevent Child Abuse America, Chicago, IL.

Zellman, G. L., & Antler, S. (1990). Mandated reporters and CPS: A study in frustration. *Public Welfare, 48*(1), 30.

## ADDITIONAL READING

Levine, M. & Doueck, H. J. (1995). *The impact of mandated reporting on the therapeutic process.* Thousand Oaks, CA: Sage.

Newburger, E. H. (1983). The helping hand strikes again: Unintended consequences of child abuse reporting. *Journal of Clinical Child Psychology, 12*(3), 307–311.

Swan, N. (1998). Exploring the role of child abuse on later drug abuse: Researchers face broad gaps in information. *NIDA Notes, 13*(2). National Institute on Drug Abuse, National Institutes of Health, Washington, DC.

# 2 The Social Worker As Mandated Reporter

Writing a book to educate social workers of their responsibilities as mandated reporters of child abuse and neglect presents a unique difficulty. Social work as a profession is very diverse. Knowledge assumedly known by some social workers would be foreign to other social workers. For instance, social workers in practice with children and families may understand instinctively the limitations of recall with young children, whereas social workers who work primarily with the elderly may not understand this and may see a young child's difficulty recalling an incident as an attempt to hide abuse or a symptom of head trauma.

This chapter explores the diversity of the social work profession in an effort to identify the skills that each specialization brings to the process of determining if a report of suspected child abuse or neglect needs to be made.

## WHAT IS THE PROFESSION OF SOCIAL WORK?

The profession of social work encompasses many different professional roles, but there are certain characteristics of all social work roles that unify the profession itself. Social work is a profession for those who have a strong desire to help improve people's lives. The primary mission of the social work profession is to enhance human well-being and help meet the basic needs of all people, with particular attention to the needs and empowerment of people who are vulnerable, oppressed, or living in poverty. An historic and defining feature of social work is the profession's focus on individual well-being in a social context and the well-being of society. Fundamental to social work is attention to the environmental forces that create, contribute to, and address problems in people's living circumstances.

Social workers promote social justice and social change with and on behalf of clients. As a term, *client* is used here inclusively to refer to individuals, families, groups, organizations, and communities. Social workers need to be sensitive to cultural and ethnic diversity and strive to end discrimination, oppression, poverty, and other forms of social injustice. They may pursue these activities through direct practice, community organizing, supervision, consultation, administration, advocacy, social and political action, policy development and implementation, education, research and evaluation, or some combination of these activities.

Social workers seek to enhance the capacity of people to address their own needs. Social workers also seek to promote the responsiveness of organizations, communities, and other social institutions to individuals' needs and social problems.

The mission of the social work profession is rooted in a set of core values. These core values, embraced by social workers throughout the profession's history, are the foundation of social work's unique purpose and perspective: service, social justice, dignity and worth of the person, importance of human relationships, integrity, and competence (National Association of Social Workers [NASW], 1999). This constellation of core values reflects what is unique to the social work profession. Core values, and the principles that flow from them, must be balanced within the context and complexity of the human experience. The primary responsibility of social workers is to promote the well-being of clients. In general, client interests are primary. However, the social worker's responsibility to the larger society or specific legal obligations may on limited occasions supersede the loyalty owed clients, and clients should be so advised. (Examples include when a social worker is required by law to report that a client has abused a child or has threatened to harm oneself or others.)

Social workers should respect and promote the right of clients to self-determination and assist clients in their efforts to identify and clarify their goals. Social workers help people function the best way they can in their environment, deal with their relationships, and solve personal and family problems. Social workers often see clients who face a life-threatening disease or a social problem, such as inadequate housing, unemployment, a serious illness, a disability, or substance abuse. Social workers also assist families that have serious domestic conflicts, sometimes involving child or spousal abuse.

As mandated reporters, social workers are often placed in a difficult situation related to reporting families to the authorities when there is reasonable cause to suspect that a child has been or is at risk of being abused and/or neglected. Using their professional judgment, social workers must act by limiting the client's right to self-determination when client actions or potential actions pose a serious, foreseeable, and imminent risk to themselves or others.

Social workers help people overcome some of life's most difficult challenges: poverty, discrimination, abuse, addiction, physical illness, divorce, loss, unemployment, educational problems, disability, and mental illness. Professional social workers are found in every facet of community life—in schools, hospitals, mental health clinics, senior centers, elected offices, private practices, prisons, military organizations, corporations, and in numerous public and private agencies that serve individuals and families in need.

## WHAT MAKES SOMEONE A SOCIAL WORKER?

In order to be considered a social worker, one must attain a specialized education. A bachelor's in social work (BSW) degree is the most common minimum educational requirement to qualify as a social worker. A BSW provides the education and experience to qualify for case management and other basic social work functions. Many entry-level government jobs in social services require (or prefer) a BSW.

Although a BSW is sufficient for entry into the field, an advanced degree has become standard for many positions, including therapeutic social work practice. A master's in social work (MSW) degree is typically required for positions in health settings. Some jobs in public and private agencies also may require an MSW. Supervisory, administrative, and staff training positions usually require the MSW degree.

Master's programs prepare graduates for work in their chosen field of concentration and continue to develop the skills required to perform clinical assessments, manage large caseloads, take on supervisory roles, and explore new ways of drawing on social services to meet the needs of clients. Such programs typically involve 2 years of full-time course work and include a minimum of 900 hours of supervised field instruction, or internship. A part-time program may take 4 or more years.

Entry into a master's program does not require a BSW, but those who hold a BSW degree from an accredited social work program may be eligible for advanced standing. Course work in psychology, biology, sociology, economics, and political science may also be eligible. In addition, a second language can be very helpful.

Beyond the MSW, doctoral-level social work study is available. Unlike other mental health professions, a doctoral-level social work degree is not considered a "clinical" degree, in that it does not prepare the social worker for advanced therapeutic training. Instead, college and university teaching positions and most research appointments normally require a doctorate in social work (DSW) or doctor of philosophy degree (PhD).

## THE SOCIAL WORKER/CASEWORKER DISTINCTION

Many jobs tout themselves as "social work" positions but do not require a BSW or MSW. Instead, these jobs often seek bachelor-level graduates with undergraduate majors in psychology, sociology, and related fields. These positions generally serve a role of basic case management.

Sometimes, the job descriptions for these positions include skills generally obtained through social work education, such as assessment. However, these positions, when filled by persons other than those holding a degree in social work, are appropriately defined as "casework" positions, *not* social work positions. Persons occupying these positions without a social work degree should be referred to as *caseworker*. Referring to such persons as *social workers* devalues the integrity of the social work profession. In fact, in many states where the practice of social work is regulated through a professional licensing system, holding oneself out as a "social worker" without the proper credentials and licensing would be considered the illegal practice of social work without a license.

As social workers, we must insist on the appropriate use of the term *social worker*.

## LICENSING AND CERTIFICATION OF SOCIAL WORKERS

All states and the District of Columbia have licensing, certification, or registration requirements regarding social work practice and the use of professional titles. Although standards for licensing vary by state, a growing number of states are placing greater emphasis on communications skills, professional ethics, and sensitivity to cultural diversity issues by requiring specific training. Most states require 2 years (3,000 hours) of supervised clinical experience for licensure of clinical social workers.

In addition to state credentials, the NASW offers voluntary credentials. Social workers with an MSW may be eligible for the Academy of Certified Social Workers (ACSW), the Qualified Clinical Social Worker (QCSW), or the Diplomate in Clinical Social Work (DCSW) credential, based on their professional experience. Credentials are particularly important for those in private practice; some health insurance providers require social workers to have them in order to be reimbursed for services.

## PRACTICE AREAS

We will now examine the various practice areas that social workers may focus on as well as how those areas relate to mandated reporting.

### Child and Family Social Work

Child and family social workers provide social services and assistance to improve the social and psychological functioning of children and their families and to maximize the family well-being of children. Some social workers in this area of practice assist single parents; arrange adoptions; or help find foster homes for neglected, abandoned, or abused children. Some of these social workers specialize in services for senior citizens— running support groups for family caregivers or for the adult children of aging parents; advising elderly people or family members about choices in areas such as housing, transportation, and long-term care; and coordinating and monitoring these services. Through employee assistance programs, social workers help workers cope with job-related pressures or with personal problems that affect the quality of their work.

Child and family social workers typically work for individual and family services agencies, schools, domestic violence or child abuse programs, or state or local governments. These social workers may be known as child welfare social workers, family services social workers, child protective services (CPS) social workers, occupational social workers, or gerontology social workers. Such social workers may be working with families already involved in the child protection system. As a result, child and family social workers in this position often believe that they do not have to report families when they have suspicions of child abuse or neglect, since the family is already under the watchful eye of CPS. This may be untrue. The social worker with reasonable suspicion of child abuse or neglect should make a report regardless of the family's previous or current involvement with CPS.

Child and family social workers have a great deal of contact with children and families and therefore are likely to report cases of suspected child abuse and neglect. Because these social workers often are working with families involved in current crises, they may discover issues of concern that were previously unnoticed, such as domestic violence. These social workers can use their practice skills and experience, along with consulting colleagues and supervisors, to make informed decisions about when to make a report.

## School Social Work

School social workers provide assistance to improve the social and psychological functioning of children to maximize the child's well-being and academic functioning. School social workers are sometimes found teaching workshops on special topics to teachers and students. They address such problems as teenage pregnancy, misbehavior, and truancy. These social workers also advise teachers on how to cope with problem students. They can often be found working with students on an individual basis as well as running specialized groups.

School social workers have much of their contact with children who exhibit signs or symptoms of distress. School social workers are often the source of a report of suspected child abuse and neglect in the educational system. For obvious reasons, school social workers are more likely to report cases of educational neglect than other types of social workers. In addition, school social workers, due to their education and experience, may be integral to the assessment of potential reports from teachers and other school personnel.

## Medical and Public Health Social Workers

Medical and public health social workers provide persons, families, or vulnerable populations with the psychosocial support needed to cope with chronic, acute, or terminal illness, such as Alzheimer disease, cancer, or AIDS. They also advise family caregivers, counsel patients, and help plan for patient needs after discharge by arranging for at-home services—from meals-on-wheels to oxygen equipment. Some work on interdisciplinary teams that evaluate certain kinds of patients, such as geriatric or organ transplant patients. Medical and public health social workers may work for hospitals, nursing and personal care facilities, individual and family services agencies, or local governments.

Social workers who work in health care settings are more likely to see serious cases of physical abuse than other social workers. Social workers are invaluable sources of information in the investigation of such cases, since they are not only knowledgeable of the health aspects of the case but also can assess the psychological and social functioning of the child and family during the crisis.

Social workers in health care settings should assert their knowledge and expertise, as their education and training makes them uniquely situated in this interdisciplinary setting.

## Mental Health and Substance Abuse

Mental health and substance abuse social workers assess and treat individuals with mental illness or substance abuse problems, including abuse of alcohol, tobacco, or other drugs. Such services include individual and group therapy, outreach, crisis intervention, social rehabilitation, and training in skills of everyday living. They also may help plan for supportive services to ease a patient's return to the community. Mental health and substance abuse social workers are likely to work in hospitals, substance abuse treatment centers, individual and family services agencies, or local governments. These social workers may also be known as clinical social workers. Social workers often provide social services in health-related settings that now are governed by managed care organizations. To contain costs, these organizations emphasize short-term intervention, ambulatory and community-based care, and greater decentralization of services.

Social workers in mental health and substance abuse treatment have specialized expertise in areas that intersect most often with child abuse and neglect. These social workers simultaneously assess client functioning and apply a diagnosis while determining if the client is a potential harm to his or her child. Since such social workers are more likely to come in contact with situations involving parental substance abuse, they need to be able to determine when the law in their state requires them to report parental substance abuse to CPS.

Similar to child and family social workers, social workers employed in mental health and/or substance abuse treatment are often exposed to families already identified by CPS for past allegations of abuse or neglect. These social workers still have a responsibility to make a report, when required to do so by law, regardless of the standing of the client's case.

## Private Practice

Some social workers go into private practice. Most private practitioners are clinical social workers who provide psychotherapy and others forms of treatment, usually paid for through health insurance or by the client themselves. Private practitioners must have at least a master's degree and a period of supervised work experience and are usually licensed by the state where they are practicing. A network of contacts for referrals is essential as well. Many private practitioners split their time between working for an agency or hospital and working in their private practice. They may continue to hold a position at a hospital or agency in order to receive health and life insurance.

Most social workers in private practice have extensive experience in other settings that is invaluable to their work as mandated reporters. Social workers in private practice do not have the institutional supports to further a report of suspected child abuse or neglect. Instead, private practitioners would be well served by creating a local professional network to turn to in cases where consultation would be appropriate and helpful. Due to the close clinical relationships developed between private practitioners and their clients, these social workers may be more likely to hear disclosures about sexual abuse perpetration or victimization.

## Probation, Parole, and Corrections

Social workers employed in probation, parole, and corrections provide services to individuals who have been arrested and are under the supervision of the court. Such services include individual and group therapy, outreach, crisis intervention, social rehabilitation, supervision, and training in skills of everyday living. They also may help plan for supportive services to ease an offender's return to the community. These services can be for juveniles or adults.

Social workers in this role are uniquely situated to assess situations of potential recurrence of abuse or neglect. At the same time, these social workers must be attuned to the stress that comes with assimilating back into one's life and family. Social workers working with this population can serve an important role in supporting successful reunification and reducing the likelihood of abuse and neglect.

## Planners and Policy Makers

Social work planners and policy makers develop programs to address such issues as child abuse, homelessness, substance abuse, poverty, and domestic violence. These workers research and analyze policies, programs, and regulations. They identify social problems and suggest legislative and other solutions. They may help raise funds or write grants to support these programs.

Although social work planners and policy makers are less likely to come in direct contact with clients that would obligate them to make a report of suspected child abuse or neglect, they must remain educated about their responsibilities. These social workers may also be uniquely situated to influence policy regarding the education and training of social workers, and other mandated reporters—a very important role for the profession and society at large.

## RESPONSIBILITIES OF THE SOCIAL WORKER

No matter what position a social worker holds, he or she should provide services to clients only in the context of a professional relationship based, when appropriate, on valid informed consent. Social workers should use clear and understandable language to inform clients of the purpose of the services, risks related to the services, limits to services because of the requirements of a third-party payer, relevant costs, reasonable alternatives, the client's right to refuse or withdraw consent, and the time frame covered by the consent. Social workers should provide clients with an opportunity to ask questions.

In instances when clients lack the capacity to provide informed consent, social workers should protect client interests by seeking permission from an appropriate third party, informing clients consistent with the clients' level of understanding. In such instances, social workers should seek to ensure that the third party acts in a manner consistent with client wishes and interests. Social workers should take reasonable steps to enhance such clients' ability to give informed consent.

Social workers should respect the client's right to privacy. They should not solicit private information from clients unless it is essential to providing services or conducting social work evaluation or research. Once private information is shared, standards of confidentiality apply. Social workers may disclose confidential information when appropriate with valid consent from a client or a person legally authorized to consent on behalf of a client. Social workers should protect the confidentiality of all information obtained in the course of professional service, except for compelling professional reasons. The general expectation that social workers will keep information confidential does not apply when disclosure is necessary to prevent serious, foreseeable, and imminent harm to a client or other identifiable person. In all instances, social workers should disclose the least amount of confidential information necessary to achieve the desired purpose; only information that is directly relevant to the purpose for which the disclosure is made should be revealed.

Social workers should inform clients, to the extent possible, about the disclosure of confidential information and the potential consequences *when feasible* before the disclosure is made. This applies whether social workers disclose confidential information on the basis of a legal requirement or client consent. Social workers should discuss with clients and other interested parties the nature of confidentiality and limitations of the clients' right to confidentiality. Social workers should review with clients circumstances where confidential information may be requested and where disclosure of confidential information may be legally required. This discussion should occur as soon as possible in the social worker–client relationship and as needed throughout the course of the relationship.

When social workers provide counseling services to families, couples, or groups, they should seek agreement among the parties involved concerning the individual's right to confidentiality and obligation to preserve the confidentiality of information shared by others. Social workers should inform participants in family, couples, or group counseling that they cannot guarantee that all participants will honor such agreements. In addition, social workers should inform clients involved in family, couples, marital, or group counseling of the social worker, employer, and agency's policy concerning disclosure of confidential information among the parties involved in the counseling.

Social workers should protect the confidentiality of clients during legal proceedings to the extent permitted by law. When a court of law or other legally authorized body orders social workers to disclose confidential or privileged information without a client's consent and such disclosure could cause harm to the client, social workers should request that the court withdraw the order or limit the order as narrowly as possible or maintain the records under seal, unavailable for public inspection. Social workers should protect the confidentiality of a client's written and electronic records and other sensitive information. Social workers should take reasonable steps to ensure that client records are stored in a secure location and that the records are not available to others who are not authorized to have access. It is important that social workers familiarize themselves with the Health Insurance Portability and Accountability Act (HIPAA) laws.

Social workers should take precautions to ensure and maintain the confidentiality of information transmitted to other parties through the use of computers, electronic mail, facsimile machines, telephones and telephone answering machines, and other electronic or computer technology. Disclosure of identifying information should be avoided whenever possible. Social workers should transfer or dispose of client records in a manner that protects client confidentiality and is consistent with state statutes governing records and social work licensure. Social workers should take reasonable precautions to protect client confidentiality in the event of the social worker's termination of practice, incapacitation, or death.

## REFERENCE

National Association of Social Workers. (1999). *Code of ethics of the National Association of Social Workers*. Washington, DC: Author.

# Defining Child Abuse and Neglect

All social workers need to be familiar with the child abuse, neglect, and maltreatment laws in the state in which they practice. Unfortunately, many schools of social work do not require graduates to complete mandated reporter education prior to graduation. Some states, but not all, require social workers to take a class on child abuse and neglect as a prerequisite to obtaining a state license in social work (see appendix A). In New York State, for example, required mandated reporter training for social workers went into effect in 2005. For all these reasons, many social workers are not as familiar with current mandated reporter laws as they could or should be. This chapter will help you understand the terms often used in child abuse and neglect cases.

## DEFINITION OF CHILD ABUSE, NEGLECT, AND MALTREATMENT

Child abuse, neglect, and maltreatment are defined in both federal and state legislation. As discussed in chapter 1, the first federal legislation, the Child Abuse Prevention and Treatment Act (CAPTA) was passed in 1974. This legislation established a minimum set of acts or behaviors that define physical abuse, neglect, and sexual abuse. The federal definition of child abuse and neglect refers to "any recent act or failure to act on the part of a parent or caretaker, which results in death, serious physical or emotional harm, sexual abuse, or exploitation, or an act or failure to act which presents an imminent risk of serious harm" (CAPTA, 1974a).

As a result of the financial incentives put forth in CAPTA for state adherence to federal standards, each state passed its own laws in compliance with federal mandates. In all states, people under the age of 18 years can be defined as an abused or neglected child. In some states, people in residential care with certain handicapping conditions are included up to age 21 years.

CAPTA, reauthorized in the Keeping Children and Families Safe Act of 2003 (Public Law 108–36), provides minimum standards for defining child abuse and neglect. As in the past, states must incorporate these minimum standards into their statutory definitions in order to receive federal funds. Under this act, child abuse and/or maltreatment is defined as "any recent act or failure to act on the part of a parent or caregiver, which results in death, serious physical or emotional harm, sexual abuse or exploitation, or an act or failure to act which presents an imminent risk of serious harm." A "child" under this definition generally means a person who is under the age of 18 years or who is not an emancipated minor. In cases of child sexual abuse, a "child" is generally one who has not attained the age of 18 years or the age specified by the child protection law of the state in which the child resides, whichever is younger.

## PHYSICAL ABUSE

CAPTA defines physical abuse as "any non accidental physical injury to the child" and can include striking, kicking, burning, or biting the child or any action that results in a physical impairment of the child (Child Welfare Information Gateway, 2007). In 36 states[1] and American Samoa, Guam, the Northern Mariana Islands, Puerto Rico, and the Virgin Islands, the definition of abuse also includes acts or circumstances that threaten the child with harm or create a substantial risk of harm to the child's health or welfare.

---

[1] Alabama, Alaska, Arkansas, California, Colorado, Florida, Hawaii, Illinois, Indiana, Kentucky, Louisiana, Maine, Maryland, Massachusetts, Michigan, Minnesota, Montana, Nebraska, New Jersey, New Mexico, New York, North Carolina, Ohio, Oklahoma, Oregon, Pennsylvania, Rhode Island, South Carolina, Tennessee, Texas, Utah, Vermont, Virginia, West Virginia, Wisconsin, and Wyoming. In addition, Arizona, Kansas, New Hampshire, Washington, and the District of Columbia address the issue of risk of harm in their definitions of neglect.

As a result, all state child abuse laws apply to specific acts and (for most states) an act of omission of the legally responsible person. *Serious injury* would best be defined when a person legally responsible inflicts (or allows to be inflicted) on the child a serious injury by other than accidental means. Serious injury includes disfigurement or impairment that is extensive and lasting, loss or impairment of a function of a bodily organ, other impairment of physical or emotional health that is extended in duration, or an injury that causes or creates a substantial risk of death. Examples of such physical injuries include but are not limited to bruises, fractures, head and internal injuries, and burns.

An act of *omission* would be best defined as where there is a danger of serious injury that is created or allowed to be created by other than accidental means, (e.g., a parent leaves a window open without a window guard, which results in a 2-year-old child falling out the window). This includes a substantial risk of physical injury to the child, which would be likely to cause death, serious or extended disfigurement, impairment, or loss of the function of a bodily organ.

## Corporal Punishment

Corporal punishment is the use of physical force in disciplining a child. Excessive corporal punishment is when the parent or person legally responsible unreasonably inflicts, or allows to be inflicted, harm, or there is a substantial risk thereof. Some questions to ask to determine whether the punishment was excessive:

- Is the punishment *cruel?*
- What is the *intent* of the act?
- Which *part of the body* is affected?
- How often does it take place?
- What is the *nature and severity* of the punishment (beyond reasonable)?
- Is the punishment *appropriate* for the age of the child, and what was the *duration* of punishment?

## SEXUAL ABUSE

The CAPTA definition of sexual abuse involves "the employment, use, persuasion, inducement, enticement, or coercion of any child to engage in, or assist any other person to engage in, any sexually explicit conduct or simulation of such conduct for the purpose of producing a visual depiction of such conduct; or the rape, and in cases of caretaker or interfamilial relationships, statutory rape, molestation, prostitution, or other form of sexual exploitation of children, or incest with children" ( CAPTA, 1974b).

All states include sexual abuse in their definitions of child abuse. Some states refer in general terms to sexual abuse, while others specify various acts as sexual abuse. Sexual exploitation is an element of the definition of sexual abuse in most jurisdictions.

Sexual exploitation includes allowing the child to engage in prostitution or in the production of child pornography.

Sexual abuse is not an easy phenomenon to define; permissible childhood sexual behavior varies in accordance with cultural, family, and social tolerances. Sexual abuse is often defined as the involvement of dependent, developmentally immature children in sexual activities that they do not fully comprehend and therefore to which they are unable to give informed consent and/or which violates the taboos of society. It can be further defined as any misuse of a child for sexual pleasure or gratification.

Sexual abuse has the potential to interfere with a child's normal, healthy development, both emotionally and physically. Often, sexually victimized children experience severe emotional disturbances from their own feelings of guilt and shame as well as the feelings that society imposes on them. At the extreme end of the spectrum, sexual abuse includes sadistic sexual behavior or sexual intercourse. These behaviors may be the final acts in a worsening pattern of sexual abuse. For this reason and because of their devastating effects, exhibitionism, fondling, and any other sexual contact with children are also considered sexually abusive. Nontouching sexual abuse offenses include indecent exposure/exhibitionism, exposing children to pornographic material, deliberately exposing a child to the act of sexual intercourse, and masturbation in front of a child.

Touching sexual offenses include fondling of child's private parts, making a child touch an adult's sexual organs, oral sexual contact, or any penetration of a child's vagina or anus by an object that does not have a medical purpose.

Sexual exploitation offenses include engaging a child for the purposes of prostitution and using a child to film, photograph, or model pornography (e.g., a parent who photographs his or her child in sexually provocative positions and sends the photos out over the internet).

Although a child, for the purposes of determining sexual abuse, is generally considered someone under the age of 18 years, the age a child can legally consent (this is covered under each state's penal laws rather than child protective laws) to sexual contact varies from state to state. For the most part, age of consent laws exist to stop young people from being exploited by adults or younger children from being exploited by older children. The age of consent is the age when the law says that a child can agree to have sex. It means that until a child reaches this age, a child cannot legally have sex with anyone, regardless of his or her age. In most states, the legal age of consent is 16, 17, or 18 years.

Until recently, in some states, the age of consent laws were different for females and males or those engaging in same-sex relationships. Lawsuits have challenged these differences. As a result, the age of consent for male–male and female–female sex are the same as the age for male–female sex in most jurisdictions. However, in other states, it is not entirely clear how the decisions will be applied to their laws. If you are unsure about the age of consent in your state, you should seek clarification from your state's CPS office.

## EMOTIONAL ABUSE

All states and territories except Georgia and Washington include emotional maltreatment as part of their definitions of abuse or neglect. Twenty-two states,[2] the District of Columbia, the Northern Mariana Islands, and Puerto Rico provide specific definitions of emotional abuse or mental injury to a child. Typical language used in these definitions is "injury to the psychological capacity or emotional stability of the child as evidenced by an observable or substantial change in behavior, emotional response, or cognition" or as evidenced by "anxiety, depression, withdrawal, or aggressive behavior." Emotional abuse is considered a pattern of behavior that can seriously interfere with a child's positive development. Emotional abuse is probably the least understood of all child abuse.

Because emotional abuse attacks the child's psyche and self-concept, the victim comes to see him or herself as unworthy of love and affection. Children who are constantly shamed, humiliated, terrorized, or rejected suffer at least as much, if not more, than if they had been physically assaulted (Korfmacher, 1998). An infant who is being severely deprived

---

[2] States that provide a definition *of emotional* abuse: Alaska, Arizona, Arkansas, California, Colorado, Florida, Idaho, Kentucky, Maine, Maryland, Minnesota, Montana, Nevada, New York, Ohio, Pennsylvania, Rhode Island, South Carolina, Tennessee, Vermont, Wisconsin, and Wyoming.

of basic emotional nurturing, even though physically well cared for, can fail to thrive and eventually die. Less severe forms of early emotional deprivation may produce babies who grow into anxious and insecure children who are slow to develop or who might have low self-esteem.

## What Are the Effects of Emotional Abuse?

The consequences of emotional child abuse can be serious and long term (Spertus, Yehuda, Wong, Halligan, & Seremetis, 2003). Research studies conclude that psychopathologic symptoms are more likely to develop in emotionally abused children. These children may experience a lifelong pattern of depression, estrangement, anxiety, low self-esteem, inappropriate or troubled relationships, or a lack of empathy (Rich, Gingerich, & Rosen, 1997; Sanders & Becker-Lausen, 1995; Spertus et al.). During their childhood, victims may fail to thrive, or their developmental progress may be halted. Some children may also become poorly adjusted emotionally and psychologically (Kairys, 2002). As teenagers, they find it difficult to trust, participate in and achieve happiness in interpersonal relationships, and resolve the complex feelings left over from their childhoods. As adults, they may have trouble recognizing and appreciating the needs and feelings of their own children and emotionally abuse them.

Other types of abuse are usually identifiable because they leave marks or other physical evidence; however, emotional abuse can be very hard to diagnose or even to define. In some instances, an emotionally abused child will show no signs of abuse. For this reason, emotional abuse is the most difficult form of child maltreatment to identify and stop. This type of abuse leaves hidden scars that manifest themselves in numerous ways. Insecurity, poor self-esteem, destructive behavior, angry acts (such as fire setting or cruelty to animals), withdrawal, poor development of basic skills, alcohol or drug abuse, suicide, and difficulty forming relationships can all be possible results of emotional abuse.

## MALTREATMENT/NEGLECT

Child neglect is the most commonly reported type of child maltreatment (over 60%), according to the 2005 statistics released by the U.S. Department of Health and Human Services, Administration for Children and Families. Unfortunately, neglect frequently goes unreported and, historically, has not been acknowledged or publicized as greatly as child abuse.

Even child welfare professionals often give less attention to child neglect than to abuse. One study found that caseworkers indicated that they were least likely to substantiate referrals for neglect (English, Graham, Brummel, Coghlan, & Clark, 2002). In some respects, it is understandable why violence against children has commanded more attention than neglect. Abuse often leaves visible bruises and scars, whereas the signs of neglect tend to be less visible. However, the effects of neglect can be just as detrimental. In fact, some studies have shown that neglect may be more detrimental to children's early brain development than physical or sexual abuse ( Teicher, 2000).

Definitions of neglect vary among states. The definitions also are used for different purposes within the child welfare field. For example, a medical doctor may view a parent as neglectful if the parent repeatedly forgets to give his child a prescribed medication. This may or may not legally be considered neglect, however, depending on the stringency of the neglect criteria of many child protective services (CPS) agencies.

Additionally, what is considered neglect varies based on the age and the developmental level of the child, making it difficult to outline a set of behaviors that are *always* considered neglect. For example, leaving a child unattended for an hour is considered neglect when the child is young but not when the child is a teenager. Some states will specifically define an age that children cannot be left without supervision; others will leave it up to the mandated reporter to determine the impact on the child.

Another issue is that many neglect definitions specify that omissions in care may result either in "risk of harm" or "significant harm" to the child. While the 1996 reauthorization of CAPTA (Public Law 104–235) narrowed the definition of child maltreatment to cases where there has been actual harm or an imminent risk of serious harm, these terms often are not defined by law, leaving the local child protective agencies to interpret them. This leads to a lack of consistency in responding to families who may be challenged to meet the basic needs of their children.

Neglect is frequently defined in terms of deprivation of adequate food, clothing, shelter, medical care, or supervision. Twenty-one states and American Samoa, Puerto Rico, and the Virgin Islands include failure to educate the child as required by law in their definition of neglect. Seven states further define medical neglect as failing to provide any special medical treatment or mental health care needed by the child. In addition, four states define as medical neglect the withholding of medical treatment or nutrition from disabled infants with life-threatening conditions.

Child maltreatment/neglect is commonly defined when a child's physical, mental, or emotional condition is impaired or is in imminent danger of impairment as a result of the failure of the parent or person legally responsible (PLR) to exercise a minimum degree of care. There is no clear definition in the federal law that defines what is meant by a minimal degree of care. Parents or PLRs are expected to provide adequate food, shelter, and clothing; adequate education according to the education law; and adequate medical, dental, optometric, and surgical care. If they are unable to provide such basic necessities, they may be found neglectful. If they are unable to provide these necessities because of lack of ability to pay for them, the law, as written, will not find them neglectful, unless they are offered financial or other reasonable means to do so and they refuse the assistance. In essence, the law attempts to protect families from a finding of neglect simply for being poor. Parents are also expected to provide the child proper supervision or guardianship.

Instances of neglect may be classified as mild, moderate, or severe. Mild neglect usually does not warrant a report to CPS but might necessitate a community-based intervention (e.g., a parent failing to put the child in a car safety seat).

Moderate neglect occurs when less intrusive measures, such as community interventions, have failed or some moderate harm to the child has occurred (e.g., a child consistently is inappropriately dressed for the weather, such as being in shorts and sandals in the middle of winter in northern states). For moderate neglect, CPS may be involved in partnership with community support.

Severe neglect occurs when severe or long-term harm has been done to the child (e.g., a child with asthma has not received appropriate medications over a long period of time and is frequently admitted to the hospital). In these cases, CPS should be and is usually involved, as is the legal system.

Viewing the severity of neglect along this continuum helps practitioners assess the strengths and weaknesses of families and allows for the possibility of providing preventive services before neglect actually occurs or becomes severe. There is some controversy over whether "potential harm" should be considered neglect, and, as with the definition of neglect, state laws vary on this issue. Although it is difficult to assess potential harm as neglect, it can have emotional as well as physical consequences, such as difficulty establishing and maintaining current relationships or those later in life. The seriousness of the neglect is determined not only by how much harm or risk of harm there is to the child but also by how chronic the neglect.

## What Is Medical Neglect?

Medical neglect generally encompasses a parent or guardian's denial of or delay in seeking needed health care for a child.

Denial of health care is the failure to provide or to allow needed care as recommended by a competent health care professional for a physical injury, illness, medical condition, or impairment. The CAPTA amendments of 1996 and 2003 contained no *federal* requirement for a parent to provide any medical treatment for a child if that treatment is against the parent's religious beliefs. However, CAPTA also designates that there is no requirement that a *state* either find or be prohibited from finding abuse or neglect in cases where parents or legal guardians act in accordance with their religious beliefs. While CAPTA stipulates that all states must give authority to CPS to pursue any legal actions necessary to ensure medical care or treatment to prevent or remedy serious harm to a child or to prevent the withholding of medically indicated treatment from a child with a life-threatening condition (except in the cases of withholding treatment from disabled infants), all determinations will be done on a case-by-case basis within the sole discretion of each state.

Delay in health care is the failure to seek timely and appropriate medical care for a serious health problem that any reasonable person would have recognized as needing professional medical attention. Examples of a delay in health care include not getting appropriate preventive medical or dental care for a child, not obtaining care for a sick child, or not following medical recommendations. Not seeking adequate mental health care also falls under this category. A lack or delay in health care may occur because the family does not have health insurance. Individuals who are uninsured often have compromised health because they receive less preventive care; are diagnosed at more advanced disease stages; and, once diagnosed, receive less therapeutic care.

## Homelessness

It is unclear whether homelessness should be considered neglect; some states specifically omit homelessness by itself as neglect. Unstable living conditions can have a negative effect on children, and homeless children are more at risk for other types of neglect in areas such as health, education, and nutrition. Homelessness is "considered neglect when the inability to provide shelter is the result of mismanagement of financial resources or when spending rent resources on drugs or alcohol results in frequent evictions" (Grayson, 2001).

## Lack of Supervision

Some states specify the amount of time children at different ages can be left unsupervised, and the guidelines for these ages and times vary. In addition, all children are different, so the amount of supervision needed may vary by the child's age, development, or situation. It is important to evaluate the maturity of the child, the accessibility of other adults, the duration and frequency of unsupervised time, and the neighborhood or environment when determining if it is acceptable to leave a child unsupervised.

Another behavior that can fall under "failure to protect" is leaving a child in the care of someone who either is unable or should not be trusted to provide care for a child, such as a young child, a known child abuser, or someone with a substance abuse problem. Examples of failure to protect include situations such as the following:

- Leaving a child with an appropriate caregiver but without proper planning or consent (e.g., not returning to pick up the child for several hours or days after the agreed on pick-up time or not giving the caregiver all the necessary items to take care of the child).
- Leaving the child with a caregiver who is not adequately supervising the child (e.g., the caregiver is with the child but, because of other responsibilities or distractions, is not paying close attention to the child).
- Permitting or not keeping the child from engaging in risky, illegal, or harmful behaviors.

Another common but complex example is single, working parents who are having difficulty arranging for appropriate backup child care when the regular child care providers are unavailable. In such an instance, a parent may leave the child home alone, and the child care provider fails to show up. The job may be lost if the parent does not go to work, creating the possibility of not being able to financially care for the child. However, if the child is left alone, the parent will be guilty of neglect. It is important that parents in situations similar to this receive adequate support so that they are not forced to make these difficult decisions.

## Environmental Neglect

Some of the characteristics mentioned previously can be seen as stemming from environmental neglect, which is characterized by a lack of environmental or neighborhood safety, opportunities, or resources. While children's safety and protection from hazards are major concerns for CPS, most attention focuses on the conditions in the home and parental omissions in care. A broad view of neglect incorporates environmental conditions linking neighborhood factors with family and individual functioning, especially since the harmful impact of dangerous neighborhoods on children's development, mental health, and child maltreatment has been demonstrated. Child protective caseworkers should be aware of this impact on the family when assessing the situation and developing case plans (e.g., a caseworker can help parents find alternative play areas in a drug-infested neighborhood rather than have their children play on the streets).

## Educational Neglect

Although state statutes and policies vary, both parents and schools are responsible for meeting certain requirements regarding the education of children. Types of educational neglect include chronic truancy (e.g., permitting habitual absenteeism from school if the parent or guardian is informed of the problem and does not attempt to intervene), failure to enroll (e.g., failing to home school, register, or enroll a child of mandatory school age, causing the child to miss school without valid reasons), inattention to special education needs (e.g., refusing to allow or failing to obtain recommended remedial education services or neglecting to obtain or follow through with treatment for a child's diagnosed learning disorder or other special education need without reasonable cause).

## Parental Substance Abuse

Parental substance abuse is an element of the definition of child neglect in some states. Circumstances involving parental substance abuse that may be considered abuse or neglect include prenatal exposure of a child to harm due to the parent's use of an illegal drug or other substance; manufacture of a controlled substance in the presence of a child or on the premises occupied by a child; allowing a child to be present where the chemicals or equipment for the manufacture of controlled substances are used or stored, sold, or distributed; giving drugs or alcohol to a child; or the caretaker's use of a controlled substance that impairs the caregiver's ability to adequately care for the child.

## Newborns Addicted or Exposed to Drugs

As of 2005, 24 states had statutory provisions requiring the reporting of substance-exposed newborns to CPS. Women who use drugs or alcohol during pregnancy can put their unborn children at risk for mental and physical disabilities. The number of children prenatally exposed to drugs or alcohol each year is estimated to be between 400,000 and 850,000 (Ebrahim & Gfroerer, 2003). One study showed that drug-exposed newborns constitute as many as 72% of the babies abandoned in hospitals (U.S. Department of Health and Human Services, 1998). Another study found that 23% of children prenatally exposed to cocaine were later abused or neglected, compared with 3% who were not prenatally exposed ( Chasnoff & Lowder, 1999).

To address the needs of these children, the Keeping Children and Families Safe Act of 2003 mandated that states include the following in their CAPTA plans:

> (ii) Policies and procedures (including appropriate referrals to child protection service systems and for other appropriate services) to address the needs of infants born and identified as being affected by illegal substance abuse or withdrawal symptoms resulting from prenatal drug exposure, including a requirement that health care providers involved in the delivery or care of such infants notify the child protective services system of the occurrence of such condition of such infants, except that such notification shall not be construed to—(I) establish a definition under Federal law of what constitutes child abuse; or (II) require prosecution for any illegal action. (iii) The development of a plan of safe care for the infant born and identified as being affected by illegal substance abuse or withdrawal symptoms; (iv) procedures for the immediate screening, risk and safety assessment, and prompt investigation of such reports.

## ABANDONMENT

Abandonment is sometimes defined as the desertion of a child without arranging for his reasonable care or supervision. Usually, a child is considered abandoned when not picked up within 2 days. Many states and territories now provide definitions for child abandonment in their reporting laws. Eighteen states and the District of Columbia include abandonment in their definition of abuse or neglect. Thirteen states, Guam, Puerto

Rico, and the Virgin Islands provide separate definitions for establishing abandonment.

In general, it is considered abandonment of the child when the parent's identity or whereabouts are unknown, the child has been left by the parent in circumstances in which the child suffers serious harm, or the parent has failed to maintain contact with the child or provide reasonable support for a specified period of time (e.g., if the parent leaves a child with a neighbor and promises to return in 2 days yet does not show up, and the neighbor then notifies the authorities because she can no longer care for child).

*Expulsion* and *shuttling* are two commonly used terms relating to abandonment. Expulsion is the blatant refusal of custody, such as the permanent or indefinite expulsion of a child from the home, without adequately arranging for his care by others or the refusal to accept custody of a returned runaway. Shuttling is when a child is repeatedly left in the custody of others for days or weeks at a time, possibly due to the unwillingness of the parent or the caregiver to maintain custody.

## The Abandoned Infant Protection Act

Under the Abandoned Infant Protection Act, a federal law, a person who is unable to care for a newborn infant not more than 5 days old may anonymously and safely leave the infant in the care of a person at a hospital, police station, or fire station or with a responsible person at another safe location. This is a defense for being prosecuted for endangering the welfare of a child. It is still a mandated report. For example, if a parent gives birth and leaves the newborn with the minister of a local church, the parent would not be criminally charged with endangering welfare of child. However, the mandated reporter would still need to notify the CPS in that state.

## EXPOSURE TO DOMESTIC VIOLENCE

According to the Child Welfare Information Gateway, in recent years, increased attention has been focused on children who may be affected by violence in the home, either as victims or as witnesses to domestic violence. Research shows that even when children are not the direct targets of violence in the home, they can be harmed by witnessing its occurrence (Jaffe & Sudermann, 1995; Singer, Miller, Guo, Slovak, &

Frieson, 1998; Strauss, Murray, Gelles, & Smith, 1990; Wolfe, Wekerle, Reitzel, & Gough, 1995). The witnessing of domestic violence can be auditory, visual, or inferred, including cases in which the child witnesses the aftermath of violence, such as physical injuries to family members or damage to personal property. Children who witness domestic violence can suffer severe emotional and developmental difficulties similar to those of children who are direct victims of abuse. The legal system is beginning to recognize the need to protect and care for these children. Approximately 21 states and Puerto Rico currently address in statute the issue of children who witness domestic violence in their homes.

A child is a witness to domestic violence when an act that is defined as domestic violence is committed in the presence of or witnessed by the child. In five states, the definition goes no further than that. In 14 states and Puerto Rico, the language used is more specific, stating that witnessing by a child occurs when the child is physically present or can see or hear the act of violence. Ohio law states that witnessing occurs when the domestic violence is committed "in the vicinity of the child," meaning within 30 feet or within the same residential unit occupied by the child, regardless of whether the child is actually present or can actually see the commission of the offense. In 10 states, the laws apply to any child who may be present or a witness to the act of domestic violence. In 10 states and Puerto Rico, the laws apply specifically to a child who is related to or is a member of the household of the victim or perpetrator of the violence. The law in Indiana applies only to the noncustodial child of a noncustodial parent.

## MUNCHAUSEN SYNDROME BY PROXY

First described in 1977, Munchausen syndrome by proxy (MBP) is a mental disorder in which a parent or guardian falsifies symptoms of physical or psychiatric illness in a child in their care to obtain medical attention. Also called Munchausen by proxy syndrome and factitious disorder by proxy, MBP is a label for a pattern of behavior in which caretakers deliberately exaggerate, fabricate, and/or induce physical and/or psychological-behavioral-mental health problems in others. This pattern of behavior constitutes a separate kind of maltreatment (abuse/neglect) that manifests as physical abuse, sexual abuse, emotional abuse, neglect, or a combination. The primary purpose of this behavior is to gain some form of internal gratification, such as attention, for the perpetrator.

## CONCLUSION

Although the precise definitions of terms relevant to the reporting of child abuse and neglect may vary depending on the state in which you live and/or practice, it is important for social workers to have a general understanding of significant terms. With a basic understanding of these important terms, it is easier for the social worker to navigate responsibilities as a mandated reporter of child abuse and neglect.

## REFERENCES

Child Abuse and Prevention Treatment Act, 42 U.S.C.A. sec. 5106 g(2) (1974).

Child Abuse and Prevention Treatment Act, 42 U.S.C.A. sec. 5106 g(4) (1974).

Chasnoff, I. J., & Lowder, L. A. (1999). Prenatal AOD use and risk for maltreatment: A timely approach for intervention. In H. Dubowitz (Ed.), *Neglected children: Research, practice, and policy* (pp. 132–155). Thousand Oaks, CA: Sage.

Child Welfare Information Gateway. (2007). *Definition of child abuse and neglect: Summary of state laws.* Washington, DC: U.S. Department of Health and Human Services, Administration on Children, Youth and Families.

Ebrahim, S., & Gfroerer, J. (2003). Pregnancy-related substance use in the United States during 1996–1998. *Obstetrics and Gynecology, 101*(2), 374–379.

English, D., Graham, J. C., Brummel, S. C., Coghlan, L. K., & Clark, T. (2002). *Factors that influence the decision not to substantiate a CPS referral. Phase II: Mail and telephone surveys of child protective services social workers.* Olympia, WA: Department of Social and Health Services, Children's Administration, Management Services Division, Office of Children's Administration Research.

Grayson, J., & DePanfilis, D. (1999). How do I determine if a child has been neglected? In H. Dubowitz & D. DePanfilis (Eds.), *Handbook for child protection practice* (pp. 121–126). Thousand Oaks, CA: Sage.

Jaffe, P., & Sudermann, M. (1995). Child witness of women abuse: Research and community responses. In S. Stith & M. Straus (Eds.), *Understanding partner violence: Prevalence, causes, consequences, and solutions. Families in focus services, Vol. II.* Minneapolis, MN: National Council on Family Relations.

Kairys, S. W. (2002). The psychological maltreatment of children—Technical report. *Pediatrics, 109*(4).

Keeping Children and Families Safe Act, P. L. 108-36, sec. 114(b)(1)(B) (2003).

Korfmacher, J. (1998). *Emotional neglect: Being hurt by what is not there.* Chicago: National Committee to Prevent Child Abuse.

Rich, D. J., Gingerich, K. J., & Rosen, L. A. (1997). Childhood emotional abuse and associated psychopathology in college students. *Journal of College Student Psychotherapy, 11*(3), 13–28.

Sanders, B., & Becker-Lausen, E. (1995). The measurement of psychological maltreatment: Early data on the child abuse and trauma scale. *Child Abuse and Neglect, 19*(3), 315–323.

Singer, M. I., Miller, D. B., Guo, S., Slovak, K., & Frieson, T. (1998). *The mental health consequences of children's exposure to violence*. Cleveland, OH: Cuyahoga County Community Health Research Institute, Mandel School of Applied Social Sciences, Case Western Reserve University.

Spertus, I. L., Yehuda, R., Wong, C. M., Halligan, S., & Seremetis, S. V. (2003). Childhood emotional abuse and neglect as predictors of psychological and physical symptoms in women presenting to a primary care practice. *Child Abuse and Neglect, 27*(11), 1247–1258.

Strauss, M. A., Gelles, R. J., & Smith, C. (1990). *Physical violence in American families: Risk factors and adaptations to violence in 8, 145 families*. New Brunswick, NJ: Transaction Publishers.

Teicher, M. D. (2000). Wounds that time won't heal: The neurobiology of child abuse. *Cerebrum: The Dana Forum on Brain Science, 2*(4), 50–67.

U.S. Department of Health and Human Services. (1998). *1998 national estimates of the number of boarder babies, abandoned infants and discarded infants*. Washington DC: U.S. Government Printing Office.

Wolfe, D. A., Wekerle, C., Reitzel, D., & Gough, R. (1995). Strategies to address violence in the lives of high risk youth. In E. Peled, P. G. Jaffe, & J. L. Edleson, (Eds.), *Ending the cycle of violence: Community responses to children of battered women*. New York: Sage Publications.

## ADDITIONAL READING

Graham-Bermann, S., & Seng, J. (2005). Violence exposure and traumatic stress symptoms as additional predictors of health problems in high-risk children. *Journal of Pediatrics, 146*(3), 309–310.

Spilsbury, J. C., Kahana, S., Drotar, D., Creeden, R., Flannery, D. J., & Friedman, S. (2008). Profiles of behavioral problems in children who witness domestic violence. *Violence and Victims, 23*(1), 3–17.

# 4  Risk Factors: The Potential for Child Abuse or Neglect

Social workers are employed in such a wide variety of settings that they will inevitably encounter situations in which the potential for child abuse or neglect exists even where there is no identifiable reason to suspect that it has yet actually occurred. State hotlines are set up to receive reports where there is reasonable cause to suspect that child abuse or maltreatment has occurred or that there is reason to believe that a child is at imminent risk of harm. However, there is no method of reporting the *potential* for abuse or maltreatment. For this reason, it is important that social workers keep in mind the risk factors associated with child abuse and neglect as well as a strategy to help caretakers avoid neglectful or abusive behavior.

First, a word of caution about "risk factors." Risk factors are variables that research has discovered frequently (but not *always*) precede or accompany actual child abuse or neglect. They are not causes, so it is important to understand that the discovery of risk factors in a family does not alone validate the existence of child abuse or neglect. Researchers develop risk factors retrospectively by listing the descriptors that most often coexist with a particular variable. For example, research shows that alcoholic parents are more likely to have alcoholic children than are nonalcoholic parents. However, many alcoholics do not have an alcoholic parent, and many people with an alcoholic parent never become alcoholics. So, statistically, having a parent who is an alcoholic places one at greater risk of being an alcoholic than a person who does not, but it does not assure that one will be an alcoholic.

Therefore, when we examine the risk factors for child abuse and neglect, remember that finding any such factor in a person's life does *not* guarantee that child abuse has occurred or that it eventually will occur. The existence of a risk factor only means that research has indicated that a significant portion of those who have abused a child also exhibited the characteristics in question. It is a matter of scientific principle that the identified characteristic cannot be said to cause the abuse.

Most social workers who come to discover one risk factor in a client or client's family will often discover others as well. It is intuitive to conclude that multiple risk factors increase the risk of abuse or neglect, and there is possibly some validity to this presumption. In a large number of cases of neglect and abuse, several identified risk factors existed. Nevertheless, it may not automatically be concluded that once a certain threshold for number of risk factors is reached, child abuse or neglect *must* be occurring. Instead, knowledge of risk factors should help social workers tune their professional senses and offer services appropriate to the family's circumstances. Such an action may, in itself, prevent a situation from becoming abusive or neglectful.

It is essential that risk factors not be confused with reasonable suspicion. "Reasonable suspicion" is exactly that—a preliminary conclusion based on doubt that is not far-fetched or biased and that the social worker concludes, based on a combination of training, professional judgment, and experience, is not readily refuted by an alternate explanation. The discovery of risk factors of abuse or neglect by themselves should not be confused with reasonable suspicion.

There is a natural risk that statistics are accepted as proof simply because they are statistics. Research data gathered about child abuse and neglect, like that resulting from any other social phenomenon, is highly structured and filtered according to the biases of researchers and the theories they are attempting to prove. In addition, even allowing for skew based on biases, we can only know about what has been studied, not about the part of the population that is not included in the study. The only absolute about data concerning child abuse and neglect is that there is no absolute data available. All statistics should be reviewed with some healthy scientific skepticism.

Finally, social workers should not only evaluate risk factors but also the particular *strengths* a client or family possesses. For example, both poverty and pregnancy early in the life span are risk factors for child abuse or neglect. However, a young mother from a poor family with an infant may, on closer examination, be found to have strong social supports or a high level of resiliency. The discovery of such strengths is worthy of support and may mitigate the risk factors to a certain extent.

Some other risk factors, however, such as substance abuse or domestic violence, certainly call for a service needs assessment and close monitoring—even though they may not be clear cause to suspect child abuse or neglect. Often, risk factors serve as access points or portals to the acceptance of services by parents.

## ENVIRONMENTAL RISK FACTORS

### Poverty

While research shows that child abuse and neglect exists across all socioeconomic levels, children in poverty are disproportionately abused and neglected (Slack, Holl, McDaniel, Yoo, & Bolger, 2004). This is due in part to the fact that poor and disadvantaged populations are both more likely to come to the attention of mandated reporters and, therefore, are more likely to be reported to hotlines as a result of this attention. However, other factors associated with poverty may contribute to this disproportion. These factors include overcrowded living conditions, large sibling groups, substandard housing, exposure to violence and crime in substandard neighborhoods, lack of education and life skills, cultural isolation, inadequate medical care, unstable relationships, underdeveloped language skills, drug or alcohol dependency, malnourishment, unemployment or underemployment, and mental or emotional difficulties (depression, anger, anxiety). Indeed, while not every poor family will necessarily experience all these circumstances, poverty as a stressful condition might result in the family being identified with more risk factors that will be considered individually in this chapter.

## PARENT/CARETAKER RISK FACTORS

### Intimate Partner Violence

The existence of domestic violence is another risk factor for child abuse and neglect (Herrenkohl, Sousa, Tajima, Herrenkohl, & Moylan, 2008). Research shows that where domestic violence exists in a household with children, there is an increase in risk of child abuse and neglect. "Domestic violence" describes a relationship between intimate partners in which physical violence, sexual violence, manipulation, intimidation, and/or other coercive methods are employed.

Researchers are increasingly aware that there are numerous patterns in violent relationships. The traditional pattern involves one partner controlling and abusing the other. However, more recent research has found that bidirectional violence (where both partners are violent) is most common. Violence may be asymmetrical, where both partners are violent, but one partner is more violent than the other.

In the context of child abuse and neglect, we need to consider situations ranging from couples who are quick to resort to shouting, shoving, and hitting when disputes arise to more serious situations where violence is used to maintain control and power in the relationship.

Violence may be frequent, infrequent, or only occur once. Episodes of violence may come and go; in between these events, the couple might appear to function. For many reasons, ranging from intimidation to pride to denial, the problem may not be recognized by any of the family members. In many cases, the victim will exert much energy to hide the problem even after its existence is clear.

Introducing a child or even a pregnancy into this scenario will not likely improve it. In fact, the pregnancy may make the situation worse. For the abuser, pregnancy can be a way of placing the victim in a more compromised and dependent position—one in which her need of his presence is more pronounced and her willingness or ability to leave is diminished. For the victim, the pregnancy may be thought of, at least partially, as a method of appeasing the abuser as well as a form of protection against the abuse.

On the other hand, pregnancy may have the opposite effect. If the abuser does not welcome the pregnancy, he may see it as further indication of his partner's incompetence or defiance. Sometimes, the pregnancy (or, eventually, the child) will be used as grounds to accuse the victim of infidelity.

The eventual arrival of a child is likely to increase the abuser's need to control rather than reduce it. The new individual in the family sometimes presents an expansion of the territory that the abuser must now control, and this challenge may be met by escalating methods of enforcement. At the same time, the presence of the child complicates the victim's choices. She may feel more reluctant to leave him now than before the child arrived, yet now she must not only try to protect herself but the child as well.

The mother's least suggestion that priority be extended to the needs of the infant—the need for a layette, for quiet, for time to rest, for separate space, for propinquity, for toys, for food—may be experienced by the abuser not as the ordinary needs of an infant but as the mother's way to challenge his ability or willingness to provide them. These needs may be denied or thwarted by the abuser, with harm resulting to the infant.

Child abuse professionals and domestic violence advocates have historically found themselves in opposing camps, and only in the past few years have there been efforts on both their parts to work cooperatively. Early in the age of mandated reporting (beginning in the early to mid-1970s), child abuse authorities made little connection between domestic violence, or partner abuse, and child endangerment, usually getting involved only where overt violence between parents actually injured or threatened injury to children who were present. Domestic violence workers, on the other hand, hardly considered child protective services (CPS) to be a resource for their clients. In their view, the domestic violence victim was placed in an impossible position and was victimized again by the system when she was named, along with the perpetrator, as a neglectful or abusive parent on the assumption that she was indifferent to her children's need for protection from the perpetrator.

When child abuse authorities began to take more notice of domestic violence in the 1980s and early 1990s, their approach emphasized the responsibility of the victim parent (usually the mother) to protect the children in the family from the violence of the abusing parent. Sadly, this policy was insensitive to the plight of the adult victim. Domestic violence specialists and others in the community believed it only further victimized the victim, and, worse, painted her as passive and insensitive to the needs of her children.

For the past few years, CPS and domestic violence service providers, even though they may not always see this problem in entirely the same way, have begun to develop working partnerships. CPS has recognized that a child's mere presence in a family marked by frequent violence presents risks even when the child is not the direct victim of violence. CPS investigators in many jurisdictions have access to a domestic violence specialist for consultation and sometimes for joint home visits to clients in the midst of a violent relationship.

## Substance Abuse

Parental use of drugs or alcohol is yet another risk factor for child abuse and neglect (Ammerman, Kolko, Kirisci, Blackson, & Dawes, 1999). Most states require that the substance abuse interferes with the ability to meet the minimal requirements of parenting before a child abuse or neglect report can be indicated. It can be easy to infuse substance abuse behavior with legal and moral issues. It should be kept in mind that it is not the role of child abuse authorities to address the legality of drug use or whether it violates social norms. Instead, the role of CPS is to determine if the substance-using behavior is preventing the parent or caretaker from recognizing or meeting the child's needs for food, shelter, clothing, supervision, medical care, mental health services, and protection.

The potential risks presented to the child in cases where a parent or parents are using drugs or alcohol are many—often less obvious than might be assumed. They extend beyond the possibility that the parents are so intoxicated that they neglect their children's everyday needs. Children in this scenario often have to fend for themselves—eating what they can manage to scrape together, barely attending school, spending their time sleeping or watching television, and indulging in unsupervised activities.

Beyond this lack of supervision and guidance, parents who use alcohol and other intoxicating substances also place their children at risk of automobile accidents, fires due to carelessness, and other household accidents.

Not surprisingly, parents whose lives are consumed with drugs may drift into a life that is surrounded by a drug culture. Drugs may be ever present in the child's environment, available for either accidental or experimental ingestion. The parents may become involved in dealing drugs, thereby inevitably exposing their children to both addicted individuals who enter the household to complete transactions and to the possibility of persons arriving in the household intent on stealing the drugs or the drug proceeds. Indeed, drug-dealing parents may arm themselves against such an event, now exposing their children to the obvious risks presented by the presence of firearms in the home. Other ancillary environmental risks that may develop include the risks attendant to manufacturing some drugs (e.g., methamphetamine) as well as associated antisocial behaviors, including prostitution, shoplifting, robbery, and the like.

## Parent/Caretaker History of Abuse or Neglect as a Child

A high percentage of parents who abuse or neglect their children were themselves abused or neglected as children, often in ways quite similar to the ways they neglect or abuse their own children (World Health

Organization, 2002). Research does not provide reliable statistics to describe this phenomenon, but a considerable proportion of parents reported to child abuse hotlines were abused or neglected by their own parents. This should not be surprising. From the beginning of history, the family has been the main conduit for the transmission of culture from one generation to the next. Just as we typically mold many of our religious practices, political views, traditions, and language from our parents, we also imitate their methods of disciplining children. What is surprising is that in many such cases, parents recognize the inappropriateness of the punishments used by their own parents and sometimes vow not to perpetuate their use with their own children yet do so anyway. It is wise to pay close attention when a parent tells you, "I would never do that to my child—it was done to me, and I hated it." Indeed, the majority of parents who were abused or neglected as children have successfully avoided treating their own children in the same way they were treated. It should also be kept in mind that parents who were neglected or abused as children may take the opposite approach by providing little structure and few boundaries in the family rather than to replicate their own experience as a child.

## Adolescent Parents

Child abuse or neglect is more of a risk when the parent is extremely young (World Health Organization, 2002). It is, by now, a cliché: Adolescent parents are "kids who have kids." Adolescence is, by definition, a time in the life span when the person has not yet attained emotional, psychological, or social independence. It is a time, therefore, where one is expected to experiment with various roles, make errors, change direction and, above all, is not expected to commit. Neither pregnancy nor parenting fits this picture well.

Adolescents who become pregnant are far less likely to reside with their partner before pregnancy or plan for the pregnancy. This in itself is not necessarily a risk factor for abuse or neglect. However, adolescent mothers, especially those who do not have the emotional and material support of their parents, may be poorly prepared to take on the responsibilities involved. Adolescent mothers are often so preoccupied with their own needs that it is difficult for them, even when they are well intentioned, to place the infant's needs above their own.

The adolescent mother is also less likely to have the education that an older mother would have. This places the mother at direct disadvantage in terms of lack of information about infants and their needs—on both a physical and social level—as well as at a reduced ability to be employed. Of course, having the child may prevent or hinder the mother's ability to complete an education.

Research in this area reveals other common assumptions on the part of the pregnant adolescent. Many adolescents mistakenly believe their new role as parent will help them escape situations that are, at least at the moment, subjectively unendurable: a violent or unhappy family, overly strict parents, the pressures of adolescence, or school. Many adolescents recognize that their parents have done a less than enviable job raising them and believe that this will be their opportunity to correct the mistakes their parents have made.

An even worse scenario is one in which the adolescent believes, perhaps only vaguely, that the infant will somehow provide the love, recognition, and appreciation that she never received from her own parents, partner, or teachers. This may be only the first in a long list of unrealistic expectations that the mother will invest in the child. Of course, when the baby arrives, it is quite incapable of providing anything and will not be so equipped for some time to come. So, quite the opposite is true— the baby needs constant, recurring, seemingly unending attention and is quite thankless. One of the aspects of adolescence that is so maddening is the sense that time moves very slowly, so the mother, especially if alone, may soon feel that she is hopelessly and eternally trapped in her parenting role. The baby may be resented and even hated. The mother may feel exponentially less fulfilled than she was during her pregnancy. She is at high risk of becoming depressed. She may constantly leave the infant in the care of others, some of whom may not be appropriate caretakers, increasing the likelihood of stress and contention in her relationships as well as increasing the potential for social isolation and reduced self-esteem. She may ignore the baby or even lash out at it physically. The infant may be deprived of sensory stimuli and proper nourishment—two vitally important factors required for neurologic development.

Just plain lack of experience and good information about parenting can also contribute to unrealistic expectations about the baby's behavior, abilities, and rate of development. She may be disappointed when the child does not speak after a few months. She may have inaccurate ideas about when a child can be reasonably expected to smile, crawl, walk, and become toilet trained. The latter is a particularly important risk factor itself—parents of any age can find themselves enraged when confronted with an excrement-smeared crib or wall or even a dirty diaper. Children in the midst of toilet training are at great risk for being handled roughly, slapped, shaken, or scalded. This risk is greatly increased when the child is being handled by a parent who due to immaturity never thought through what this experience would be like or, worse, on some emotional level regards it as a sign of disrespect or lack of self-discipline on the part of the child.

Adolescent or immature fathers need mention here as well. Many young males are extremely frustrated by the demands of an infant and are less able to cope than more mature fathers with the competition for mother's attention that the infant represents. Not only are the toileting needs of the infant difficult for the young male, so is the infant's crying. Infants under a year old are at particular risk of being shaken in response to these events, with disastrous consequences (death, permanent brain damage, blindness). These acts are more often committed by young parents, especially young men. Many are not the baby's biologic fathers—a factor that may predispose them to such an episode.

## Parental Mental Illness

Behaving as a neglectful or abusive parent is not a psychiatric condition or diagnosis. Nor is there a specific psychiatric diagnosis that is consistently associated with the abusive or neglectful parent. However, a larger percentage of parents who are abusive or neglectful are more likely to display some psychiatric problems than the general population. It can be difficult to establish the direction of causality, though, when the many other risk factors for abuse and neglect are taken into account.

For example, many abusive or neglectful parents suffer from some level of depression. But this is hardly surprising when it is realized that many of the other identified risk factors, such as poverty, substance abuse, domestic violence, family crises, and lack of education, are also consistently associated with depression.

Some of the other problems that are often found concurrent with child abuse or neglect are parental low self-esteem (in fact, many adolescent parents—a large risk factor—appear to become pregnant in large part to compensate for a lack of self-esteem), excessive dependency, poor impulse control, and inadequate coping skills. Intellectual deficits are also commonly found among many parents who are identified as abusive or neglectful. Again, this should not be surprising considering that most low IQ scores in the United States are not caused by organic difficulties but by social deprivation.

## Situational Stresses and Family Crises

When a crisis strikes a family, the risk of child abuse or neglect increases considerably, even if there was low risk prior to the crisis (World Health Organization, 2002). Events that could fit this description are numerous: unemployment, serious illness or disability (of either a child or a parent), death of a family member (particularly a suicide or homicide), fire, or a serious natural disaster. Some more typical and predictable family "crises" that have become so familiar that we may not always think of them as "crises" include divorce, remarriage, pregnancy, or a military family member being posted to a war zone. Some crises may be "invisible," meaning that they are a family secret that may not be obvious to an outsider: a family member has an abortion, is the victim of a crime, gets arrested, becomes the respondent in a legal action, or gets discovered in a marital infidelity. Ordinary events such as members leaving or entering the family increase risk, no matter how welcome these events may be otherwise.

When the events occur, the coping ability of all family members is challenged. Parents may become considerably distracted from their parenting roles, leaving children in the family with less attention than they are accustomed. Sometimes, crises may have the opposite effect: They cause the parents to invest more attention in their children than they had before. In either case, the family's equilibrium is disturbed. Children's behavior may change, or they may become depressed or anxious. Their school attendance or academic performance may suffer. Sibling relationships may change. Children may increase their competition for parental attention as they feel their parents' energy being redirected. They may withdraw or become aggressive. They may suddenly choose a social group that is unacceptable to their parents. They may experience a shift in identity that escapes the parents' attention until the crisis as abated and which, when noticed by the parent, is unwelcome and perhaps difficult to deal with or define.

To make matters worse, when the crisis unfavorably alters a child's behavior, some parents may see the child using the crisis to "get what she wants" or to "get back at me." They may feel betrayed and use punishment as retaliation instead of discipline.

Social workers who are working with families in crisis need to pay careful attention to the heightened risk of child abuse or neglect.

## CHILD SEXUAL ABUSE RISK FACTORS

Any discussion of sexual abuse risk factors needs to be preceded by an acknowledgement of some of the difficulties encountered when these suspicions arise in the mind of the mandated reporter. First, it is entirely normal for those who begin to suspect that a child is the victim of sexual abuse to want to be quite sure of their suspicions before making a CPS report. This is a very serious charge, and potential reporters fear the embarrassment they will experience if they are wrong, the pain that will be caused for both the victim and the incorrectly alleged perpetrator, and the disruption that will likely be caused in the family. Many persons who contemplate reporting their concerns confess reluctance to report without clear evidence or an outright accusation for the above reasons and also because they fear perhaps their suspicions indicate that they have a "dirty mind" or that their suspicions will be so regarded by others. Many nonprofessional persons familiar with situations where the relationship between the perpetrator and the child seem "not quite right" have secretly harbored such hunches for years due to these sorts of concerns, only to be horrified when they learn that sexual abuse was eventually exposed when someone else made the report.

The risk factors described here are *not* proof that sexual abuse is occurring or even, in most cases, sufficient cause in and of themselves to regard suspicions as "reasonable." The reader is reminded that these risk factors have been developed retrospectively through exhaustive research applied to those who have been through the experience, either as victims, perpetrators, or other family members, particularly mothers of victims. The presence of these descriptors should increase vigilance. Children often say things, act things out, or display signs that may not be thought of as reasonable cause to suspect sexual abuse by themselves. But in the presence of other factors described in the Findelhor Precondition Model the statements or behavior may be seen as more reasonably suspicious and, therefore, are reportable.

A further note is inserted here but pursued in more detail in chapter 5: There are also a number of common errors that those who suspect child sexual abuse often commit as they make, or set out to make, the report to a child abuse hotline. Some of these might be looked on as relatively unimportant in lesser cases of child abuse or neglect, but in a case of sexual abuse, they can lead to severe complications.

## Research on Child Sexual Abuse

In the past generation, several researchers in the area of child abuse have developed ideas that have had an enormous influence in the field of incest sexual abuse, which was largely a marginalized cultural secret before the mid-1970s.

Suzanne Sgroi (1979), a pediatrician, wrote *A Handbook of Clinical Intervention in Child Sexual Abuse* in 1979. This important and ground-breaking book made several urgent points to professionals involved in the field. First, Sgroi emphasized that in most cases of familial child sexual abuse, the abuse was not confined to single event but may have occurred over a period of many years guided by a perpetrator (usually a male) who carefully and gradually crafted a sexual relationship with a child under his control (usually a female), while being extremely careful to maintain the child's silence and having ready a credible explanation for his behavior in the event he would be exposed.

Second, Sgroi pointed out that in such cases, there often was scant or nonexistent evidence that the abuse had occurred, even when it had been going on for years, because the victim often was not vaginally penetrated, and there was no torn clothing, semen specimens, or eyewitnesses. Therefore, Sgroi urged those involved after claims of sexual abuse arose not to dismiss the claim due to a lack of physical evidence.

Third, Sgroi taught those who come into contact with the potential victims how to recognize signs and warned them that disclosure could be either purposeful or accidental at *any* point during this long cycle. However, in either circumstance, disclosure was often overlooked because the possibility of sexual contact by the perpetrator seemed inherently implausible due to the child's age, the perpetrator's standing, the lack of evidence, the outlandishness of the idea that one would initiate sexual activity with a young child who is a member of their own family, and so on.

## Research on Child Sexual Abuse Perpetrators

Nicholas Groth (1979) conducted much research on the psychological makeup of perpetrators and in the 1980s generated what subsequently became a controversial theory. He proposed that most perpetrators of sexual activity between themselves and children could be divided into two basic categories: the pedophile, or "fixated" or "preferential" offender, and the incest, or "regressed" or "situational" offender.

At the time, there was a widespread tendency on the part of case-workers, police, prosecutors and even psychotherapists to classify incest child abuse perpetrators as pedophiles. Pedophilia is a specific diagnostic category in the American Psychiatric Association's *Diagnostic and Statistical Manual of Mental Disorders* (*DSM*). It is placed in the category of "paraphilias," a group of disorders in which the patient suffers from recurring sexual urges and fantasies involving sexual arousal in response to nonhuman objects or nonconsenting human victims, often to the exclusion of normal sexual arousal. A few other disorders in this category include voyeurism, fetishism, exhibitionism, and sexual sadism.

Groth asserted that his research supported the idea that "fixated" and "regressed" perpetrators were usually categorically different in terms of their motives, their behavior, and their choice of victim. To begin with, he noted, the fixated perpetrator is often very childlike himself. He has difficulty establishing adult relationships and is often more at ease when relating to children. He often works at jobs and serves as a volunteer in a field that places him in frequent contact with children. On the other hand, the regressed perpetrator more often is able to function in adult relationships and is often married. While the fixated perpetrator is sexually aroused by prepubescent children, often of a specific gender and age, the regressed perpetrator is primarily sexually aroused by adults but can be aroused by an opportunity to relate sexually to a child, especially if his life situation is frustrating.

The specific behaviors of each are born of different psychological motivations. A somewhat oversimplified description is that the fixated perpetrator becomes a child by indulging in childish sexual activities with children, usually outside of his own family, because he has no taste for ongoing, adultlike relationships, preferring those that can be easily jettisoned. Sexual contact is usually limited to a small number of occasions with many victims and may involve no more than genital exposure, fondling, or masturbation. The fixated perpetrator is likely to reject his victims as they approach puberty and is sometimes repulsed by them once they have reached it.

On the other hand, the regressed perpetrator attempts to transform a child into an adult. Incest victims are often told by the perpetrator how "big" they are or how "pretty and grown up" they are becoming. They may become interested in their victims for their adultlike physical characteristics or are first sexually aroused when they notice their physical development. Incest victims have often been found to be so-called adultified children, performing household chores, caring for younger siblings while the mother works and waiting on the father or stepfather. While the regressed perpetrator may initiate sexual contact with the child prior to the child reaching puberty, sexual intercourse, if it occurs, is most often postponed to the advent of puberty or later. As the child reaches puberty, the perpetrator may become very possessive over the child, developing feelings of jealousy about her that one would more likely expect to find in an adult relationship. This relationship, barring disclosure or discovery, is long term, and while the perpetrator may turn to other children in the family, especially if his chosen victim learns to resist him, rarely will he stray beyond the immediate family to seek a sexual relationship with a child.

Groth termed the pedophile a *fixated offender,* meaning that he had never really developed past childhood in terms of his personality or social abilities. He is emotionally dependent and frightened. However, his sexual desires are powerful, often extremely difficult to control, and may be extremely difficult to successfully treat. While he may feel guilty about his behavior, the compulsion is extremely overwhelming, and he may find it extremely difficult to control himself when he experiences sexual urges. These perpetrators often have high rates of recidivism.

Incest offenders are described by Groth as "regressed" or "situational." This is a somewhat complex idea but in its simplest form means that the incest perpetrator prefers adult relationships. However, he experiences frustration when he is not in control of the relationship. The main attraction in the child is, beyond the simple fact of her availability, not so much her lack of physical development as it is her lack of sophistication: She admires and obeys him, and she complies with his sexual attentions without imposing on the relationship any of her own wishes or expectations. The incest perpetrator is more likely to exhibit shame than guilt and, at least theoretically, may be more responsive to treatment.

Since Groth's work first appeared in the 1970s, it has served as the basis for a large number of modifications. While it was an important new way to conceptualize child sexual abuse, it has also been widely seen as too simple. One movement that that has evolved within the law enforcement community (Lanning, 2001) prefers to view perpetrators as either "situational" or "preferential." While situational abusers are much like regressed offenders, more emphasis is placed on the availability of targets rather than regressive coping. It is pointed out that they often sexually molest other opportune targets besides children (hospital patients, inmates, the elderly). They become involved because their victims are available and vulnerable. Preferential perpetrators, like Groth's fixated pedophiles, are exclusively attracted to children and have specific individual preferences in terms of age, gender, and physical appearance. These perpetrators do not wait for an opportunity to abuse; they create their own opportunity. Others theorists have grouped perpetrators as "morally indiscriminate" (deeply antisocial human beings who abuse everyone in their lives by lying, cheating, stealing, sexually exploiting, etc.), "sexually indiscriminate" (willing to try anything sexual with anyone who is willing), and "inadequate" (suffering from serious psychological or psychiatric problems).

## The Four Preconditions Model

David Finkelhor (1984), currently a professor at the University of New Hampshire, may be the most recognized and influential theorist in the area of child sexual abuse. He has spent many years researching this phenomenon by interviewing both victims and perpetrators. He has written extensively about the problem, but his landmark work is *Child Sexual Abuse: New Theory and Research,* published in 1984. Not satisfied with Groth's dichotomous view of the offender, Finkelhor developed a broad model that he felt better accounted for the wide variety of types of child sexual abuse perpetrators that he called the Four Preconditions Model. In explaining this model, Finkelhor, more clearly than any other expert in this field, identified a list of eight risk factors that correlate highly with sexual victimization in childhood. Perhaps equally important, he established that these are cumulative, meaning that as more risk factors can be listed within a family, the likelihood of there being a sexual abuse victim in the family increases. Finkelhor's risk factors include the following:

1. Having a stepfather.
2. Living without a mother in the household for an extended period of time.
3. Having an emotionally distant relationship with one's mother.
4. Having a mother who did not finish high school, especially if the father did.
5. Having a mother with punitive attitudes toward the daughter's sexual curiosity.
6. Having a father who is not physically affectionate.
7. Living in a low-income family.
8. Having two or fewer friends in childhood.

It is important to clarify and expand these risk factors somewhat and to realize that it is not always clear *why* these factors increase a child's risk of being the victim of sexual abuse.

*Having a stepfather.* Finkelhor's research indicated that girls who spend time in a family in which there is a stepfather (or paramour of the mother) were more likely to have been sexually abused as children. Part of the reason for this is that, as one might suspect, stepfathers are less restrained in making sexual or quasi-sexual approaches to their stepdaughters. But Finkelhor found that this, in and of itself, did not entirely account for this risk factor. For reasons not clearly understood, girls who live for an extended period of time with stepfathers are more likely to be sexually abused not only by their stepfathers but also by a variety of adult males.

*Living without a mother in the household for an extended period of time.* This may not be surprising when it is considered that it relates to two of the other risk factors on Finkelhor's list (emotionally distant relationship with one's mother and having a mother with punitive attitudes toward the daughter's sexual curiosity). Indeed, isolation from one's mother appears in many subtle ways to leave the child vulnerable and without defenses. When the mother is absent for a long period of time, depending on who else is in the household, there is clearly no check on the formation of an overly intimate relationship between the child and the father.

*Having an emotionally distant relationship with one's mother.* As mentioned in the last paragraph, having a mother who is emotionally distant isolates the child from a person who might otherwise serve to counter the child's vulnerability. It also needs to be considered that it is not unusual for a perpetrator to foment poor mother–daughter relations. This is achieved through subtle manipulations: by misrepresenting the mother's wishes when punishing the child, by presenting himself as the child's defender and champion when the mother wishes to deny her a privilege or a treat, by secretly soothing her when she and her mother have an argument, by making it appear that the mother favors other children in the family over her, by reporting to the child any critical comment the mother has made and never reporting a compliment, and so on.

*Having a mother who did not finish high school, especially if the father did.* The greater the difference between the parents' education where the father has more education than the mother, the higher the risk of sexual abuse. The reason for this is not clear, but it appears to be related to a power imbalance in the family. In many families where there is sexual abuse, the father is the more controlling person in the household (see Trepper, 1986, for a different point of view on this).

*Having a mother with punitive attitudes toward the daughter's sexual curiosity.* As mentioned above, this risk factor is not especially surprising since it is yet one more form of the daughter suffering isolation from the person who could more likely than anyone in the family serve as a foil to her abuse. There are several apparent reasons for this. First, a mother who displays a condemning attitude about sex will probably decrease the daughter's willingness to ask her for information about sex or to confide in her any doubts she may have about having received "bad touches" from an offender. Another possible scenario in this circumstance is that the offender may successfully appeal to the child that her mother does not like sex and that his seeking it from the daughter instead of from someone outside the family is acceptable, thus contributing to her belief that her victimization is "keeping the family together."

*Having a father who is not physically affectionate.* This is a risk factor that surprises some people. Many conceptualize incest sexual abuse as "affection that got out of control." However, with some thought, this situation can be seen differently. Fathers who are comfortable with appropriate physical affection with their daughters automatically teach their daughters, by example, the limits of touching. A girl who has experienced appropriate physical affection from her father from a young age is not as easily confused about the boundaries between normal and sexual touching by the time she has reached the age of 6 to 8 years. She may be shocked at the least attempt by any male to push this boundary and feel confident in her rejection and reporting of it to a trusted adult. A girl who is not accustomed to male affection may be more vulnerable to the offender implying or saying that "all little girls do this with their daddies."

*Living in a low-income family.* Here, we find once again the correlation between poverty and child abuse. In the instance of sexual abuse, the precise reasons for the correlation are unclear. In many such families, perhaps children have not learned to expect inhibitions from the adults in the family. Also, the overall educational level may be quite lower than in middle-class families, or the child may spend so much less time in school that there is less exposure to peers and school personnel whom he or she might come to trust and confide in.

*Having two or fewer friends in childhood.* This is, of course, one more form of isolation. Being isolated from other human beings is the most common, if most general, risk factor for all forms of child abuse and neglect. People, including children, who do not have regular human contact tend to keep to themselves and feel that they need to solve their problems on their own (this presupposes that they even recognize their problems, since we often only come to realize that something about our lives is "abnormal" when we discover that we know of no one else in our circumstances).

## CHILD RISK FACTORS

### Children With Disabilities

Children with disabilities are at a higher risk of abuse or neglect by not only their parents and guardians but also by other caretakers. In many ways, disabled children are at risk of abuse and neglect for the same reasons as younger children (under age 3 years): They are more isolated, they may have limited communications skills, and they may not understand that they are victims.

In a 1991 incident study, Westat, Inc., using the definition of disabilities provided in the Americans with Disabilities Act, concluded that disabled children were 1.7 times more likely to be maltreated than children without disabilities. Disabilities included mental retardation, hearing problems, vision problems, speech impairments, serious emotional disturbances, orthopedic impairments, or learning problems. A 2005 UNICEF international study of disabled children found an even more pronounced differential and pointed out that disabled children are also more vulnerable than nondisabled children to bullying, exploitation, abuse, and neglect outside their own homes as well (Groce & Paeglow, 2005).

There are many reasons for this disparity. In some cases, a child's disability may itself have been caused by neglectful or abusive conditions either early in life or during the mother's pregnancy. The mother may not have received prenatal care, or she may have ingested drugs or alcohol during pregnancy. If there is domestic violence in the family, she may have been abused while she was pregnant. During infancy, the child may have been malnourished or seriously neglected, resulting in neurologic disadvantages. The infant might also have been handled roughly or shaken, which could result in both neurologic and visual impairments.

Whether or not these conditions are present, parents can find it highly stressful to manage a child with disabilities. They may not feel as bonded or attached to a child who is less responsive, or they may become impatient with a child who is impossible to comfort. In many areas, services for such children, as well as respite for their parents, are lacking or overtaxed, resulting in parents who may be left to provide care the best they can on their own. As the child ages, he or she may not be able to recognize the parent's behavioral cues that indicate that they are in danger. As well, they often have a limited ability to defend themselves by either getting out of the way or by modifying their behavior before the parent loses patience. Their disability may cause them to spend more time at home and in the caretaker's presence than children without disabilities, increasing both parental stress and risk to the child. Even if they gain an understanding of their status, seriously impaired communications or cognitive skills may prevent the child from informing someone outside the family that he or she is being abused or neglected.

Parental neglect is also more likely for disabled children (Groce & Paeglow, 2005). The physical demands of caring for a disabled child sometimes causes the parent to skip some of the required care regimens. Medical care may be sporadic, prescriptions may not be filled on time, and physical therapy appointments may be skipped. Some disabled children may need to rely on parents or other caretakers for virtually all their maintenance needs, placing them in such extremely dependent circumstances that they are virtually powerless to report mistreatment or gain autonomy. They may have a great deal of anxiety that the parents will abandon their care to an institution, even further increasing their vulnerability.

Assistance to care for disabled children in the home can be difficult to obtain. Because of this, there is a risk that sometimes parents who have managed to secure some assistance to care for disabled children may be unwilling to speak out when they suspect that their children are being abused or neglected by these caretakers. In addition, the presence of a child with a disability can introduce stresses in the family that often complicate the issue of the child's treatment. Caretakers will often be siblings or other family members informally arranged by the parent. These caretakers may be resentful and take this out on the child. The parent may be unwilling to vigorously confront family members on these issues, partly because of fear of losing the help but also for more complicated emotions, including guilt and depression.

Professionals who work with disabled children and their families need to keep a close eye on their own reactions when working with families with disabled children. Empathy for the difficulty of the parents' situation, while ordinarily commendable, may also result in tolerating a lower standard of protection for disabled children than we would expect for children who do not have disabilities. Social workers, teachers, medical personnel, and even CPS staff may intervene less strenuously than they would otherwise, feeling that the parents "have enough stress already" and "I am not sure if I could properly handle that situation." On some level, some professionals may also realize that if they did press the issue to the point of necessitating the child's removal, finding a resource for the child would be difficult if not impossible.

## Children Who Are Infants or Not Attending School or Day Care

As noted previously, children who are home alone most or all of the time with their caretakers may be at increased risk of being abused or neglected mostly due to their isolation from anyone, mandated reporter or otherwise, who might encounter and report signs of the abuse or neglect. Most caretakers who subject children to harm or its risk are aware that their actions are improper, socially unacceptable, or illegal. When the child leaves the home on a nearly daily basis and spends time with others who have the opportunity to interact on a fairly intimate level with the child, the caretaker may be more reluctant to inflict abuse or neglect or even to use corporal punishment excessively.

Similarly, the younger the child, the less developed is his or her capacity to interact verbally with others—a 1 year old obviously cannot report to anyone that she has been slapped hard across the face. Even older preschool children may not have sufficient language power to describe what they have experienced. In addition, preschool children and infants have not reached a level of cognitive functioning that allows them to clearly understand that what has happened to them is inappropriate or wrong since they have not yet formed concepts of personal responsibility and victimization.

The natural behavior of younger children is also somewhat more likely, however inadvertently, to provoke the parent or caretaker. Colicky infants who cry incessantly may be extremely trying for the parent, and children who are not yet toilet trained often provoke rage through either ordinary soiling of diapers or with less usual events, such as smearing or ingestion of feces. Toileting accidents and potty-training events can be monumentally exasperating to even the calmest parent. Experienced CPS investigators have seen a range of child abuse in response to these behaviors, from bruises and spiral fractures sustained as an angry parent strongly grips and twists the child's hip during a diaper change to serious scalding when the "dirty" child is "cleaned" by being dipped or splashed in hot water. Shaken baby syndrome is often a result of incessant crying or soiling incidents.

Children who have already been toilet trained but have not yet entered school are also at increased risk as a result of their behavior. This is an age when children are ambulatory, quite active, and curious. They have not yet developed the ability to obey the rules of the household, and their curiosity often leads them into forbidden places and adventures. Their behavior may frighten and alarm the parent, such as when they go outdoors without permission, climb high furniture in the house, or torment household pets or younger children in the household. The result may be that the parent lashes out with a slap, a spanking that is too severe, or a whipping. Children this age are also famous for resisting bedtime by getting out of bed, calling repeatedly for water or milk, or displaying tantrums. Frustrated caretakers may punish or "train" children inappropriately by tying them to the bed, taping their mouths, rigging tight netting over their beds or cribs, or locking their doors from the outside.

## Children Who Are Placed in Foster Care or Adopted

Children who are placed with foster parents or adopted are clearly not in precisely the same category legally or filially, but there are important similarities and overlaps between them. For example, many people are under the impression that the great majority of children who are adopted are adopted as infants. However, exactly the opposite is true: Most children who are adopted have spent time in foster care before they were adopted; many spent time in foster care after they were removed from their families of origin, usually due to abuse or neglect; and most are not infants at the time of adoption. Many children who are adopted from foster care are adopted by their foster parents.

In fairness, it is necessary to point out that there indeed exists a harshly negative stereotype of foster parents. It would be very unfortunate to have any statements listed here validate or amplify that stereotype. The great majority of foster parents, especially those who have been carefully selected and trained by licensed child-caring agencies and departments of social services, competently and lovingly fulfill one of the most important (if not *the* most important) needs in the child welfare system. More often than not, fostering can be a difficult, stressful, and emotionally exhausting job, but most people who undertake it have been motivated by a deep sense of community service and commitment to and love for children in need.

The heightened risk of abuse and neglect to foster children is largely a result of the very aspects of fostering that make it difficult. To begin with, most children in foster care have already suffered a great deal, first by being neglected or abused by their parents and then by the very painful separation from them that follows. The doubt, confusion, and uncertainty occasioned by these kinds of events in the life a child often result in "acting out." The child may be aggressive with other children; may steal or lie; may run away; may challenge the authority of the foster parent; may exhibit tantrums, sleeplessness, or nightmares; may attempt suicide or use drugs or alcohol; may vandalize the home or the neighbors' homes; may sexually seduce other children or even attempt to seduce one of the foster parents; or may refuse to go to school or get into trouble there. The foster child may require frequent trips to doctors, therapists, court appointments, probation officers, and parental visits. After each such event, the acting out is likely to intensify. In some situations, the more obvious the display of love and attention from the foster parent, the more determined is the child to demonstrate his or her unworthiness of it (probably because the urge to reciprocate stirs guilty feelings of disloyalty to the parents).

The foster parent may commit years to the child only to see the child returned to the abusive or neglectful parent by the courts. This often results in anger and frustration for the foster parent, who cannot understand the reasoning of a system that would return a child to such a negative environment. The foster parents may feel that all efforts and devotion have been futile, especially when they receive a call from the caseworker 2, 3, or 6 months later to advise that the discharge did not work out, followed by a request for the foster parents to accept the child back into their home. Trying to reestablish a positive relationship with the child may now be very difficult because the foster parents have already dealt with their own feelings of separation and loss and must now confront the child's feelings about why there is a need to return to foster care.

It does not take much imagination to understand how stressful all this can be, even for the hardiest of souls. Foster parents are as subject to "burnout" as anyone else in the child welfare system, but they have the child in the next room and do not get to go home for the weekend. Foster parents sometimes succumb to the temptation to use overly forceful or harsh methods of discipline that they hope will counter some of the above behaviors. Or, they may defend themselves emotionally by becoming cold and aloof in their interactions with their foster children—a state of mind that sometimes finds its eventual expression in isolating the foster child: feeding the child separately from the family, confining the child to a separate part of the house, and segregating the child from family life.

Policies concerning the use of corporal punishment on foster children by foster parents is often a source of confusion. Most jurisdictions strictly forbid a foster parent to utilize corporal punishment in the course of disciplining a foster child. The use of noninjurious corporal punishment to discipline a child does not meet the definition of child abuse or neglect; therefore, the foster parents who use corporal punishment on their foster children may be violating the rules, but they are not, per se, abusing or neglecting the foster child. The same CPS definitions that apply to parents apply similarly, no more and no less, to foster parents.

It may also be worthwhile to note that foster parents tend to be "subjects" of child abuse reports—and therefore investigations—more often than parents. The reason for this is that it is relatively common for natural parents to interpret the foster parents' discipline of their child as neglect or abuse. The natural parent may then report the foster parents to the child abuse hotline or to the foster care caseworker who, in turn, makes a report to the hotline. (It would be a mistake to assume there is always a natural rivalry between the child's natural parents and the foster parents, but it is not rare for there to exist a certain level of resentment and jealousy.)

The increased risk for adopted children exists partly for the reasons identified for foster children, although the constant pull of the child in two directions—foster (adoptive) parent and natural parent—will almost always be absent, relieving the relationship of much of the stress described previously. Also, there is no difference between the legal rights of the natural parent and the adoptive parent. However, even where a child has been adopted as an infant, the adoptive parents have often created a complex conglomeration of expectations and dreams. Disappointment may be no more likely for them than it is for natural parents, but for adoptive parents, such disappointments may ultimately be blamed on the fact that the child is adopted rather than "natural," and the child may become scapegoated as a result. Another risk with adoption is that adopted children may undergo a pronounced "identity crisis" later in life, even if their initial adjustment to learning that they are adopted was successful. This may result in some of the same sort of acting out that is described above, with similar challenges to the parents' ability to cope.

## REFERENCES

Ammerman, R. T., Kolko, D. J., Kirisci, L., Blackson, T. C., & Dawes, M. A. (1999). Child abuse potential in parents with histories of substance use disorder. *Child Abuse and Neglect, 23*(12), 1225–1238.

Finkelhor, D. (1984). Child sexual abuse: New theory and research. *Family Process, 24*(2), 292–293.

Groce, N. E., & Paeglow, C. (2005). *Violence against disabled children.* New York: UNICEF.

Groth, A. Nicholas, with H. Jean Birnbaum. (1979). *Men who rape: The psychology of the offender.* New York: Plenum Press.

Herrenkohl, T. I., Sousa, C., Tajima, E. A., Herrenkohl, R. C., & Moylan, C. A. (2008). Intersection of child abuse and children's exposure to domestic violence. *Trauma, Violence, and Abuse, 9*(2), 84–99.

Lanning, K. V. (2001). *Child molesters: A behavioral analysis* (4th ed). Alexandria, VA: National Center for Missing & Exploited Children.

Sgroi, S. (1979). *Handbook of clinical intervention in child sexual abuse.* New York: The Free Press.

Slack, K. S., Holl, J. L., McDaniel, M., Yoo, J., & Bolger, K. (2004). Understanding the risks of child neglect: An exploration of poverty and parenting characteristics. *Child Maltreatment, 9*(4), 395–408.

Trepper, T. S., & Barrett, M. (Eds). (1986). *Treating incest: A multimodal systems perspective.* New York: Haworth.

World Health Organization. (2002). *World report on violence and health.* Geneva, Switzerland: Author.

## ADDITIONAL READING

American Academy of Pediatrics. (2001). Assessment of maltreatment of children with disabilities. *Pediatrics, 108*(2), 508–552.

# 5 Signs of Abuse and Neglect

As we turn our attention to the signs of child abuse and neglect, we differentiate "signs" from "risk factors." A common mistake made by reporters of child abuse is to fail to understand what is occurring in all but the most obvious situations. We certainly do not advocate that social workers incorporate into their practice a constant suspicion of maltreatment that becomes the guiding factor in all their professional dealings with parents or children—that would be the opposite problem. However, it is equally important that the social worker not adopt a naive approach in which only the most severe and obvious signs of abuse or neglect raise suspicion.

Risk factors, as described in chapter 4, are descriptive characteristics that have been noted by researchers to accompany the presence of child abuse or neglect with some frequency. Observing risk factors should sharpen the potential reporter's sensitivity to the possibility that child abuse or neglect is occurring. Signs, on the other hand, are observable elements presented by the child and/or the parents/caretakers that should, combined with the reporter's knowledge, training, and experience, stimulate and shape reasonable suspicion. Signs are more pronounced than risk factors, demanding clear and credible counters before they can permit a suspicion to be dismissed as either not reasonable or erroneous.

Therein lies one of the problems for potential reporters. Those who encounter signs of child abuse or neglect do not have the responsibility to invest more than the slightest effort in developing countering explanations for the signs. Mandated reporters are cautioned not to "preinvestigate" or undertake the endeavor to examine every possible alternative explanation for what they have encountered. Overcompensating with countering explanations can be a trap, particularly where the potential reporter is familiar or sympathetic with the parent/guardian or family. In many states, subscribing to an alternative but obviously less reasonable explanation for the observed sign might be considered "willful failure" to report suspected child abuse.

The other factor that often causes potential reporters to err in the direction of preinvestigation is the uncomfortable sense that making a child protective services (CPS) report based on mere suspicion is somehow "sneaky" and that fairness would require one to have clear proof that an act of abuse or neglect has occurred before the report is made. State reporting systems take into account the possibility that the suspicion is incorrect by relieving the reporter of legal responsibility in the event the investigation fails to produce credible evidence. Personnel who staff the state hotlines (who often have field experience themselves) are trained to separate reasonable suspicion from unreasonable suspicion and are thereby available to serve as the potential reporter's conscience should such misgivings arise.

An age-old conflict for social workers involved in providing psychotherapy or others who are involved in a constructive relationship with their clients is the destructive effect reporting may have on that relationship. In virtually all state reporting systems, mandated reporters have the right to have their identity held confidential, but this is, of course, of nearly no significance if their relationship with their client is close, as the client will easily recognize where the report originated. When this happens, it can often be more damaging to the relationship for the social worker to remain closed mouthed about his or her role in the report. In the end, this relationship does not excuse the social worker from the mandate to report suspicion. Each professional must decide the best approach to utilize with the client. During the initial intake process, it is recommended that the social worker explains in detail the limits of his or her confidentiality. Experts in the field believe that a frank discussion with the client about the social worker's legal requirement, along with assurances that the client–reporter relationship remains important, is the best action.

If the social worker has been working with the client for some time, it is quite possible that a positive and trusting connection has been established. This type of relationship will probably withstand the stress of a CPS report. However, it is probably more likely that the social worker is going to learn of abuse or neglect in the early part of the relationship. Realizing this, it is tempting to delay the report until more is known and the relationship has had time to develop some strength. This would be a mistake. Aside from the facts that mandated reporters are required to make their reports "immediately" and that a delay would present risk of further harm to the child, making the report later might cause the client to wonder to ask "why now?" On the other hand, if the client decides to terminate the relationship at some time after the disclosure but before the report, a report might appear to be punitive.

Another source of reluctance for some potential reporters is their prior experience with CPS authorities. Perhaps they have made many reports that have ultimately turned out to be unfounded, or they have made reports that are indicated but in which they witness little or no change in the pattern of abuse or neglect.

The most obvious advice in situations such as this, and they are many, is that mandated reporters are not excused from the requirement to report reasonable suspicions even if their doubt concerning the efficacy of the system is well founded. These attitudes do not justify a failure to report, nor will they be a viable defense either legally or psychologically if further harm befalls the child. However, there is an additional step that reporters in this position can take, and that is to become constructively involved in the case. Call CPS and speak with the assigned caseworker. If this does not result in a satisfactory experience, ask to speak with the caseworker's supervisor. CPS organizations are bureaucracies with many levels of authority. Keep moving up the lines of authority until you believe that you are being heard.

Three cautions are offered along with this advice. First, remain patient, polite, and friendly at every step of the way. You will be dealing with human beings. Most staff members are accustomed to being shouted at, threatened, accused, or manipulated, and they have developed immunity to these approaches. They are probably overwhelmed and weary. Many will be quite pleased to hand you off to their supervisor. As you work your way up the bureaucratic hierarchy, you will inevitably encounter someone who responds on a very human level to your patience, politeness, and respect.

Second, maintain an awareness that CPS staff are thoroughly trained in confidentiality. Their first reaction to your attempt to be involved, no matter how polite you are, will be to keep information to themselves. The best way to approach this is to provide information. Information is currency. If you give information about the child or the situation you have reported, you will probably get information in return, just in the process of human communication. You may have to listen closely for it, but you will hear it when the person you reach attempts to clarify and refine what you are offering.

Third, and probably most important, you should convey that your most important concern is for the child's best interests. In fact, this aspect of your involvement with CPS is so important that you probably should be very sure in your own mind that the information is true before you even begin your contacts. Concern for the child you have reported is what gives you credibility and makes the time that child protective personnel spend in contact with you worth the time it takes from their many other cases.

## CATEGORIES OF ABUSE AND NEGLECT

The mistreatment of children is usually broken down into two categories: child abuse and child neglect. Child sexual abuse is usually considered to be a subcategory of child abuse, but many discussions in this field treat it as a third category. For the purposes of this chapter, we will treat these as three separate categories; however, it needs to be understood that a categorical approach, while providing some convenience in describing and understanding child abuse and neglect, is somewhat artificial in that real-life events do not conform so neatly to clear tracks. A child may be exposed to a combination of all three types of mistreatment at the same time or to different categories at different times in his or her development. So, as a precaution, the mandated reporter should keep in mind that there is an area of overlap between situations that might be classed as child neglect (or maltreatment), child abuse, and child sexual abuse.

To a considerable extent, the mandated reporter can ignore the precise difference in terms of the legal definitions of abuse and neglect. In most cases, the decision to classify an act as one or the other is going to be made either by or with the assistance of hotline interviewers. In a less precise sense, the differences between the two broad categories of "abuse" and "neglect" (maltreatment) can be thought of by utilizing the following two rules of thumb. First, child abuse is usually—although not always—an act of commission, while child neglect is usually an act of omission. Second, acts of child abuse either place the child at risk of serious permanent injury or death or actually cause serious or permanent (or protracted) injury. Neglect is far more common than abuse and constitutes the great majority of reports phoned in to child abuse hotlines (American Journal of Family Law, 2000).

## Corporal Punishment

Another aspect of these definitions that occasionally confuses potential reporters is how acts of corporal punishment fit into the definitions. Corporal punishment—the use of painful stimuli to discipline a child—is generally legal. However, employing corporal punishment to excess (too often or too strenuously), in a manner that is injurious, or primarily as a means of expressing the displeasure or anger of the disciplinarian (parent or caretaker) rather than as a measure that will correct future behavior is considered to be child neglect. Corporal punishment that strays too far outside these parameters may even constitute criminal assault. But many lesser injuries that a child sustains as a result of corporal punishment may be considered maltreatment, even if they do not rise to the definition of abuse.

Abuse places the child at risk of serious or permanent injury or death. Spanking a child on the buttocks, slapping the child in the face, grabbing the child by the bicep, and pulling the child's hair are not ordinarily acts of "abuse," although they may well meet the definition of "neglect." When thinking in terms of neglect as an act of omission by the caretaker, what has been omitted by employing these measures, if they are sufficiently severe, is good judgment and self-restraint with resulting detriment to the child. A child who is occasionally spanked on the buttocks and suffers no bruises or marks would not be described as neglected. On the other hand, if the same child is spanked in a similar manner constantly, multiple times per day, day in and day out, then the child may be neglected. A child who is suddenly grabbed in anger by the biceps without leaving a mark is probably not neglected. Yet, if the grab is so severe as to leave a bruise, an investigator may find it to be neglectful. As well, if the child is grabbed simultaneously by both biceps and then shaken with force, the child may even be considered to be abused, since such punishment places the child at risk of injury to the central nervous system. Lesser injuries such as bruises, welts, abrasions, and small lacerations that result from parental efforts to discipline children comprise a great percentage of events that are reported to child abuse hotlines. They are usually placed in a category of child maltreatment called *excessive corporal punishment*.

## DISCLOSURE OF ABUSE

Before we discuss the signs of abuse, it is important to understand how to react if a child discloses abuse. When a child begins to share a history of abuse, it is critical to be sensitive to the child's needs. Start off by taking a deep breath. You and the child will get through this. Here are a few suggestions:

- Have the discussion in a safe, private space.
- Remain calm, and allow the child to say what he or she needs to without questioning.
- Listen empathically and without judgment. Remember that the child may be telling about abuse by someone he or she knows and loves, possibly a family member. The child may be concerned that no one "gets into trouble."
- Reassure the child. Realize that the child may have been building up to a disclosure for some time; say that you appreciate his or her courage in telling you. Affirm that the child is right to talk about the abuse. Let the child know that you are sorry this happened.
- Reassure the child that it is not his or her fault. Children do not make abuse happen. It was not anything that he or she did. You may also say that this has happened to other children. He or she is not the only one.
- Do not promise to keep the abuse secret, as you cannot. In fact, do not make any promises about what will happen. You really do not know how the process will unfold.
- Explain clearly and honestly what the next steps will be. There are people who help children to whom this has happened. You will help by contacting those people who can best help the child. Offer to remain with the child, if possible.
- After you have taken care of the child, it is time to take care of yourself. Listening to a child talk about abuse is emotionally draining. Talk with a colleague and/or professional who can help you.

## SIGNS OF NEGLECT OR MALTREATMENT

### Physical Signs of Neglect

*Neonate drug toxicology.* When toxicology tests on a newborn child show that the child's system contains metabolites of addictive drugs or if the child is addicted to drugs, a CPS report should be made. When these tests are positive, it is a sure indication that the mother who gave birth used drugs during pregnancy. Of course, this is not proof that the mother will continue to use the drugs—or that she will use them to the point that they will interfere with her ability to adequately parent the child— now that the baby is her day-to-day responsibility, but it is sufficient reason for CPS to investigate whether the circumstances place the child at risk.

*Infant failure to thrive.* In the few days following birth, a neonate will naturally lose a small percentage of its birth weight, then gain it back. From that point on, the baby should continue to gain weight at a regular pace through infancy and toddlerhood. Failure to gain weight—or worse, losing weight—is termed *failure to thrive*. In some cases, this condition is due to medical problems, but it is more likely that the mother is not providing adequate care for the infant—not feeding often enough, not feeding a correct diet, leaving the baby alone for lengthy periods of time, or ignoring the baby's needs.

*Developmental lags.* Social workers and other professionals whose practice brings them into contact with children should have a good awareness of the general developmental expectations for a child at various ages, especially in the first 5 years of life when a child may be isolated, unaware of its own needs, and inexperienced at communicating. This includes physical development, language development, cognitive development, social awareness, and life skills. When one, and often more, milestones are reached late or not at all, there could be trouble for the child. In the first 3 years of life, growth of the central nervous system requires lots of protein nourishment and sensory stimulation. If these are not available, the child could suffer permanent damage. Developmental lags may be due to medical conditions that are not recognized by an inexperienced caretaker. However, they may also be due to inadequate care—not feeding the child enough or not spending time with the child. Even when a child is well fed and has its physical needs met, if left alone for long periods of time every day, it may suffer developmental lags.

*Hunger and malnourishment.* A child who is hungry all the time and is obviously malnourished may be neglected.

*Poor hygiene and improper clothing.* Children who are not bathed and shampooed regularly and provided with minimal care in terms of haircuts, clean and trimmed nails, brushed teeth, and clean clothing do not develop these skills and tend to grow up in a constant state of poor hygiene. Not only is this condition a health risk, it can also cause severe social problems for children. They may be shunned by peers, teased mercilessly, and often rejected by adults as well. While a parent's choice not to keep his or her child scrubbed up constantly and always well dressed is certainly not child neglect, parents need to be taken to account when a child's poor hygiene is so noticeable that peers react.

As with other potential signs of neglect, parents are held to the minimum standard in these areas, not the maximum. A parent is not expected to provide a child with designer clothing, for example, but the clothing that is provided must be reasonably clean, of suitable size, and appropriate to the season.

*Unattended dental, medical, or prosthetic needs.* Parents and other caretakers have a responsibility to provide their children with dental care, eyeglasses, corrective surgery, crutches, braces, and so on. Again, this is not a "zero tolerance" issue. A child who is noted to have cavities for a few weeks before they are addressed or the child who loses a pair of glasses and does not immediately have them replaced is not neglected if these needs are met within a reasonable time. The principle of minimal need also applies here. While dental cavities and corrective lenses must be addressed, especially after the need has been brought to the parent's attention, expensive braces and fashionable glasses are not required.

*Bruises, welts, and lacerations.* As explained previously, not all marks or injuries are necessarily categorized as abuse. Many, if not most encountered in the CPS realm, are the result of neglect. The difference is that inflicted injuries that are serious, life threatening, or permanent are abuse, while lesser, more common injuries may be classified as neglect. The parent who bruises a child's buttocks in the course of a spanking or who leaves a red mark on the side of the face as a result of a slap with an open hand is not ordinarily considered to be abusive but could be neglectful. Children who display these marks have often sustained them as a result of parental attempts at discipline. This is especially true of bruises to the back of the body such as the buttocks, the back of the legs, and the shoulders. It is also true when the injuries appear in the shape of an implement, such as a looped electrical cord (see section on physical signs of abuse.)

## Behavioral Signs of Neglect

*Overdependency on adults.* Children who are neglected by their parents may appear overly eager to please other adults. Their behavior may be overcompliant to the extent that they impress as needy. They may seem to prefer the company of adults over the company of other children. They may seem eager to demonstrate that they are "good" children and may simultaneously be quick to perceive criticism as rejection. They seem socially awkward and have a hard time relaxing or letting themselves go.

*Aggressive behavior.* On the other hand, neglected children may exhibit behavior that constantly challenges the authority of adults outside their families. They may be purposely disobedient or aggressive. They may pick fights with adults or peers.

*Passive or depressed behavior.* A third set of behaviors often displayed by children who are chronically neglected is passivity or depression. Passivity includes apathy about whether the child is liked by peers or other adults and a lack of motivation to perform a task or work in a team with others. The passive child shows neither enthusiasm nor fear. Punishment or rejection is accepted with a shrug of the shoulders. Depression is exhibited in the form of apathy and a lack of joy as well as a consistently negative view of the child's own abilities and a sense of being resolved to the fact that he or she will never succeed at anything. The depressed child has a very low sense of self-worth. Rarely, he or she may make self-destructive or suicidal comments. (Obviously, such events must be promptly attended, and the professional should be careful to gauge the parents' reaction to such remarks, as neglectful parents often minimize the importance of self-destructive comments and behavior.)

*Begging or stealing food.* The child who begs food from peers, other adults, neighbors, stores, and such is very likely being neglected. The same can be said for the child who steals food from peers, shops, and so on. When this behavior is discovered, it is often useful to ask about the parents' role, as it is not unusual to discover that the neglectful parent is not only aware of this behavior but encourages it and sometimes compels the child to beg or steal.

*Evidence of unsupervised and/or dangerous activities.* Social workers and other professionals who work with or around children should be careful to listen to them, both when they speak directly to the professional or when they speak among themselves. Children's conversations usually provide rather complete descriptions of how they spend their time and what activities they enjoy, and in this way, neglectful patterns of family interaction may come to the social worker's attention. For example, a child who is often noted to be sleepy and inattentive may comment about something he saw on a late night television show, or a child may reveal in conversation that she is burdened with unusual responsibilities in the household, such as cooking meals or supervising siblings on a regular basis. Children may be worked to exhaustion in family businesses or be required to perform tasks that are illegal or beyond their developmental capabilities, and perhaps blamed when they prove incapable.

If children describe activities that are risky or dangerous, their caretakers may not be providing adequate supervision. Description of activities such as roaming the streets late at night, operating motor vehicles without a license, drinking, breaking into buildings, hitchhiking, climbing tall structures, and so forth, especially if indulged in on a regular and continuous basis, need to be investigated. Of course, there is the possibility that the parent genuinely has no way of knowing that these adventures are occurring, but a mandated reporter needs to examine if there is reasonable suspicion to believe that the parents know, or should know, what their children are doing and proceed to make a CPS report for lack of supervision if it is concluded that the suspicion is reasonable.

*Chronic truancy.* Chronic absence from school is a classic sign of neglect. A truly chronic situation is almost impossible not to attribute to parental neglect of one type or another. Even a large number of absences for which the parent has provided excuses may be considered neglectful, especially if there is a negative effect on the child's academic performance. If the parent does not know about the absences, the school will soon make the parent aware. The notified parent has a responsibility to correct the child's behavior, even if it means cooperating closely with school and court or probation officials. Parental involvement in truancy ranges widely from tacit approval of the child's absences to apathy about whether the child is in school to a complete inability to exercise authority over the child to keeping the child home to help with household tasks or just to keep the parent company.

*Use of alcohol or drugs.* Substance use in adolescence is a widespread problem not always directly attributable to parental shortcomings. Indeed, much of it is peer driven and not chronic. However, when this problem is encountered, it should not be assumed that the parent has no culpability. Parents who are made aware of this problem with their child are expected to take forthright steps to address the issue. However, some parents will not treat alcohol and drug use by their child as a serious problem; to many it is little more than teenage tomfoolery, even after repeated events. Further along the spectrum is the parent who is apathetic about the problem or too preoccupied with other problems in life to pay attention. As well, there are parents who believe that the best defense is to "keep the problem at home" and who supply their children and their children's friends with alcohol with the proviso that they drink on premises. Anything short of the forthright corrective response can be considered neglectful.

*Runaway behavior.* Children who run away from home—in particular, "chronic absconders"— arc often neglected. To be sure, there are often times when, to the adolescent mind, leaving home without parental permission seems to be an effective method of declaring one's independence and doing as one pleases. However, there are also many times when leaving can be seen as a healthy response to an unhealthy family situation, especially when the child chooses to go to a "sensible" place, such as a youth shelter, or the home of a trusted relative, such as a grandparent or an aunt or uncle. Family tension brought on by marital discord, illness, financial or job difficulties, and overcrowding sometimes becomes so intense that the child seeks relief by leaving. However, in a different vein, it is not unusual for a neglectful parent to largely ignore their child's behavior, good and bad, until suddenly one day the child is nowhere to be found. Anger and panic often ensue, and the child, when located, receives heaps of blame and punishment. Ironically, in this situation, the running behavior is rewarded with attention and, therefore, is likely to be repeated in the future; so, indeed in some families, running away, or the effective threat of running away, gives a child much power.

*Delinquency.* Children who are involved in criminal activity often live in neglectful homes. Breaking into houses and commercial enterprises may begin because there is no supervision at home and children are able to roam at will, with no accountability as to their whereabouts or as to how they come to possess certain items. Similar neglect may result in the child forming an alliance with a gang that replaces its alliance with its family. Many delinquent adolescents are duplicating behavior they have seen all their lives at home: drug dealing, burglary, petty thievery, scamming, stealing automobiles, or mugging.

## Environmental Signs of Neglect

Another area of concern about which there is often confusion involves conditions in the family's household. A frequent category of reports to child abuse hotlines is "dirty house" cases. Mandated reporters are frequently uncertain about what standard to apply in deciding to make such a report. The principle of minimal standards again serves to guide us. A house that is not vacuumed on a regular basis and has accumulated numerous "dust bunnies" would not ordinarily be reportable because there is no identifiable risk of harm to the children who reside there. Dirt and disorder that present no clear risk to the occupants of the home are not the concern of child protective authorities. On the other hand, if one of the children who reside there has a serious bronchial allergy to dust, the situation might be considered neglectful.

A frequent concern in this area is the presence of household pets and their debris. A house in which there regularly is an accumulation of fecal matter that is not promptly cleaned up would usually be considered to be a neglectful circumstance. Other conditions that might be included in this area of concern are inoperable toilets, accumulations of rotting food, unattended carcasses of animals, and vermin or insect infestation (particularly fleas and bed bugs). The presence of various poisonous compounds, drugs, or other noxious substances would also be neglectful.

Structural shortcomings also need to be considered. The absence of doors or windows that cause the child to be exposed to the elements (rain, snow, cold) would be considered neglectful. Jagged broken glass, slippery surfaces, dilapidated stairs, floor or landings that are about to give way, items that are about to fall, unprotected pools, and lack of railings on upper decks might all be considered dangerous and, therefore, neglectful, especially if the parent has made no effort to correct them.

It is not necessary that these conditions be observed personally in order to be reported. The conditions may even be described by the parent themselves but are more often described by the child. The child may display physical signs, such as injuries, insect bites, or illness, that resulted from one of the conditions described.

Parents or caretakers are also expected to exercise reasonable precautions to safeguard their children's health and safety. Some failures in this regard are obvious: The parent who drives while intoxicated with a child in the vehicle is unquestionably neglectful, perhaps even abusive. Yet, mandated child abuse reporters often overlook the neglect that is involved, such as when a toddler has fallen down a flight of stairs where a safety gate across the top of stairs would have provided for the child's safety. Similar situations abound—children who are injured in house fires; who drown, or nearly drown, in swimming pools; who are struck by an ice cream truck; or who are injured in automobile accidents because the parent did not use proper safety restraints. Reporters may be particularly unmindful of the need for a CPS report if the parent is demonstrably regretful or in mourning.

## SIGNS OF PHYSICAL ABUSE

Some signs of abuse may appear at first to be the same as those for neglect. Keep in mind that there is a great deal of overlap between these somewhat artificial "categories" as well as the important difference of severity. Child neglect so severe that it endangers the child's life or permanent health is no longer neglect, it is abuse.

### Physical Signs of Abuse

*Head injuries.* Injuries to the head, just by virtue of the risk to the child's life that they present, are most often classified as abuse. Spanking an infant's buttocks for crying all night is neglect; grabbing the same infant by the shoulders and shaking him is abuse, because it presents a great chance of causing injury to the brain, retinas, and spinal cord (shaken baby syndrome). Similarly, slapping an older child in the face might not cause significant injuries and would likely be classed as neglect, but similarly slapping a baby may cause serious injuries. Sometimes, the injuries point to the event. For example, attempting to smother a child with a pillow will likely rupture the frenulum (the skin tissue that connects the inside of the lips and cheeks to the gums). Punching a child in the mouth may loosen or break teeth or risk the loss of vision in an eye. Cuffing the ears may cause damage to the child's hearing.

*Injuries to the scalp.* Children who are slapped about the head may display huge areas of bruising in the scalp. Bald spots may indicate that hair has been pulled out violently.

*Serious injuries such as fractures.* Serious injuries to a child must always be regarded with careful attention. Listen for conflicting stories or explanations that do not make sense. Breaks and fractures of the bones need to match the explanation. For example, a spiral fracture of the leg in an infant in diapers frequently results from the caretaker violently (and often angrily) twisting the child's leg while changing a diaper. Skull and rib fractures need to be carefully matched with the explanation that is provided. Those sorts of injuries are so severe that they are almost always classified as abuse.

*Burns.* Burns constitute some of the most serious injuries children can suffer, both because their skin is delicate and burns more easily than adult skin and because any burn they sustain will occupy a larger percentage of skin area just by virtue of their smaller size. There is a wide variety of types of burns: scalds, contact, exposure to flame, chemical, and exposure to the sun. Some burns, such as sun exposure, will result from neglect. This makes them no less serious a threat to a child's health. It may seem incomprehensible, even to some seasoned CPS investigators, that anyone would purposely burn a child, but it happens all the time. Be on the lookout for immersion burns, such as "stocking" or "glove" burns that result when, usually as a form of punishment, a child's foot or hand is thrust into scalding water, leaving severe burns that are defined by a clear cutoff line at the wrist or ankle. Parents may claim that a child inadvertently stepped into a hot bathtub, but this is an extremely remote possibility because most such burns result from hot water that one would reflexively recoil from, and if one did accidentally thrust a limb into such a hot liquid, he or she would immediately splash around wildly, causing a poorly delineated burn.

Burning a child with the end of a cigarette or cigar is a frequently encountered form of punishment, and cigarette burns, once they begin to heal, can be difficult to distinguish from insect bites, even for medical professionals. When in doubt, report. Another somewhat rare practice, but one seen more than once, is the practice of "tipping"—touching a child with the point of a hot iron, a method that often leaves a pattern burn that matches the iron used. There is also the often-heard practice of teaching a child the danger of operating the cooking range by placing the child's hand on a hot burner—another type that often leaves a telltale pattern of burns. Be aware also that when parents purposely burn children, they are less likely to seek medical care for fear of being discovered.

*Bruises, welts, and lacerations.* These have already been presented in the section on physical signs of neglect, but their more serious forms may also be found in situations where a child has been abused. Striking a child with a stick, branch, bat, or belt can leave extensive, deep bruising that should receive medical attention. Due usually to anger, some parents go overboard once they have an implement in their hand and begin hitting a child. They are not receiving the kind of tactile feedback that spanking with a hand provides, and they may hit much harder than they realize many more times than they would with their hand. Lacerations may result that require stitches. A repeated switching to the back and the back of the legs can cause welts that bleed. Again, telltale scarring patterns may be present—a bruise in the shape of a belt buckle, a welt in the shape of a looped electrical wire that was used as a whip, or a hand-shaped bruise on the arm or the side of the face.

*Bites.* It may not be surprising that some parents bite their children playfully or affectionately, but it is not unheard of for parents to bite children in anger or even sexual passion. Bites can be serious injuries, particularly if the skin has been broken. Any part of the body might be bitten, but the buttocks, back, neck, face, and arms are most often targeted. Parents may claim the bites were inflicted by an animal, but human bite marks are quite distinguishable from animal bites: They are crescent shaped rather than pointed and leave compression marks, whereas animals tear the skin when they bite.

*Induced illness.* This sort of abuse was comparatively recently discovered in the 1970s and has only slowly been understood in the medical community. The most common psychiatric label is Munchausen syndrome by proxy, which is a factitious disorder. In this disorder, a person gains notoriety and the satisfaction of a sort of an intimacy with medical professionals by using the illness of someone in their care as their "admission ticket," although the "symptoms" have been created by their own furtive actions.

In child abuse, the parent or caretaker induces symptoms in the child in a variety of ways—pricking a pin smeared with fecal matter under the child's skin to produce a raging, and inexplicable, sepsis; adulterating an intravenous drip with some sickening matter; partially smothering a child with a pillow to temporarily stop breathing, and so forth. There is a nearly infinite variety of methods available to a caretaker who spends much time alone with the child.

In these cases, the caretaker often has had some medical training or had a desire for such a career that was somehow cut short or a history of holding the medical community in awe. These caretakers seem to gain a lot of satisfaction by focusing almost exclusively on their child's symptoms, sometimes with the same glee that most parents display when they are proud of their children's accomplishments. They may take it upon themselves to study various possible diseases and sometimes become quite expert amateurs. There may be a tendency for them to focus on very rare disorders and syndromes. Characteristically, they present as unusually dedicated, sometimes remaining with the child around the clock, day after day. When finally presented with allegations, they often exhibit exaggerated indignation and fierce denial. Some of their actions may well place the child at risk of permanent damage or even death. Munchausen syndrome by proxy is a medical diagnosis that can only be officially attached to a person by a physician or nurse practitioner.

## Behavioral Signs of Physical Abuse

*Social anxiety.* Many abused children live in fear and may develop apprehension and fearfulness around adults other than their caretakers. In general, they may be withdrawn or even secretive. Some may seem to have very little self-confidence or self-esteem. They may seem surprised if someone appears to like them. Reflexive flinching in the presence of someone who moves suddenly is often observed.

 *Aggression and bullying.* It is common, and probably not very surprising, for children who are the victims of abuse at home to display abusive behavior against others in their social environment. Physically teasing and torturing other children, in particular those less able or willing to defend themselves, may be observed. They may intimidate their peers into giving them their money or "loaning" them their belongings. They may destroy property and vandalize their surroundings for no apparent reason other than the pleasure it provides. They may try to provoke adults into physical confrontations or use their bullying to force other children to indulge in antiauthoritarian acts. Much of this behavior is typical of what is termed a *conduct disorder*—a childhood psychiatric condition that may become "antisocial personality disorder" when the child reaches adolescence or early adulthood.

 *Chronic running away.* This behavior was discussed earlier as a possible sign of neglect, but it is another of those overlapping characteristics. Running away for the abused child is much more obviously a method of avoiding pain and could probably be thought of as an "adaptive" response. With the abused child, absconding is more likely to be a chronic problem, particularly where the parent is accustomed to using physical violence to express anger and is likely to be calmed down by the time the child shows up at home.

 *Fear of going home.* Not all children have the boldness to abscond. However, they may fear going home to an abusive parent and may, therefore, dawdle or otherwise find ways to delay going home. The child who seems to be misbehaving because he wants to be kept after school or the child who is reluctant to have a club meeting or a therapy session end may be trying to avoid going home. This behavior may be linked to specific events, such as the arrival of a report card at home or a call made to the home by a therapist or a truant official. If this behavior is suspected, the child should probably be asked directly if there is apprehension about going home.

*Self-blame.* Children who are abused may have difficulty assigning blame for the abuse to their parents. Often, when abused children are directly asked if they were hit or otherwise hurt, they will not answer directly but will instead make a comment such as "it is my own fault—I broke the rules," "I deserved to be hit—it is no big deal, it happens all the time," or "I'm lucky, my brother gets it worse than me." Abused children often become so accustomed to their abuse that they develop a stoic "I can take it" approach to the problem.

*Hiding injuries.* It is a mistake to believe that children do not understand that their caretakers are wrong to have abused them or that the caretaker risks getting into trouble for his or her actions. Abused children may "conspire" with their caretakers to hide what is going on. They may wear seasonably inappropriate clothing—long sleeves, turtlenecks, and such—to hide bruises or marks. Makeup may have been applied to cover up injuries or marks. This should not, by the way, be construed to mean that children never simply stand up for themselves, report their abusers, and insist that action be taken to defend them, as this also occurs, especially for older children who have more mature reality testing skills to understand their situation and their rights. However, when this sort of demand does not occur, the child's complicity may be due not only to self-blame but also to deep uncertainties about the unpredictable outcomes that may result if they disclose. They may have been well schooled by their parent that they will be placed in foster care, away from their friends and school; that they will bring shame and embarrassment to the family; or that a parent will lose a job.

*Depression, low self-esteem, and suicide attempts.* Abused children are often depressed as well. They may display very little motivation in their schoolwork, have no hobbies or interests, and few if any friends. Their outlook on life may be noticeably pessimistic. They may not participate in outings, athletics, or extracurricular activities. This is often the result of the fact that the abuse does not follow a rational pattern; thus, it becomes impossible for the child to succeed. Even if the abuse, unacceptable as it may be, nevertheless only follows certain forbidden behaviors, then the child can succeed by avoiding those behaviors. However, often abusive caretakers, no matter what they may claim, are not truly trying to discipline their children but rather are taking out their anger and their frustration on them. Chronic depression will often be the child's reaction. In serious cases of depression, the child may speak of suicide or actually attempt suicide. These actions must be taken seriously, and responses must be immediate. If child abuse is suspected, do not trust that the parents, once informed of the problem, will take immediate or proper action. In fact, they may even punish the child for "exposing" the family's troubles.

## SIGNS OF SEXUAL ABUSE

There is no area of child welfare more difficult than child sexual abuse. The difficulties are everywhere in this most complex problem: Good statistics are difficult to find and sometimes appear to contradict each other; the act defies imagination and, often, empathy; definitions vary; outcomes are not reliably predictable; the causes defy simplifying; prosecutors find them to be an overwhelming forensic challenge; and hysteria often reigns and various factions are ever at odds with each other over the proper design of research methodologies, effective intervention, and public policy.

The best starting point is probably to put aside the numbers and theories for a moment and understand a simple and painful truth: Adults from all walks of life impose their sexual will on children every day, everywhere. It is happening as you read this sentence, perhaps closer to you than you realize, perhaps where you least expect it. And if you have not received some training in this field, many of your most logical and professionally based assumptions about the phenomenon are probably wrong. In fact, perhaps no one completely knows the "correct" assumptions to use when confronting this phenomenon. As a society, our awareness of this problem is in its historic infancy, and formulating widely constructive responses will probably evolve as research continues to be developed and there is a better understanding of it.

### Categories of Child Sexual Abuse

There are many categories of child sexual abuse, and many types of offenders: the pedophile with a preference and numerous unrelated victims over a period of time, the sexual opportunist who seduces young and naive victims, the sadistic child rapist, the family tyrant who forces sex on all family members of all ages and both genders, or the "regressed" offender who forms a sexual relationship with a child in his care or custody that occurs over many years in what amounts to a lengthy seduction.

For the purposes of this chapter, the focus will be on adults who indulge in sexual behavior with children for whom they have some parental or parentlike responsibility. This behavior is usually termed *incest child sexual abuse* or *intrafamilial child sexual abuse*. Definitions may vary in terms of specific ages used to define *children* or role descriptions used to define *custodial responsibility*. In the child protective world, the great majority of these offenders, or perpetrators, are biologic parents, stepparents, or paramours to parents. Less commonly, they may be grandparents, older siblings, boarders, or members of the extended family (especially who reside in the child's household) as well as babysitters or day care providers.

Many children have been the unfortunate recipients of the sexual attention of adults in other roles, to be sure, such as scout leaders, teachers, clergy, school bus drivers, older peers, and so on. However, these events are not the topic of discussion here, although it is better to understand that they are not entirely an unrelated sociocultural phenomenon. Also, in relation to these types of sexual perpetrators, it should be kept in mind that when someone outside the family sexually abuses a child, the child's parent might be considered neglectful if there was sufficient cause to suspect that permitting the child to be with this person exposed the child to such risk.

The great majority of incest sexual abuse cannot be explained in terms of one main, clearly describable (and therefore predictable), pathologic process. While all such activity can be aptly described as *rape* (a legal term used to define any sexual act involving two or more persons in which at least one of the persons has not consented—and children are legally incapable of consent), events of incest are less likely to fit the picture of what most people think of as rape: a sexual event in which a perpetrator uses overwhelming force or intimidation to compel his victim to submit to sexual intercourse. Attacks such as these would almost certainly be reported or detected almost immediately. The victim would probably recognize clearly that she is a victim and, therefore, be more willing to tell about the event and seek protection. There would often be ample medical and physical evidence of the attack (injuries, torn clothing, semen). This kind of evidence is often very lacking in child sexual abuse, the great majority of which is a process that occurs over a long period of time, involves a victim who does not recognize her victim status until the process is well under way, and leaves little or no physical evidence (many cases never involve sexual intercourse even though a large number of sexual interactions may take place over many years).

## The Stages of Child Sexual Abuse

Perhaps the largest percentage of sexual abuse, however, is a process, guided by the perpetrator, that occurs in stages over a long period of time, perhaps many years. Douglas Pryor called this "turning the victim out" (Pryor, 1996, p. 150). This process is subtle in the beginning, and in these early stages, it is difficult for an observer to differentiate from normal parent–child interaction. Indeed, one of the great puzzles of sexual abuse within a family is how other family members could not be aware of what is occurring in their midst. Certainly, part of the reason is that suspicions formed early in the process are not easily voiced because one fears the embarrassment of being seen as jealous, irrational, or overly suspicious when expressing discomfort about, for example, the amount of time a 4- or 5-year-old girl spends on her father or stepfather's lap or the number of times he checks on her in her bed during the night.

Sexual abuse usually begins secretly in the mind of the perpetrator. For purposes of this example, imagine a male perpetrator and his young daughter. Long before any "inappropriate" touching occurs, the perpetrator experiences sexual arousal in response to the child, sometimes when she is quite young. He may seize every opportunity to have her sit in his lap, put her to bed, or bathe her. He may work to form a special relationship with her—subtly isolating her from her mother, being her friend, providing emotional support for her, and getting her used to the idea of sharing secrets with him. He may encourage her mother to take a job or go to school in the evening and then volunteer to care for the child during the absence he has created.

If there are other siblings, he may give the target child special privileges and elevated status, sometimes behind the scenes. He may allow her to stay up later to watch television with him, to play cards, or talk. While the mother is absent from the home (indeed, sometimes when she is not), the target child, who is often the oldest girl in the family, may take on an almost spousal role with the perpetrator—waiting on him, cleaning house, and supervising her younger siblings.

After months or years of building this relationship and keeping his sexual impulses to himself while spending as much time as he can cuddling, caressing, or massaging the child, the perpetrator may escalate the process by arranging to have the child accidentally see him naked. He may set up a situation in which, for example, it feels comfortable and "normal" for him and the child to habitually be in the bathroom at the same time. By this time, the child may be anywhere between the ages of 4 and 7 years. It is often at this stage that the first sexual touching occurs. It may begin with the perpetrator requesting that the child wash his back while he is in the tub or shower. The washing may escalate to washing the whole body, including the perpetrator's genitals. Eventually, he will probably reciprocate. Or, he may begin by touch the child legs, arms, back, or feet while watching television together, then escalate the touching to include the buttocks and, if he encounters no resistance, her chest and vagina; or he arranges for the child feel that he has an erection while she sits in his lap. This is an important point in the process, because there is now no doubt that the relationship has become sexual, even though the child may be too naive to be aware of this.

In retrospective interviews, many perpetrators report that if the child had rebuffed them at this point, they would not have continued their attempts (Pryor, 1996, p. 123–155). There are reasons to doubt such claims. First, this behavior is so obsessive that its voluntary cessation seems unlikely. However, this also serves the perpetrator's need to believe that the actions have not caused any real harm to the victim. The statement that victim resistance would have prevented further sexual abuse allows the perpetrator to tell himself that the victim really was in charge of events and that real harm could only have resulted from forcefully overcoming such resistance. In this way, perpetrators convince themselves that their behavior may have been aberrant, but it was not abhorrent. This is a subtle blaming of the victim and expecting the victim to take the adult role of making a decision about sexual contact.

Thus, most perpetrators interpret a lack of resistance to their escalations as an indication that the child is interested in his continuing. In reality, however, there are many other reasons the victim may not resist at this point. The child may not understand that the touching is sexual. Or, the child may find the attention and the sensations pleasurable, especially if the perpetrator has carefully nurtured a relationship that is close and trusting, without any real idea where the attention is likely to lead. At this point, child victims may vary in their responses. Some, especially those who are isolated from supportive mothers or other sources of alternative relationships, may passively accede to these advances for some time without openly complaining or resisting. Others, after a brief period of cooperation with the perpetrator's advances, begin to feel uncomfortable and either resist, complain, or avoid the perpetrator. Few children (usually, at this stage, they are under age 9 or 10 years) have the power to stand firmly before the perpetrator and say "No! Stop!"

At this stage, there may be some perpetrators who are sufficiently conscientious to recognize the horror of the path they have chosen and either stop themselves or slow their advance. But a considerable number of them (it seems doubtful that researchers can say with certainty how many, but probably most) will be firmly determined to continue and expand their actions even if the victim expresses discomfort or outright resistance.

The methods used vary. The perpetrator may simply resort to his authority and order the child to comply and keep quiet about it. However, this approach carries the risk of destroying the relationship the perpetrator has spent so much time cultivating. Most perpetrators employ a combination of manipulation, intimidation, and blackmail. If the child appears uncertain, frightened, or resistant, the perpetrator may retreat temporarily or try subtly to convince the child that nothing untoward occurred. The perpetrator may remind the victim that she used to find the actions enjoyable.

In many instances, the perpetrator may easily convince the child that she, after all, initiated the behavior (indeed many perpetrators are apparently convinced of this themselves). If this can be accomplished, the perpetrator has a powerful and ironic advantage over the child, who may now be manipulated by a threat to reveal her "seductiveness" to others, especially her mother. Generally, the often-repeated message is that if the secret is discovered, everyone will blame her, and his version of events will be believed over hers.

The perpetrator may tell the child that he knows what he is doing is wrong but that he cannot help himself because of her beauty or her sweetness. He may pretend to throw himself on her mercy, perhaps promising that "this will be the last time." Some will even claim to be in love with the child and to need her—indeed, some perpetrators report that they were "in love" with the victim.

Some perpetrators have told older children that the child's mother is no longer interested in sex and that a doctor advised him that he risks becoming ill if he goes too long without sexual contact. This reasoning may lead the child to conclude that she is preventing her father or stepfather from an act of infidelity that would endanger the very existence of the family, placing responsibility for keeping the family intact on her. The perpetrator may tell the child that the behavior is so serious that he risks going to jail, indicating how important the behavior is and how vital her silence is as well as effectively implying that she may face a similar risk.

The perpetrator's pursuit may continue for some time, occupying a major portion of the victim's childhood. The sexual contacts may be frequent or infrequent, but they gradually escalate. Secrecy is maintained by the methods described above, but it may also involve giving the child extra privileges, defending her against her mother (while simultaneously working quietly to perpetuate animosity or estrangement between the child and her mother), permitting her to stay home from school, or purchasing her the things she wants. Manipulations will also continue; she may be told that if she tells, her friends will shun her, she will be placed in foster care, her mother will hate her, and boys will never be interested in her.

Intimidation may also be subtle or open. Even after years of acquiescence, as the child matures and develops better reality-testing skills, she may begin to resist involvement. The perpetrator must now either desist or escalate his actions. At this point, he may threaten to harm the child, her siblings, or her pets. He may threaten to destroy her property or take things or privileges away from her. Sometimes, the perpetrator will even threaten to expose the relationship himself in order to embarrass and humiliate the child, sometimes feigning remorse. If she continues to refuse his advances, he may tell her "Okay, I understand. I guess I am going to have to go to your little sister."

By the time the child reaches adolescence, she is firmly ensnared in a trap—the horror of which can only be imagined. By now, the perpetrator's sexual acts, if they have not progressed to sexual intercourse (most do not reach this level—another fact perhaps attributable to the perpetrator's need to believe that he has caused no real harm) are advanced and most often regarded as thoroughly loathsome by the victim. She may be permitted no privacy or boundaries. Her father may exercise complete control over her life, imposing strict rules and demanding to know her every thought, action, and social contact. He may either flatly refuse to allow her to date, or he may exhibit obvious jealousy and distrust about her dates. In some cases, the opposite may be true—the perpetrator encourages dating and sexual activity and then exhibits a leering and voyeuristic interest in her dating and her sex life. Occasionally, he may force her to trade off certain freedoms, including dating, for sexual favors.

The victim may utilize several forms of defense. She may avoid the perpetrator, threaten to expose him, fake menstrual periods, keep busy outside the home with extracurricular and social activities, or keep friends with her constantly (some perpetrators will exhibit flirtatious and seductive behavior with the victim's friends). However, the resistance or defense may take more pathologic or self-sacrificial forms. She might lapse into poor hygiene so that the perpetrator is less interested. She may adopt a tough and unpleasant personality. She may constantly provoke chaos in family relations, providing somewhat of a shield and simultaneously gaining some measure of control. She may try to escape by running away, using drugs or alcohol, becoming promiscuous, getting in trouble at school or in the community, or failing her courses. She may employ irrational methods, like dressing in layers of baggy clothing or by being masculine.

However, the opposite may be true. As touched on previously, the victim may become an almost spousal figure in the home. She may clean house, prepare meals, supervise younger siblings, and wait on the perpetrator. Many victims feel that they are protecting the family and perhaps their younger siblings from the perpetrator's attentions by taking on such a role. A psychoanalytic interpretation of such behavior may be that the child is unconsciously compensating for the guilt she feels for what she believes to be her betrayal of her mother.

## Sexual Abuse of Girls Versus Boys

Throughout this section, we have consistently referred to the perpetrator as "he" and to the child victim as "she." This is not accidental. The great majority of victims of incest child abuse are female, and the great majority of perpetrators are male. Incident studies are markedly inconsistent since definitions of *childhood, sexual contact, male family member*, and similar variables may differ among various research projects. However, with that in mind, retrospective studies indicate that as high as 25% to 30% of women report some form of unwelcome sexual attention from an adult male family member at least once during childhood. Most experts conclude that about 10% to 15% of all women have received some form of sexual attention during their childhood from a stepfather, father, paramour of mother, grandfather, or older brother (Finkelhor & Hotaling, 1990).

Boys are not exempt from such attention. Early in our awareness of this family problem in the 1980s, it was believed that boys were seldom victims. However, more recently, it appears that boys are more often the victims of incest abuse than once believed. Fewer statistics are available concerning the prevalence of sexual abuse for males, but it may be that more than 10% of boys have been the recipient of sexual attention from an adult male during childhood (Finkelhor & Brown, 1988).

It is possible also that male victims are underreported for other reasons. When boys are sexually abused by fathers or stepfathers, which certainly appears to occur far more often than by mothers or stepmothers, there may be an element of shame—beyond the shame in heterosexual child abuse—in admitting the occurrence of "homosexual abuse." This shame may apply to both the perpetrator and the victim and may extend to retrospective studies in which adults are asked to remember childhood experiences. It should be noted as well that most fathers or stepfathers who sexually abuse their male children are apparently not homosexuals (Men Can Stop Rape, 2007).

## Females As Perpetrators

While it appears that it is rare for mothers or stepmothers to actively sexually abuse children of either sex, reliable data is not readily available. Child protective statistics do not always provide a good measure, because most states list the mother as a perpetrator even when her involvement has been passive—often her "involvement" is no more than the fact that she should have known that the male in the household was sexually abusing her child. Indeed, there are numerous incidents where the victim claims to have "told" mother what was occurring, only to have mother insist that the child should not have such "dirty" thoughts, that the perpetrator's intentions were misunderstood, or that the perpetrator was lying. Many victims report that when they told their mothers of the abuse, it stopped temporarily but then resumed, resulting in their loss of faith in the efficacy of such telling. However, for a mother to actively sexually abuse a daughter or stepdaughter appears to be rare. There may be a small percentage of boys, usually adolescents, who are sexually abused by their mothers or stepmothers, although often the abuse is limited to one or a small number of occasions. There are signs that this type of abuse may be on the increase.

## Causes of Childhood Sexual Abuse

What motivates the violation of trust related to childhood sexual abuse? Again, simple explanations are not satisfying. Perhaps the nature of the deviance defies any satisfactory explanation. Over the years, it has been frequently stated that the perpetrator's motivation is not sexual but rather is the need to dominate or control (Men Can Stop Rape, 2007). Some multifactor or family systems theories have been developed over the years that have some appeal. Nicholas Groth developed a framework for understanding the psychological motivations of perpetrators by dividing them into two broad classifications: the "fixated" and the "regressed" offenders (also discussed in chapter 4) (Groth & Birnbaum, 1979).

The fixated offender is the almost stereotypical pedophile, who is only able to experience true sexual arousal with prepubertal children, who typically has numerous victims of either sex, and who shares childish preoccupations and pleasures with his victims and attracts them with toys and sweets—who, in short, is a child at heart. The regressed offender, more likely to be found in the world of incest sexual abuse, is excited by "normal" sexual relations with a recurring partner but is psychologically threatened by the demands of a sexual relationship with another adult. Frustrated by the transactions inherent in the adult relationship, this offender regresses to a sexual relationship with a child whom he targets for the cultivation of an adultlike sexual relationship. However, other theorists point out that many perpetrators are sexual opportunists who seek out vulnerable victims who can be easily exploited or compelled (Lisak & Miller, 2002).

## Disclosure of Childhood Sexual Abuse

While disclosure of abuse has been discussed earlier in this chapter, there are certain aspects of disclosure specific to sexual abuse that must be discussed here. The social worker needs to understand that child sexual abuse may be encountered at *any* stage in the process. It has already been pointed out that there are certain risk factors that should demand careful attention. Beyond those, certain signs may appear that require one to ask very direct questions, or, perhaps more often, to make the CPS report.

Certain assumptions are often made, and they are often incorrect. For example, for many reasons, most victims will *not* readily seek out someone to confide in, and if they do, it is more likely to be a peer or a trusted family member. Not only have perpetrators probably employed some or all of the previously described methods to have their victims maintain secrecy, but most victims sense from the earliest advances made by the perpetrators that what they are experiencing is weighty and private. Perpetrators often report retrospectively that they took no conscious measures to maintain silence because their victims "just knew" that this type of behavior is not discussed (Pryor, 1996). A great level of trust would be required for victims to reveal their experiences to anyone, especially when they are younger and the process has only begun, when it is indiscernible and difficult to describe.

It should also be understood that even if a child does choose to confide in someone about his or her victimization, it will usually not be revealed in a direct and forthright statement, especially if the child is young. It is difficult enough for adults to confide their sexual doubts and secrets to their closest friends. For children, who lack experience, vocabulary, and sexual maturity, it is impossible to know where, or even if, to begin.

In fact, to a significant extent, what—if anything—is revealed to others about the victim's experiences is related to the victim's age. Younger victims, having no comparative measure, may initially assume that their experience is no different than that of any other child. After some time, many young victims begin to wonder about this, and it is frequent that sexual abuse at this stage is accidentally disclosed when a victim innocently asks a trusted friend a question such as "Does your daddy's pee-pee get big when you touch it?" The shocked friend then blurts out the question to the teacher, a parent, or other kids in the class.

By the time the victim is a little older, perhaps a preadolescent, social reality testing has developed sufficiently that he or she is probably aware that what is happening is not a common childhood experience. In addition to all the dire consequences her perpetrator has enumerated, this very fact may discourage her even further. At this age and older, the victim may have observed the experience of a classmate or friend whose victimization was revealed, and sadly, she may have witnessed that many of the perpetrator's predictions for her indeed happened to her friend (shame, humiliation before peers, anger from other family members, placement in foster care, etc.). Also, her sexual involvement with the perpetrator may extend to her earliest memories, and at this age, she is fully capable of predicting the questions she will be asked if she reveals her abuse—"Why did you let it go on so long without telling someone?"

## SIGNS OF CHILD SEXUAL ABUSE

### Physical Signs of Sexual Abuse

*Bruises, lacerations, or bleeding in the genital or anal area.* It is, of course, possible for injuries to the genital or anal area to be sustained in an accidental manner. However, explanations for such injuries that are not reasonable or that have no witnesses should be assessed carefully, especially if such injuries occur more than once. Ultimately, these injuries should be examined by a physician or nurse practitioner, preferably one who has received specialized training in this area and who is skilled at using special diagnostic instruments, such as a colposcope.

*Pain or itching in the genitals.* Pain or itching in the genitals is another possible sign of sexual abuse but by no means certain. Children with a diaper rash, for example, may suffer such problems, and some children's bubble bath products may cause an allergic reaction. This is again an area that requires medical assessment, although one should not expect that a doctor would necessarily be able to state with certainty the source of these problems.

*Repeated urinary tract infections.* Urinary tract infections, especially when recurring, are another possible rather than definite sign of sexual abuse. Of course, this is an area in which the professional opinion of a physician should be sought. If there are other reasons to suspect sexual abuse, these should be brought to the physician's attention. (This discussion specifically excludes sexually transmitted diseases, discussed later.)

*Injuries to the mouth or palate.* Many perpetrators of sexual abuse orally rape a child in the belief that such contact will be less likely to leave evidence. However, such contact may leave injuries to the hard or soft palate or the inside of the mouth as well as bruising on the lips. Any age child may be such a victim.

*Difficulty walking or sitting.* Penile, finger, or oral contact with a child's anal or genital area can cause soreness and swelling that makes it painful for a child to sit. In situations where a child is in such pain or discomfort and has chosen not to tell anyone about the problem, this type of discomfort may be observed. If it is observed, the child should be taken aside and asked privately what is causing the difficulty. As in each of these signs, a physician or nurse practitioner should be consulted.

*Pregnancy.* Pregnancy, in particular pregnancy that occurs at a very early age, may have resulted from contact with a sexual perpetrator. This possibility needs to be taken into consideration especially when a child is not fully sexually mature and is not involved in a sexual relationship. Even if a young child has not been impregnated by a parent, caretaker, or perpetrator, her pregnancy may lead to a question as to how she became sufficiently sexually experienced to have sex with a peer.

*Sexually transmitted diseases.* When children, especially young ones, are diagnosed with sexually transmitted diseases, the possibility of sexual abuse needs to be considered. This is always a consideration for the prepubertal child.

## Behavioral Signs of Sexual Abuse

*Advanced sexual knowledge for age.* When young children display advanced knowledge of sexual behaviors such as oral sex, sexual positions, sexual slang, and sexual behavioral dynamics, close attention needs to be paid. It is possible that the child has learned some of this from pornographic materials in the home or from peers or from listening to, or even observing, adults. Even so, this exposure may be due to parental neglect. However, when children pick up information from such activities or materials, it may be quite incomplete and may be displayed with bravado among peers. When it is the result of parental instruction, the instruction is likely to be displayed in a very academic way that may be accurate but has no sense of authenticity. But when children obtain this knowledge from experience, it is likely to have the feeling of accuracy to it, and it may be exhibited in a matter-of-fact or even reticent way. Sometimes, it may be displayed with great naivete, as when one child asks a friend if her sexual experiences with her father are similar to her own. In any case, the child should be discreetly asked about it.

*Seductive behavior.* Children who are the victims of sexual abuse may learn early that their sexuality has value and that it may be used to be liked, favored, or in exchange for something. Such children may exhibit seductive behavior with peers or adults. They may display poor physical boundaries in that they stand or sit too close, touch too often or at inappropriate times, or expose body parts.

*Statements or descriptions.* While sexually abused children may well keep their secret, sometimes they do the opposite: They select someone to tell their secret to or talk out loud about their experiences with anyone who is available. When children describe their experiences, adults, especially professionals, need to listen and validate. Hearing what the child has to say can be embarrassing and anxiety provoking. Some adults have a tendency to deny what they are hearing and discourage the child by saying things such as "Well, I am sure that is just your imagination" or "It is impolite to say things like that." When a child describes any type of victimization, become a listener. Do not display shock or revulsion; keep your remarks to a minimum. Do not attempt to be empathetic by making remarks such as "Your daddy is a bad man, and he will go to jail." Remain calm, and assure the child that you have heard many stories from children over the years. Ask only sufficient questions to clearly establish what you are being told. Do not venture into the area of a "forensic interview."

*Depression and other emotional problems.* Chronic or persistent depression, anxiety, and anger can all be related to the child's victimization. Of course, none of these emotional problems indicates absolutely that the child has been sexually abused. But the possibility needs to be taken into consideration, especially if combined with some of the other signs mentioned here.

*Promiscuity or prostitution.* Children who act out in the form of sexual promiscuity or prostitution may be the result of having become "sexualized" by their experiences as victims of sexual abuse. As with sexually transmitted diseases, the younger the child, the more likely it is that this behavior is a sign of sexual abuse.

*Chronic running away.* Leaving home may be a very effective way for the child to avoid unwelcome sexual contact, although it should not be considered an absolute indicator.

*Reluctance to undress.* Children who are victims of sexual abuse often feel great discomfort about undressing in front of other people, such as in gym class or in front of roommates on an outing. Occasionally, a specific incident of refusal to undress may be rooted in a fear that injuries caused by sexual abuse may be revealed.

*Sudden changes in social or academic functioning.* Sexual victimization should be considered in situations where a child's grades suddenly deteriorate or where they suddenly and without explanation curtail friendships or drop out of a circle of friends and isolate themselves.

*Resistance to being left alone or other activities with certain adults.* Pay careful attention when children demonstrate firm opposition to being left alone with a particular adult for babysitting, tutoring, or any other activity. The same holds true if, for example, children express fear or apprehension about a particular person tucking them in at night, having them sit on their lap, taking them for a ride in the car, or attending an event with them. It is possible that the child merely does not like the person or feels that the person is too strict or disinterested, but the child's feelings should be discussed rather than dismissed, and the reason for the resistance should be understood.

*Poor hygiene.* Older children and adolescents may purposely neglect their hygiene in an attempt to make themselves less desirable to the perpetrator.

*Sleep problems.* Problems sleeping, particularly repeated nightmares and insomnia, may be due to many causes, but one of them may be that the child is being sexually victimized. This may not be terribly surprising when it is realized that a considerable number of sexual abuse victims are abused in their own beds, often in the middle of the night while everyone else in the family is sleeping.

*Chronic incorrigibility.* General incorrigibility, including truancy, disturbed relationships with peers/parents/authority figures, petty thievery, drug or alcohol use, smoking, violating curfew, acts of vandalism, disobedience, fighting and academic failure, and disrespect, is a problem exhibited by some adolescents. Very often, incorrigible adolescents come from families with problems. In some cases, the problem in the family is sexual abuse, and incorrigibility is seen as the child's way to express rage, take revenge, and stake out an area of life that only he or she can control.

*The "adultified" child.* Sometimes, children of either gender in homes where there is abuse or neglect react by being overly responsible, obedient, and sensitive to their caretaker's needs, wants, and moods. One form of this response to sexual abuse is the female child who appears to have become the female head of the household. She is often responsible for seeing to the needs of younger children; takes care of household tasks such as cooking, cleaning, and laundry; and spends time and energy anticipating the whims of her father, making him comfortable on his arrival home from work (bringing him his slippers and a drink, etc.). Home responsibilities may keep the child from optimum school attendance, and school and relationships with peers are often of minimal importance to her.

## WHAT TO DO WHEN SEXUAL ABUSE IS SUSPECTED

Any social worker whose professional activities involves a fair amount of contact with children over a period of time will, sooner or later, be confronted with reasonable suspicion that a child is being sexually abused. It is important to be aware of several fairly common errors that are inadvertently made by mandated reporters when confronted with these suspicions, particularly when the child has made a disclosure to either a peer or an official. Suspicions of sexual abuse need to be handled differently from suspicions of neglect or physical abuse.

First, no matter how shocking or repulsive you find what you are discovering, do not let the child see your disgust. It is of utmost importance at this stage to realize that the child is extremely nervous about how her experience is going to be regarded by others. She almost certainly will have ambivalence about what has happened to her, about the perpetrator, and about telling. It will take very little for her to retract her story. She is not sure if others will at least partly blame her for what has happened. She is not sure if she is ready for a fight with the perpetrator. She is not certain how the rest of the family, especially her mother, will regard it all. She is extremely anxious about all the dire predictions her father/stepfather/perpetrator has uttered. Above all, you should be aware that you are probably only being told an infinitesimally small portion of what has happened to her. The first thing that will validate her doubts and cause her to retreat is the discovery that someone she has trusted enough to disclose this story to is repulsed by it, especially when she knows there is so much more to tell. At the first sign of trouble, she may claim that she was misunderstood, that she lied, or that she meant to say it was a story about her friend, and so on.

Second, an otherwise noble impulse of many recipients of a sexual abuse disclosure is to mobilize support for the child by saying things such as "Don't you worry, we are going to make sure that evil man gets arrested and goes to jail for a very long time." This is a very frightening statement for the child to hear. It confirms one of the warnings that have undoubtedly been given by the perpetrator. Again, it places the child in a position of active opposition to the perpetrator—something she deeply fears she will be unable to pull off. At the point of disclosure, children usually do not want what you may project that they want— escape, retribution, or outside help. Sometimes, all the victim wants is to discover if what is happening in her family is normal. More often, she simply wants the activity to cease, not total disruption of her family. The victim's feelings about her perpetrator will fall anywhere in a continuum that extends from fear to hatred and ambivalence to love. Remember that most perpetrators seem, until discovered, to be ordinary and normal. Many of them, aside from their awful acts of sexual exploitation, are otherwise endearing, funny, sociable people.

Third, do *not* "overinterview." This is a piece of advice that is probably widely known in the world of the mandated reporter, but there is confusion about the reasons for it. There are many. The primary reason is for the sake of the child's emotional state. Here, it is again important to realize that in most cases, the child has a very long story to tell. At disclosure, she is in a turmoil of anxiety and doubt. As people commence to interview her, she begins to anticipate the next questions that will be asked. Her mind is probably a clash of muddled memories. Often, children remember the lengthy development of the forced sexual relationship in a series of shocking memories rather than as a continuing series of events. Asking her questions may confuse and alarm her and make it appear that she is inventing things when she is actually remembering them out of order or because of her lack of sexual sophistication may be inaccurate about some of the things that the perpetrator did with her.

This leads us to the fact that there is an important forensic reason not to interview more than is necessary to make a report. Anything the child says is subject to a formal statement that may be later submitted as evidence in court (both criminal court and family court). Not only should these statements be prepared by those who have been specially trained in the forensics of such statements, but the more people who interview the child, the more difficult it may be for the district attorney to assemble a meaningful prosecution. There also is the issue of the child's opportunity to heal. Many people mistakenly believe that it is mentally or developmentally damaging for a victim of sexual abuse to talk about her experiences. Of course, the fact is that healing will occur, to a significant extent, through talking about her experiences. But that talking needs to occur in a quiet, therapeutic environment at a pace that is comfortable for the victim and in a setting that is protected by confidentiality and absent of piercing cross-examination. Permitting one well-intentioned professional after another to interview her on disclosure only causes her to feel uncertainty, confusion, humiliation, fear, and perhaps further victimized.

Fourth, the child's disclosure needs to occur in an orderly atmosphere. As soon as it becomes likely that a disclosure of sexual abuse is imminent, the child should unobtrusively be brought to a place that is private and quiet, where she will not be overheard, interrupted, or distracted. One person should be selected to speak with the child (note I have not used the word "interview"), and there should be another person present who serves as a witness. If at all possible, at least one of these people should be someone the child knows and trusts. Do not bring several persons in and out of the room or move the child from one place to another. Do not leave the child alone. Do not discuss strategy or emotional reactions or editorialize in the presence of the child. Never speak as if the child is not in the room. Adopt a sympathetic and reassuring tone with her. She should be assured that her classmates will not be informed of what is happening, that the interviewer has met other children who have had this kind of experience, and that the interviewer understands how difficult it is to talk about or think about these experiences.

Fifth, *never* assume that the nonoffending parent in the family will come to the child's aid or serve as the child's support. Such an assumption, especially if it is followed with an immediate notification to that parent, can be disastrous. Usually, this person will be the child's mother. In many cases, the mother's initial reaction, once she is over her initial shock, is sadness and empathy—and she comes immediately to the child's emotional aid. However, in a considerable percentage of cases, the mother's initial reaction will be shock and rage. Often, the child, even though a victim, may be included as a target of that rage. In rare cases, the child may be the exclusive target of the rage. Aside from the irrationality that may be experienced in a situation like this, keep in mind that often the perpetrator has for years fomented and capitalized on alienation between mother and daughter, so they may not be close to begin with. For this reason, victims—especially adolescents—may have been seen for years by their mothers as frustrating problems in the family because they have they have exhibited seemingly endless problems: academic failure, incorrigibility, running away, alcohol use, self-mutilation, defiance, and depression. At the time she learns of the disclosure, it may seem to her that these problem behaviors are the cause of the sexual contact between the perpetrator rather than the result. Leave the matter of informing the family to the authorities.

## Involving Law Enforcement

Most forms of child physical and sexual abuse and even some forms of child neglect are not only child welfare and family issues but also are crimes, sometimes rather important felonies. Discussion of police involvement is thoroughly addressed in chapter 11.

## FREQUENTLY ASKED QUESTIONS

**Q.** I am a social worker in a contract agency counseling a 14-year-old girl who is on probation as a repeat runaway. She is a very angry child who lives with a father who is very controlling and suspicious and a mother who seems distant and apathetic. Her father constantly yells at her, and she reports that he recently told her that if she runs away again, it doesn't matter what the probation department does because he will "beat her until she bleeds." I strongly suspect that this girl is being sexually abused by her father, but I would like to talk to her mother and hear what she thinks before I make a report to the child abuse hotline.

**A.** There are several parts to this problem that you need to sort out and place in their proper sequence. First, you are required to make a report as soon as you reasonably suspect neglect or abuse. At the moment, your suspicions of sexual abuse are too vague to be considered reasonable, but the father's threat to "beat her until she bleeds" is certainly reportable. Once you have made the call to the hotline, you can discuss with the interviewer all your suspicions and the degree to which they are reasonable. Last, your impulse to discuss your concerns with the child's mother should be approached with the utmost caution. Such a step should not be taken without letting the child know, and it should probably wait until you have earned more trust from the child and spoken to her directly about your concerns. If you do discover that the child has been sexually abused by her father, notify CPS and the police, and let them handle notifying *both* parents.

**Q.** I am a social worker at a county clinic. A 4-year-old boy was brought in by his grandmother when she discovered an extremely large area of bruising on his buttocks, legs, and back. There are apparently several sets of bruises in various stages of healing. The physician referred the situation to me after treatment to make a CPS report and coordinate the case with the police. I believe that this case fits the definition of neglect, but the doctor says it is abuse.

**A.** This lack of agreement about the classification of the abuse should not be permitted to delay calling in a CPS report to the child abuse hotline. Ultimately, the staff at the hotline will make the decision whether to classify the case as abuse or neglect.

**Q.** I am a school social worker who has been assigned to work with a 9-year-old boy who needs eyeglasses and who has several cavities in his teeth. I am reluctant to make a CPS report because his parents are quite poor, and I am sure they cannot afford either glasses or the cost of the dentist.

**A.** You may be correct about the inability of his parents to pay for these needs, but first, you should hear from them that this is their perception of the situation rather than hearing it just from the child or some other source. You should get in touch with them and discuss their son's needs. First, be sure that they are even aware of the needs. Then, if they are in need of assistance, work with them to secure assistance from a public child health plan or a charitable organization. As long as the parents recognize their son's needs and work with you to secure help, they are not neglectful. However, if your contact finds that either they actually do have the means but have ignored his needs or that they are apathetic about securing assistance or fail to act after the assistance has been arranged, then they should be reported to the child abuse hotline as neglectful.

**Q.** I am a social worker with a client who is a 7-year-old boy named Sam. Even though he vehemently denies it, I believe that Sam has been sexually abused, as he is an extremely sexualized child. He appears to know all about sexual practices and the slang names for various sexual body parts and sex acts. He will constantly proclaim, for example, that he is "horny," and he masturbates compulsively. I have reported this situation twice to CPS, and both times they have determined the case to be "unfounded." They will not discuss their reasons for this decision.

**A.** As a person mandated by law to report child abuse, reporting your suspicions was the correct action to take. Furthermore, if your suspicions increase as the result of new information, you should report again. Keep in mind that to report, you need only to have reasonable suspicions. However, to indicate the investigation, CPS needs to have credible evidence and, if they pursue the case in court, a fair preponderance of evidence. In situations like this, if the suspected child victim and the parents all firmly deny the allegations and there is no physical evidence or witness, CPS has no choice but to close the case unfounded.

## REFERENCES

Groth, A. N., & Birnbaum, H. J. (1979). *Men who rape—The psychology of the offender.* New York: Plenum Press.

Lisak, D., & Miller, P. M. (2002). Repeat rape and multiple offending among undetected rapists. *Violence and Victims, 17*(1), 73–84.

Men Can Stop Rape. (2007). Retrieved July 3, 2008, from http://www.mencanstoprape. org

Pryor, D. W. (1996). *Unspeakable acts: Why men sexually abuse children.* New York: New York University Press.

## ADDITIONAL READING

Barnett, O., Miller-Perrin, C. L., & Perrin, R. D. (2005). *Family violence across the lifespan* (2nd ed.). Thousand Oaks, CA: Sage.

Finkelhor, D. (1979). *Sexually victimized children.* New York: The Free Press.

Finkelhor, D. (1984). *Child sexual abuse—New theory and research.* New York: The Free Press.

Finkelhor, D., & Williams, D. (1988). Sexual abuse in a national survey of adult men and women: Prevalence, characteristics, and risk factors. *Child Abuse and Neglect: The International Journal, 14,* 19–28.

Sgroi, M. D., & Suzanne, M. (1982). *Handbook of clinical intervention in child sexual abuse.* New York: Free Press.

# 6  When Is a Report Required?

All states require certain designated professionals to report (or cause a report to be made) if they have a suspicion that a child has been abused or neglected. When information comes to the attention of these mandated reporters in their professional capacity that a child has been abused and/or neglected, all states require that child protective services (CPS) be notified. This chapter will discuss who is required to report, when there is enough evidence to report, and against whom a report can be made.

## WHO IS REQUIRED TO REPORT?

Many states have exceptions to the list of professionals who are required to report. For example, defense attorneys are exempt in some states, as are members of the clergy if they are acting in a religious capacity. On the other hand, some states, like North Dakota and New Mexico, do mandate the clergy. (See appendix A for a list of mandated reporters by state.)

Social workers in all states—whether employed in schools, health or mental health settings, social service agencies, substance abuse programs, or in private practice—are considered professionals that are required to make reports of abuse and neglect. In addition, all states have provisions related to confidentiality, failure to make a report, or penalties for making a false report. (See appendix A for a complete summary of state laws.) Social workers need to be aware that failure to report abuse and neglect could subject them to both civil liabilities and criminal prosecution as well as cause them to lose their state license. This is covered further in chapter 10.

Most states require that mandated reporters make reports when they are acting in their professional and/or official capacity. This means if mandated reporters are not working in their professional capacity, they do not have a legal mandate to make a child abuse and neglect report. A question that often arises concerns the requirement for mandated reporters who become aware of a possible abuse or neglect situation when they are not officially working. For example, suppose a school social worker is approached in a shopping mall on a Saturday afternoon by a student at the school where she is employed. The student reports being abused by a parent. Even though the social worker is not officially working, she should make a mandated report. It should be noted that even if such a report is not legally required, there is a moral and ethical argument to be made for a report to be entered by the social worker. The social worker could make the report in a nonmandated capacity. Many states have a separate hotline number for nonmandated reporters.

New York State recently passed a law that further broadens the circumstances under which a mandated reporter must act. This law, entitled Xctasy's law, requires all social service workers to make reports of child abuse and neglect even in situations where they learn about the abuse and neglect *from other parties*. The legislation was named for 4-year-old Xctasy Garcia. In spring 2007, a patron at a motel where Xctasy was staying with her parents heard screams and loud noises coming from an adjoining room. He reported this to the manager of the motel, saying that he believed a "man might be harming a child." The manager twice called the county department of social services to report these concerns, but there was no follow-up investigation. Two weeks later, parishioners at a nearby church found Xctasy severely beaten and badly burned with bleach. They quickly rushed her to a local hospital. Only then did a child abuse investigation begin. If the Xctasy law was in effect at the time of the original call, the social service worker who received the call from the hotel manager would have been mandated to notify the New York State Child Abuse Hotline.

## WHEN IS THERE ENOUGH EVIDENCE TO REPORT?

For social workers who are mandated by law to make CPS reports, a report is required as soon as there is reasonable suspicion that a situation about which they have knowledge constitutes child abuse or neglect in accordance with the definitions set forth by the law in the jurisdiction in which they practice. This requirement seems simple enough, but it bears some reflection. Often, mandated reporters are confused about the difference between reporting based on *reasonable suspicion* versus reporting based on a *minimal degree of evidence*. This confusion is quite understandable, since a common ethical norm in democratic societies is the idea that one must be accused based on evidence rather than feelings or opinions. It is best to keep in mind that in making a CPS report, one is not "accusing" or "charging" someone but rather is registering reasonable suspicions in order that a formal organization, founded and designed for this specific purpose, may examine the situation to determine if accusations or charges may be in order.

Note also that the requirement is that one's suspicions be reasonable. This means that suspicions must withstand self-scrutiny to match a test in which they "make sense" based on the potential reporter's education, training, professional experience and common sense. Reasonable suspicion may begin with an intuition that "all is not right with this child," but such a gut feeling, in the absence of all other reason to suspect, is not in and of itself "reasonable." It is instead a departure point to begin examining one's doubts or further exploring the situation.

The mandated reporter must be careful not to form immediate, unreasonable suspicions as well as not rule out otherwise reasonable suspicions because the situation seems "normal," the parent seems "not like the kind of person who would abuse or neglect a child," or one is readily able to empathize with the parent's frustration or temporary loss of control due to a stressful home situation. What is required in this process is for mandated reporters to objectively identify and examine their biases and overcome those that might interfere with the obligation to report.

Self-examination in this matter may seem counterintuitive, but the degree of objectivity required is no more elaborate than that required by a juror who is admonished by a judge to "disregard" improper information that comes to his or her attention in a courtroom. There is a risk that mandated reporters who are uncomfortable with their suspicions will expend time and energy searching for information to confirm their suspicions or worse, begin a series of informal consultations with peers in an effort to feel supported in their suspicions. The problem here (aside from the loss of time) is that mandated reporters begin venturing into two areas that may compromise their role: First, they are conducting an investigation; second, they may be violating the right of the subject's family to confidentiality.

## Reasonable Cause to Suspect

States differ on the terms used to define the threshold for reporting. In Wisconsin, for example, mandated reporters must make a report when, in the course of their professional duties, they have *reasonable cause to suspect* that a child has been abused or neglected or when, in the course of their professional duties, they have *reason to believe* that a child has been threatened with abuse or neglect or that abuse or neglect will occur.

Most states use terms such as *reasonable cause to suspect* or *reasonable cause to believe*. Some states, like Wisconsin, use both terms in their definition. Ohio and Alabama use the terms *know* or *suspect,* and New Mexico uses the term *reasonable suspicion* (Child Welfare Information Gateway, 2006).

*Reasonable cause* can be defined as when a mandated reporter can entertain the possibility of a child being abused and/or maltreated based on what he or she has observed or has been told and when this, combined with the reporter's training and experience, leads the reporter to feel that the child may be harmed or is in imminent danger of being harmed. Mandated reporters need to be sensitive to explanations that are inconsistent with their observations, experience, and/or knowledge. Therefore, social workers do not need to be *sure* that child abuse or maltreatment has taken place. Once social workers have assessed that there is *reasonable cause* to suspect or believe that a child has been abused and/or neglected, they need to understand the reporting procedures in their state.

Social workers will find that some cases are not that difficult to assess for abuse and neglect. However, for others—especially those involving potential neglect—it is often difficult for mandated reporters to determine whether the information they have obtained has reached the threshold to report. It is important for social workers to understand that it is not their responsibility to know or prove that a child has been abused or neglected but to only have reasonable suspicion that abuse or neglect has occurred. Again, remember that a report is not an accusation but rather a request for an investigation of a suspicious situation.

## Legal Burdens of Proof

One way of understanding the term *reasonable cause to suspect/believe* is to explore the different standards of proof in our legal system, which employs different levels of evidence (otherwise known as the standard of proof or burden of proof). The standard of proof is the level of proof required in a legal action to convince the fact-finder (usually the judge or jury) that a given allegation is true. The degree of proof required depends on the circumstances of the allegation and in part on the risk the respondent or defendant faces as a result of an adjudication or conviction. Charges that carry mild consequences, such as a fine for a traffic ticket have lower burdens of proof and therefore are easier to prove than those that carry serious consequences, such as a jail or prison sentence for an assault charge.

The highest standard of proof is used in criminal cases. In most of these cases, the prosecution must prove that the defendant committed the crime "beyond a reasonable doubt." This means that there can be no reasonable doubt in the mind of a reasonable person that the defendant is guilty. There can still be a doubt, but only to the extent that it would *not* affect a reasonable person's belief that the defendant is guilty. If the doubt that is raised *does* affect a reasonable person's belief that the defendant is guilty, the jury is not satisfied beyond a reasonable doubt (Kagehiro & Stanton, 1985).

For example, if a parent is charged with serious physical abuse or child sexual abuse and the case goes to trial in a criminal court, the judge will instruct the jury to use the standard of beyond a reasonable doubt when determining the parent's guilt or innocence. Most experts will advise that under these circumstances, before the jury members can vote for conviction, they need to be close to 100% sure that the parent committed the crime, based on the evidence presented.

For cases in civil court, including family or juvenile courts, the standard most often used is "a fair preponderance of the evidence." Legal manuals describe this level as evoking "belief produced by ascertaining the greater or weightier evidence. The trier of fact must believe that it is more probable that the fact is true or exists than it is that it does not exist" (see Gellhorn, Byse and Strauss, 1979, p. 270).

For example, if a parent is alleged to have neglected a child and the matter is brought to the attention of family court, the judge determines whether the parent should be held responsible for the neglect. The judgment is made by determining whether the evidence presented against the parent indicates that the parent more likely (with a greater than 50% likelihood) neglected the child than not.

Some states use preponderance of the evidence as the standard of proof for substantiating child protection cases after investigation. However, most states use a less rigorous standard of proof—"some credible evidence." This is the level that many states require CPS to apply when determining if a case is indicated/substantiated or unfounded/unsubstantiated. "Some credible evidence," as used by CPS, is a lower standard than "preponderance of the evidence" as used by the civil courts. Whereas preponderance requires at least a 50% likelihood of guilt, most experts would measure some credible evidence at about 35%.

As compared with the levels discussed previously, "reasonable cause to suspect/believe" as required by most mandated reporters is even lower than "some credible evidence" and could perhaps be quantified at around 10% to 15%. The reason lawmakers keep this standard so low is to initiate interventions whenever there is a suspicion that a child is being abused and/or neglected. Better to err on the side of protection of children was the reason behind the low standard being used.

Thus, if a social worker has reasonable cause to suspect or believe, he or she should make a report to alert the child protective authorities. If the allegation and subsequent investigation results in a "finding" or "indication" of possible abuse or neglect, then often additional services are offered to the parent and the family to alleviate the problem and assure that the child is safe and protected. If the degree of abuse and/or neglect is a major concern and the ongoing safety of the child is questionable, a petition against the parent may be filed in family/juvenile court. The parents may lose temporary custody of the child. If the allegations indicate a crime may have been committed, the parents may also be arrested and prosecuted in criminal court. At each stage, a different level of proof is required to initiate action on behalf of the child and against the accused abuser.

## WHO CAN BE THE SUBJECT OF THE REPORT?

All states define a "child" as an individual from birth to the age of 18 years as well as those with a handicapping condition who are in the care of a specialized residential facility between the ages of 18 to 21 years. Therefore, as a mandated reporter, you generally cannot report abuse or neglect against anyone older than the age of 18 years. You cannot report prenatal harm, but most states will require the mandated reporter to notify CPS if a child is born with a positive toxicology, indicating drug use.

With regards to allegations of severe child abuse and/or sexual abuse that are made once a child reaches his or her 18th birthday, any abuse investigation no longer falls under the responsibility of CPS—even though the abuse happened when the person was a child. If the allegation is related to severe abuse, then it may be a criminal or civil matter depending on the statue of limitations in that state related to criminal or civil actions.

The definition of who can be the subject of a report varies across states (see appendix A). For instance, in some states, all suspected abuse or neglect of children must be reported, regardless of who is suspected of causing the abuse or neglect (parent, guardian, or any other adult).

In other states, mandated reporting legislation limits the requirement of a report to cases in which the suspected abuse or neglect is caused by a parent or other adult who has custodial responsibilities for the subject child. The custodial responsibilities of the nonparent subject of the report do not have to be full-time, or long term. For instance, a parent's paramour who has regular contact with the child may be the subject of a report in certain jurisdictions.

There are a few justifications for limiting the scope of mandated reports to cases in which the suspected abuse or neglect is caused by parents or other responsible adults. First of all, the purpose of mandated reporting legislation was to bring to light cases of abuse and neglect at the hands of family members, as these instances were not otherwise being brought to the attention of CPS. Historically, parents raised their children in private, with little or no opportunity for intervention from the outside. Professionals were wary of intruding into the private sphere of family functioning. Therefore, there was little voluntary reporting of suspected child abuse or neglect. Mandated reporting laws were passed in an effort to bring these cases to light so that intervention could be provided for these families and children's safety could be secured.

Cases of abuse or neglect at the hands of nonparents were less likely to be shielded from government intervention. In fact, parents themselves are often the ones who seek government intervention when their children are harmed by others (such as teachers, coaches, or other adult figures). Thus, it was not deemed necessary to provide a requirement for the reporting of such behaviors.

As well, in order to receive a socially appropriate response to abuse or neglect by persons other than parents or custodians, police intervention—as opposed to CPS intervention—is warranted. A report to CPS prompts an investigation of family functioning and assessment as to the need for family-related services. CPS workers themselves cannot institute criminal penalties for child endangerment. Assessment and provision of family services may not be appropriate in cases where the person responsible for abuse or neglect is not a family member (or similar person). Instead, the involvement of law enforcement would be the appropriate response. Although the law in your particular state may not mandate you to report such instances of abuse or neglect to CPS, a report to the police may be justified after careful consideration of your ethical and moral concerns.

## REFERENCES

Child Welfare Information Gateway. (2006). *Long term consequences of child abuse and neglect.* Washington, DC: U.S. Department of Health and Human Services, Administration on Children, Youth and Families.

Gellhorn, W., Byse, C., & Strauss, P. (1979). *Administrative law 916* (7th ed.). New York: Foundation Press.

Kagehiro, D. K., & Stanton, W. C. (1985). Legal vs. quantified definitions of standards of proof. *Law and Human Behavior, 9,* 159–178.

# 7 How to Make a Report

As discussed in previous chapters, all states require mandated reporters to make reports of child abuse and neglect. Furthermore, all 50 states, the District of Columbia, American Samoa, Guam, the Northern Mariana Islands, Puerto Rico, and the U.S. Virgin Islands have laws and policies that specify procedures for making and responding to reports of suspected child abuse or neglect. This chapter will discuss the general procedures involved. For more specific information, consult your organization's policies and/or local child protective services (CPS), police, or child advocacy center.

## TO WHOM IS THE REPORT MADE?

In all jurisdictions, the initial report may be made *orally* to either the CPS agency or a law enforcement agency. In all states, there is a single phone number through which mandated reporters can make a report of suspected child abuse or neglect. In some states, that phone number routes the call to a centralized government agency that receives all reports of suspected child abuse and neglect throughout the state; this entity is sometimes known as the state central register (see chapter 1 for a discussion of state central registers). In other states, that central phone number may route the call to the local CPS unit, usually at a regional or county level.

In all states, the person receiving the mandated reporter's call is a trained government employee. Similar to an emergency services (911) operator, the employee is trained to handle stressful situations. Such an operator may be simultaneously speaking with the reporter and inputting information into a computer system. Supervisors are available for consultation or clarification. The operator should have a professional demeanor. If you are not satisfied with the operator's response, you should ask to speak to a supervisor.

## WHAT YOU SHOULD KNOW BEFORE YOU REPORT

You should have readily available to you as much information as you can gather before you call the CPS hotline. Most states require that the actual hotline oral report by a mandated reporter be followed up with the submission of a written form that verifies the report. You should review that form prior to calling in a report, as the form generally provides guidance on the important information that the hotline interviewer will need to set up the case for investigation.

Figure 7.1 is a sample of a CPS reporting form that is required to be used in New York State. This form, called the DSS-2221-A, provides spaces for the person who makes a report to the child abuse hotline to list all the identifying information concerning the case they have reported. There is also space for a brief narrative description of the circumstances that lead to the report. For example, this form must be completed, signed, and mailed to CPS within 48 hours after the hotline conversation, if you are a mandated reporter making a report in New York State. The form also provides useful information that the CPS investigator will use and also documents that the mandated reporter completed a referral. Each state has its own method for verifying the hotline report in writing; check with your local CPS for the procedure in your state.

It is quite possible that you will not have all the information called for on the form, and it is not your job to get this information if you do not have it readily available or if it is not information that you would normally gather in connection with your professional role with the child or the family.

Most CPS hotlines will require a minimum level of information before they will register the call for an investigation. The reporter will be

LDSS-2221A (Rev. 9/2007) FRONT

NEW YORK STATE
OFFICE OF CHILDREN AND FAMILY SERVICES
**REPORT OF SUSPECTED
CHILD ABUSE OR MALTREATMENT**

| Report Date | Case ID | Call ID |
|---|---|---|
| Time ☐ AM ☐ PM | Local Case # | Local Dist/Agency |

### SUBJECTS OF REPORT

List all children in household, adults responsible and alleged subjects.

| Line # Last Name | First Name | Aliases | Sex (M, F, Unk) | Birthday or Age Mo/Day/Yr | Race Code | Ethnicity (Ck Only If Hispanic/Latino) | Relation Code | Role Code | Lang. Code |
|---|---|---|---|---|---|---|---|---|---|
| 1. | | | | | | ☐ | | | |
| 2. | | | | | | ☐ | | | |
| 3. | | | | | | ☐ | | | |
| 4. | | | | | | ☐ | | | |
| 5. | | | | | | ☐ | | | |
| 6. | | | | | | ☐ | | | |
| 7. | | | | | | ☐ | | | |

☐ MORE

| List Addresses and Telephone Numbers (Using Line Numbers From Above) | (Area Code) Telephone No. |
|---|---|
| | |

### BASIS OF SUSPICIONS

Alleged suspicions of abuse or maltreatment. Give child(ren)'s line number(s). If all children, write **"ALL"**.

____ DOA/Fatality
____ Fractures
____ Internal Injuries (e.g., Subdural Hematoma)
____ Lacerations/Bruises/Welts
____ Burns/Scalding
____ Excessive Corporal Punishment
____ Inappropriate Isolation/Restraint (Institutional Abuse Only)
____ Inappropriate Custodial Conduct (Institutional Abuse Only)

____ Child's Drug/Alcohol Use
____ Poisoning/Noxious Substances
____ Choking/Twisting/Shaking
____ Lack of Medical Care
____ Malnutrition/Failure to Thrive
____ Sexual Abuse
____ Inadequate Guardianship
____ Other (specify) ____

____ Swelling/Dislocation/Sprains
____ Educational Neglect
____ Emotional Neglect
____ Inadequate Food/Clothing/Shelter
____ Lack of Supervision
____ Abandonment
____ Parent's Drug/Alcohol Misuse

State reasons for suspicion, including the nature and extent of each child's injuries, abuse or maltreatment, past and present, and any evidence or suspicions of "Parental" behavior contributing to the problem.

(If known, give time/date of alleged incident)
MO
DAY
YR
Time : ☐ AM ☐ PM

☐ Additional sheet attached with more explanation.　The Mandated Reporter Requests Finding of Investigation ☐ YES ☐ NO

### *CONFIDENTIAL*　SOURCE(S) OF REPORT　*CONFIDENTIAL*

| NAME | (Area Code) TELEPHONE | NAME | (Area Code) TELEPHONE |
|---|---|---|---|
| ADDRESS | | ADDRESS | |
| AGENCY/INSTITUTION | | AGENCY/INSTITUTION | |

**RELATIONSHIP**

____ Med. Exam/Coroner ____ Physician ____ Hosp. Staff ____ Law Enforcement ____ Neighbor ____ Relative ____ Instit. Staff
____ Social Services ____ Public Health ____ Mental Health ____ School Staff ____ Other (Specify)

| For Use By Physicians Only | Medical Diagnosis on Child | Signature of Physician who examined/treated child X | (Area Code) Telephone No. |
|---|---|---|---|
| | Hospitalization Required: ☐ None | ☐ Under 1 week ☐ 1-2 weeks | ☐ Over 2 weeks |

| Actions Taken Or About To Be Taken | ☐ Medical Exam ☐ Photographs | ☐ X-Ray ☐ Hospitalization | ☐ Removal/Keeping ☐ Returning Home | ☐ Not. Med Exam/Coroner ☐ Notified DA |
|---|---|---|---|---|

| Signature of Person Making This Report: X | Title | Date Submitted Mo. Day Yr. |
|---|---|---|

**Figure 7.1** New York State's DSS-2221 is one example of a reporting form.

LDSS-2221A (Rev. 9/2007) REVERSE

**TO ACCESS THE LDSS-2221-A FORMS: Via Internet: http://www.ocfs.state.ny.us/main/forms/cps/**
**Via Intranet: http://ocfs.state.nyenet/admin/forms/SCR/ or**

**TO ORDER A SUPPLY OF FORMS:** access **(OCFS-4627) Request for Forms and Publications**, from either site above, fill it out and send to: **Office of Children and Family Services, Resource Distribution Center, 11 Fourth Ave, Rensselaer, NY 12144.**
If you have difficulty accessing this form from either site, you can call **The Forms Hot Line at 518-473-0971.** Leave a detailed message including your name, address, city, state, what form number you need, how many and a phone number in case we need to contact you.

## NEW YORK STATE OFFICE OF CHILDREN AND FAMILY SERVICES

| RACE CODE | ETHNICITY CODE | RELATION CODES FAMILIAL REPORTS *(Choose One)* | | ROLE CODE *(Choose One)* | LANGUAGE CODE *(Choose One)* | |
|---|---|---|---|---|---|---|
| **AA**: Black or African-American | *(Check Only If Hispanic/ Latino)* | **AU**: Aunt/Uncle | **XX**: Other | **AB**: Abused Child | **CH**: Chinese | **KR**: Korean |
| **AL**: Alaskan Native | | **CH**: Child | **PA**: Parent | **MA**: Maltreated Child | **CR**: Creole | **MU**: Multiple |
| **AS**: Asian | | **GP**: Grandparent | **PS**: Parent Substitute | **AS**: Alleged Subject | **EN**: English | **PL**: Polish |
| **NA**: Native American | | **FM**: Other Family Member | **UH**: Unrelated Home Member | (Perpetrator) | **FR**: French | **RS**: Russian |
| **PI**: Native Hawaiian/Pacific Islander | | **FP**: Foster Parent | **UK**: Unknown | **NO**: No Role | **GR**: German | **SI**: Sign |
| **WH**: White | | **DC**: Daycare Provider | | **UK**: Unknown | **HI**: Hindi | **SP**: Spanish |
| **XX**: Other | | **IAB REPORTS ONLY** | | | **HW**: Hebrew | **VT**: Vietnamese |
| **UNK**: Unknown | | **AR**: Administrator | **IN**: Instit. Non-Prof | | **IT**: Italian | **XX**: Other |
| | | **CW**: Child Care Worker | **IP**: Instit. Pers/Vol. | | **JP**: Japanese | |
| | | **DO**: Director/Operator | **PI**: Psychiatric Staff | | | |

### Abstract of Sections from Article 6, Title 6, Social Services Law
### Section 412. Definitions
1. **Definition of Child Abuse,** (see also N.Y.S. Family Court Act Section 1012(e))
   An "abused child" is a child less than eighteen years of age whose parent or other person legally responsible for his care:
   1) Inflicts or allows to be inflicted upon the child serious physical injury, or
   2) Creates or allows to be created a substantial risk of physical injury, or
   3) Commits sexual abuse against the child or allows sexual abuse to be committed.
2. **Definition of Child Maltreatment,** (see also N.Y.S. Family Court Act, Section 1012(f))
   A 'maltreated child' is a child under eighteen years of age whose physical, mental or emotional condition has been impaired or is in imminent danger of becoming impaired as a result of the failure of his parent or other person legally responsible for his care to exercise a minimum degree of care:
   1) in supplying the child with adequate food, clothing, shelter, education, medical or surgical care, though financially able to do so or offered financial or other reasonable means to do so; or
   2) in providing the child with proper supervision or guardianship; or
   3) by unreasonably inflicting, or allowing to be inflicted, harm or a substantial risk thereof, including the infliction of excessive corporal punishment; or
   4) by misusing a drug or drugs; or
   5) by misusing alcoholic beverages to the extent that he loses self-control of his actions; or
   6) by any other acts of a similarly serious nature requiring the aid of the Family Court; or
   7) By abandoning the child.

**Section 415. Reporting Procedure.** Reports of suspected child abuse or maltreatment shall be made immediately by telephone and in writing within 48 hours after such oral report.

**Submit the written paper copy of the LDSS-2221-A form originally signed to: the County Department of Social Services where the abused/maltreated child resides.**

**Residential Institutional Abuse Reports: Submit a paper copy of form, LDSS 2221A, originally signed. It must be submitted directly to the Office of Children and Family Services (OCFS) Regional Office, associated with the county in which the abused/maltreated child is in care.**

**NYS CHILD ABUSE AND MALTREATMENT REGISTER: 1-800-635-1522 (FOR MANDATED REPORTERS ONLY)**
**1-800-342-3720 (FOR PUBLIC CALLERS)**

**Section 419. Immunity from Liability,** Pursuant to Section 419 of the Social Services Law, any person, official, or institution participating in good faith in the making of a report of suspected child abuse or maltreatment, the taking of photographs, or the removal or keeping of a child pursuant to the relevant provisions of the Social Services Law shall have immunity from any liability, civil or criminal, that might otherwise result by reason of such actions. For the purpose of any proceeding, civil or criminal, the good faith of any such person, official, or institution required to report cases of child abuse or maltreatment shall be presumed, provided such person, official or institution was acting in discharge of their duties and within the scope of their employment, and that such liability did not result from the willful misconduct or gross negligence of such person, official or institution.

**Section 420. Penalties for Failure to Report.**
1. Any person, official, or institution required by this title to report a case of suspected child abuse or maltreatment who willfully fails to do so shall be guilty of a class A misdemeanor.
2. Any person, official, or institution required by this title to report a case of suspected child abuse or maltreatment who knowingly and willfully fails to do so shall be civilly liable for the damages proximately caused by such failure.

LDSS-2221A (Rev. 9/2007) ATTACHMENT

STAPLE TO LDSS-2221A *(IF NEEDED)*

**REPORT OF SUSPECTED
CHILD ABUSE OR MALTREATMENT**

**(Use only if the space on the LDSS-2221A under "Reasons for Suspicion" is not enough to accommodate your information)**

| Report Date | Case ID | Call ID |
|---|---|---|
| Time    ☐ AM <br> :    ☐ PM | Local Case # | Local Dist/Agency |

**PERSON MAKING
THIS REPORT:** _____

**Print clearly if filling out hard copy.**

| *Continued:* State reasons for suspicion, including the nature and extent of each child's injuries, abuse or maltreatment, past and present, and any evidence or suspicions of "Parental" behavior contributing to the problem. | (If known, give time/date of alleged incident) <br> MO <br> DAY <br> YR <br>      Time    :    ☐ AM ☐ PM |
|---|---|
| | |

asked to provide as much information about the child's situation as possible, including the name and address of the child and the child's parents or other persons responsible for the child's care, the child's age, conditions in the child's home environment, and the nature and extent of the child's injuries.

You should provide a definite location for the family. This will usually be an address, or even an automobile license plate or a specifically described location ("a yellow house, the third house on the left after you turn onto Smith Street"), but not a vague reference ("somewhere in the Scenty Pines subdivision").

If a family does not all live together in the same location, do your best to provide all addresses and family compositions involved. This will help CPS discover if anyone involved has been or is currently involved in another CPS case. If you have phone numbers, provide them.

You should include the names and ages of everyone in the family. If you do not have formal names and dates of birth, provide nicknames and approximate ages. If you do not have information about other family members, do not let this delay your report—call and provide what you do have.

The next most important data set is the allegations. Take a moment before you call to organize what you want to say. It is not unusual for reporters to pour out a complex mix of facts, unrelated information, opinions, and assumptions. You will help by presenting a clear and organized narrative.

Be clear in your language. Rather than say, for example, "his mother emotionally abuses him all the time," say, "when the mother picks him up after our counseling sessions, she constantly tells him that all the family's problems are due to his being a 'sicko.'" Or, instead of saying "the house is a pigpen," say "when I visited the house last Friday, there were several piles of dog feces in the living room and kitchen and quite a number of empty pizza boxes and dirty dishes all around the house, and there was a foul odor."

Use the words that the child has actually used. Rather than say "his father abuses him," say "yesterday I noticed a bruise on his arm, and he told me he got it when his father punched him with a closed fist during an argument."

Try to provide as much information as you can that will assist the investigation or even protect the CPS investigator. If you know that the house contains weapons, vicious dogs, dangerously dilapidated steps, vermin infestation, and so on, tell the interviewer. If a family member has a history of violence, or if someone has said something like "if you send a CPS worker around here again, I'm going to punch him in the face," report this information. If you have seen drug paraphernalia, large amounts of cash lying around, or evidence of a drug manufacturing operation, report this as well.

If there are other organizations involved with the child or the family, make a list of these and let the hotline know. This would include the police, probation, parole, clinics, hospitals, drug programs, parenting programs, and schools. If you know the names and contact information for others in your organization who are involved with the child or the family, provide these.

If you know of witnesses to specific events, such as beatings, neglect, anyone providing the child with drugs, anyone having sexual contact with the child, or anyone who has witnessed criminal activities, provide these to the hotline along with how the witnesses may be contacted.

Finally, let the CPS hotline interviewer know who you have informed of the report. Remember that you are ordinarily not required to let any family member, including the child, know that you made the report, but if you have opted to let anyone in the family know, pass this information on. You should also advise the CPS hotline of anyone in your organization who knows of the report. Keep in mind that once the report has been made, you should not talk about it with others unless such discussion is required as part of your professional duties.

## Documentation and Evidence

If you have documentation of your allegations or related information in the forms of reports, medical forms, x-rays or other types of medical images, drug tests, psychological tests, photographs, case notes, educational records, video or tape recordings, arrest records, and so forth, make a list of them and tell the CPS hotline interviewer that you have them. Please note that it is not always advisable to send these items in accompaniment to the written form that CPS requires you to submit, for several reasons. First, there is the possibility that they will be lost or misrouted. More important, they may be valuable evidence, and if so, they must be handled in a way that maintains the chain of custody, especially if you caused them to be created specifically due to your suspicions that the child was abused or neglected. When you hear from the CPS investigator, remind him or her that you have these materials. The person will let you know the preferred method of getting the materials into the CPS record.

Remember that mandated reporters are not investigators, and many problems can arise when mandated reporters try to investigate alleged abuse or neglect. The first is that they are most likely untrained, and untrained investigators often blunder into areas they did not expect to be and potentially find themselves in awkward situations.

Additionally, anything discovered may constitute evidence, and evidence is required to be handled in a specific way in order for it to remain forensically "pure"—in other words, usable in a trial or a hearing should one eventually be necessary. An untrained investigator may unwittingly make the evidence more difficult to use than it would otherwise have been. Worse, such efforts may render it useless or even more helpful to the defense. Or, along the same line, these actions may reduce or complicate the mandated reporter's role as a witness in a formal hearing (and make the experience of testifying very stressful).

Furthermore, depending on the mandated reporters' professional role with the family, their informal investigation may lead them to information or activities that would compromise this role or reduce their effectiveness. For example, a social worker should not be examining a child for injuries or marks, particularly if observation requires looking at or touching areas of the child's body that are normally covered with clothing. Last, if a social worker is employed by an agency or organization, conducting investigatory activities outside of one's professional realm may place the organization at risk.

It is always important for the mandated reporter to keep in mind his or her obligation to maintain the right of the subject to privacy and confidentiality. A series of inquiries among peers within the organization or, worse, among peers or others outside of one's immediate organization, runs a great risk of compromising these rights. This can be easy to forget when someone is accustomed to sharing with peers the various events of the day, both good and bad. It is probably a rare mandated reporter who does not fully realize that discussing CPS reports at a picnic or a cocktail party is an outrageous breach of ethics, but professional awareness may not be so high in the conference room or on a coffee break.

## WHAT TO DO IN AN EMERGENCY

If you are confronted with an urgent situation, especially one involving possible immediate risk to the safety of a child, you should call the CPS hotline immediately, even if you have not had time to organize yourself to present all the information listed previously. If this happens, immediately begin the call by clearly stating to the hotline interviewer, "I have an emergency." After the hotline interviewer gathers minimal information, you may be instructed to first call the police and then later complete the report.

There may be occasions, such as when a parent arrives at your location threatening immediate harm to the child and perhaps yourself, when you must call the police via 911 immediately and concern yourself with the CPS report after the child's safety is secured. Child safety is the first and foremost tenet in child protective work. If such a scene has unfolded, you should call the CPS hotline as soon as the child's safety is secured. Be sure to advise the hotline worker of what has happened, and inform the worker of any police involvement. If possible, provide a report identifier so that the CPS hotline can obtain the report. Indeed, the police are required by law to make CPS reports, but this requirement does not in any way diminish your responsibility to make the report immediately.

## HOW QUICKLY SHOULD A REPORT BE MADE?

Once suspicions have been subjected to self-examination and have been found to be "reasonable," as discussed in chapter 6, then the CPS report must be made. The mandated reporter is usually required to make the report "immediately" or "as soon as possible." Of course, these are also terms in the law that are also somewhat flexible, although obviously "immediately" may be less so than "as soon as possible." Both terms mean that the mandated reporter must commence the necessary steps to make the report without delay. It is expected that there must be an arrangement for the responsible coverage of the mandated reporter's duties during absence and that time should be taken to organize notes and other materials, get to a phone, and the like. The important point is that no other activity may be permitted to intervene prior to the report being made. The mandated reporter may not take the rest of the day to think about making the report or "sleep on it tonight" and examine if suspicions still seem reasonable the next morning. Permitting a delay in reporting, no matter how fair-minded the reason for it may be, constitutes a willful failure to report, a situation that could lead to the reporting party facing sanctions that range from being charged with a misdemeanor to the suspension of one's professional license to even a civil lawsuit for damages should the child suffer proximate damages due to the failure to make the call to the hotline.

There will inevitably be times when "immediately" will be dictated by circumstances. If a child appears to be in immediate danger, for example, "immediately" means that you will get to the phone and make the report in haste, saving organizing notes and such to a later time. In some very serious situations, you may even need to call the police *before* you call the CPS hotline, as mentioned earlier.

However, even where no such urgency is called for, if circumstances permit, it is preferable to call the report in as early as possible in the day, especially if it is believed that some contact with CPS is needed before proceeding. Most CPS jurisdictions remain primarily daytime operations, geared to an immediate or nearly immediate response during ordinary business hours. Reports made late in the day will sometimes be turned over to the emergency service operations staffed by "skeleton crews" working nights, weekends, and holidays. Even though such teams are usually composed of more experienced caseworkers or investigators, the workforce is so limited that by necessity they will need to prioritize their responses.

## CAN A CHILD BE TAKEN INTO PROTECTIVE CUSTODY?

The mandated reporter also needs to be careful to avoid being placed in an untenable position concerning the custody of the child or children in question. For example, it will not ordinarily be a problem if a school social worker makes a CPS report late in the day if the report concerns a matter that can be addressed the following day. However, in a situation where there is doubt about the safety of the child if he or she is sent home at dismissal, the reporter may be placed in a position of making a decision to either let the child leave or hold the child at the school. Once the child has been held, important questions come into play. Does the person who held the child have authority to have done so? Is the child now in the custody of the person who held him or her? Should the person who held the child have the right (or even the duty?) to transport the child to another location? What if the child is fearful and apprehensive and refuses to leave with the other pupils at the end of the day? What if the child does not wish to be kept behind at the school, day care center, or other facility?

Unfortunately, there are no ready answers to these questions, and they can mostly be avoided by deciding as early as possible the level of risk the situation presents to the particular child. The earlier the decision to report to the hotline, the sooner an investigation can begin. If these issues are present, staff at the hotline must be emphatically advised by the mandated reporter that the case involves issues of immediate safety that will need to be urgently addressed. At times like this, it becomes clear why it is a good idea to know and hopefully have a working relationship with the local CPS authorities. If such a relationship has been established, someone within the local body should be contacted as soon as possible after the CPS hotline report has been completed. Even if the CPS contact person is not the one responsible for responding, he or she can guide you to the person or unit that is responsible.

No matter how dutiful one is in attending to these issues early in the day, inevitably a situation involving serious safety concerns or a child's strong resistance to returning home is going to come to the attention of the mandated reporter near the end of the day. The answers are no more readily available! Much depends on the definitions of such legal terms as *custody, custodial interference,* and the like in your jurisdiction. The actions to take in such an event should be decided by policy or agreement well before they occur if the mandated reporter is employed by an agency or other organization. Certainly, at a minimum, no one should be left alone with a child who is fearful or at risk. Usually, it is also most advisable not to transport the child to another location, no matter how inconvenient it may be to remain at the current location. If it is absolutely necessary to move, someone else (probably best would be the police or the CPS hotline) should be advised of the departure point, the planned destination, the identity of the child, and the reason for moving.

It is probably never a good idea to take a child to your home. However, in the rare circumstance when it is necessary to do so, the person with the child should have a very clear idea of *why* this measure is necessary and should be prepared to clearly explain why other alternatives were not utilized or did not exist. It is worth pointing out again that no professional should ever be placed in this position without at least having shared the decision to take such action with another person who has some responsibility in the matter. It is extremely important that there not be a unilateral decision to take a child into one's care and control without parental permission.

Summarily taking a child into care on the spot without the intervention or involvement of a court is usually termed *protective custody*.

CPS laws clearly identify the authorities permitted to exercise protective custody of the child and what actions are required once this option has been exercised. Quite often, law enforcement officials at all levels (police, sheriffs, constabularies, etc.) or those with "peace officer" status are permitted to take a child into protective custody provided they take certain immediate actions, such as advising the local CPS or CPS hotline. CPS staff usually has the authority under the law to take a child into protective custody and must ordinarily present this decision to a court for review very soon after enacting it (e. g., the next business day). Often, a physician, hospital administrator, or other medical practitioner may be permitted to prevent a child from being taken from the immediate facility by a parent or other caretaker, provided that there is some basis for holding the child and that the police, CPS hotline, or both, are notified immediately.

## KNOWING YOUR AGENCY OR ORGANIZATION

You should familiarize yourself with the laws in your state regarding how to report suspected child abuse and neglect. If employed by an agency or organization (school, hospital, clinic, day care provider, community agency, or charitable organization), you should also check its policies and procedures. If you find they do not address how to report abuse or neglect you might consider actively suggesting that the policies and procedures be reviewed and updated. Check with the local CPS, police, or child advocacy center to ascertain if there is training or a seminar in which you and your colleagues may enroll; if appropriate, you may use the materials gathered in such a training to press your organization to formulate policies and procedures to be used when a CPS report is made or a child is stranded at your facility. In the event a child is caught in the squeeze between the time of the report and the CPS response, you will be in a far better position if you can demonstrate that your organization has procedures (in writing) and that you were following them rather than acting on your own.

Once in a great while, even with the best efforts, people and organizations may fail to prevent a child ending up unofficially and momentarily in the care of you and your colleagues. Despite the literal requirement of the law, commonsense measures undertaken to protect a child from harm will rarely cost the prudent professional more than the inconvenience of the event itself. Again, it is always advisable to know what you are doing and precisely why you are doing it. If you have a child with an injury before you, and it reasonably appears certain that the child will face further injury if required to return home, it would be quite difficult to justify sending the child home, provided you have adhered to your organization's procedures and promptly notified the authorities (CPS and the police). Indeed, if there are injuries, especially if they may be serious, you can hardly be faulted for placing the child's need for medical attention above all else. Similarly, it would be foolhardy to require a child who has refused to get on the school bus to walk home in a blizzard because you feel you do not have authority to hold the child. These are admittedly extreme examples, but they point to the need to balance adherence to procedures with reasonable concerns for a child's safety and plain good judgment.

Many social workers who work in agencies or other organizations may find that rather than an absence of procedures, there are an abundance of them. As well, they may remove much of the autonomy of making a report from the individual social worker. Organizations referred to include schools, day care facilities, hospitals, clinics, community agencies, charitable organizations, social service agencies, and the like. States differ in how they treat such organizations. Sometimes, detailed written procedures are required; sometimes, they are encouraged; and sometimes, they are vague.

Your first responsibility should be to know if your organization has a set procedure for reporting abuse or neglect. If so, they should be in writing and readily available to you and your peers. It would be best if the organization periodically trained staff in these requirements and reviewed them for necessary updates. Next, you should not assume that the procedures adhere to the provisions of the CPS laws in your state. In essence, organizations are permitted, encouraged, or required to maintain clear procedures that delineate and clarify the roles of various personnel within the organization and that permit the organization to track the reports submitted to the CPS hotline.

On the other hand, organizations are usually *not* permitted to use these procedures to "filter" CPS reports. There are times when procedures do not clearly avoid filtering. For example, if you are a social worker who is mandated to report suspected child abuse, and your organization's procedure instructs you to report your suspicions to another professional who will then decide whether to make a report, this would constitute filtering the report. Sometimes, the difference is more subtle: You may be required to "consult" with someone else in the organization prior to making a CPS report. Ordinarily, this is permissible if it does not delay reporting, but if it delays reporting or requires a joint decision to make a report, it may be considered as filtering. Organizations certainly have a right to know and keep track of CPS reports that originate from within, but the responsibility for deciding if the suspicions are reasonable and making, or causing, the report usually are responsibilities of the individual mandated reporter. In states where the mandated reporter is ultimately responsible for reporting, he/she is personally liable for willful failure to report even if his or her organization forbade or discouraged the report. This principle is so important that New York State recently passed a law requiring that the mandated reporter make the hotline call in person and that he or she must provide the names and contact information for all other mandated reporters in the organization who also know of the allegations.

## WHAT HAPPENS TO THE REPORT?

The laws and policies in all jurisdictions specify procedures for the initial response required by the agencies receiving the reports. In many states, CPS agencies have established stages for responding to child abuse and neglect allegations. The first stage is the receipt of a referral (the report) from a mandated reporter. A *referral* is the initial notification to the child protective hotline alleging abuse or neglect of one or more children.

Some referrals are screened out by the agency hotline or intake units as not being appropriate for further investigation or assessment. *Screening out* is the process of determining whether an allegation of child abuse or neglect meets the state's standard for investigation or assessment. If the standard is met, the referral then reaches the next stage—in some states called a *report*. If a referral is screened out, it means that the allegation did not meet the state's standard for an investigation.

Reasons for screening out a referral may include the following: the referral did not concern child abuse or neglect; it did not contain enough information to enable an investigation to occur; the children in the referral were the responsibility of another agency (i.e., law enforcement only); or the alleged victim was older than 18 years at the time of the report and as a result did not meet the state's definition of a child.

If a report is not screened out, CPS will either initiate an investigation or pursue an alternative response. The purpose of an investigation is to determine if the child was maltreated (or is at risk of maltreatment) and, if needed, to establish the appropriate intervention. Alternative responses emphasize an assessment of the family's needs and the prevention of future maltreatment rather than making a formal determination of maltreatment (Shusterman, Fluke, Hollinshead, & Yuan, 2005).

Regardless of which type of response the agency uses for a specific report, it must decide if further action is necessary to protect and keep the child safe. The approaches used to screen reports vary from state to state, but nearly all states utilize some type of safety assessment to determine which reports require an immediate response. Some states categorize reports based on the level of risk of harm to the child and assign different response times. Some states use differential response systems in which more serious cases are assigned to be investigated, while less serious cases are assigned to family assessments.

Investigations may be conducted by the child protective agency, a law enforcement agency, or cooperatively by both agencies, while family assessments are conducted by the child protection agency. In some states and the Virgin Islands, cases of physical or sexual abuse may be investigated by a law enforcement agency. In some states, reports are referred to law enforcement agencies when the alleged perpetrator is a person other than the parent or other caretaker. Most states also require cross reporting among professional entities. Typically, reports are shared among social services agencies, law enforcement agencies, and prosecutors' offices (Child Welfare Information Gateway, 2006).

Most states set requirements for the time period by which an investigation into a report of child abuse or neglect must begin. While some states have a single time frame for responding to reports, others establish priorities based on the information received from the report source. Of the states that establish priorities, many specify a high-priority response as soon as 1 to 24 hours. Lower priority responses range from 24 hours to 14 days. (U.S. Department of Health and Human Services, 2005). Because CPS agencies receive reports of varying degrees of urgency, average response times reflect the types of reports that are received as well as the ability of workers to meet the time standards. Some states categorize reports based on the level of risk of harm to the child; others use differential response systems in which more serious cases are assigned to be investigated, while less serious cases are assigned to family assessments.

Chapter 8 discusses what happens after a report has been made.

## FREQUENTLY ASKED QUESTIONS

**Q.** When I started work as a therapist for a small private mental health clinic, I asked about the clinic's CPS reporting procedures. I was told, "we just talk about it with Bob (the supervising psychiatrist) and then make a report. Don't worry, he never tells us not to." Is this okay?

**A.** It depends on what you mean by "okay." It may be legal, but it does not serve to protect any mandated reporter employed by the clinic, including Bob, from serious problems if harm befalls a child due to a failure to make a CPS report. For example, if an individual mandated reporter decides to make a CPS report, or not to make a CPS report, this is a system that leaves no "audit trail" if questions later arise as to the reasons underlying decisions that were made. The organization should devise a written procedure that clearly delineates duties and responsibilities that are required every time a CPS report is made or contemplated, and it should leave a record of who did what and why. It should be reviewed by an attorney to assure that it is in compliance with the CPS laws in your state. In addition, if you are covered by the clinic's malpractice insurance, you might also check to ascertain if it contains any particular requirements in this area.

**Q.** I am employed as a school social worker. In reviewing my school's written procedures for making a CPS report, I discovered that they require me to report to the school nurse rather than directly to the CPS hotline. The school nurse has had a lot of training in the area, and he has the final decision as to whether the report will be made, and if it is made, he is the one who calls. Is this allowed?

**A.** Whether it is allowed depends on the state your school is in. However, generally, mandated reporters are required to take responsibility for reporting, even if they do not actually make the report themselves. This means that if you believe a report needs to be made in accordance with the laws in your state, you are not relieved of the requirement to complete the report, or see to its completion, if the school nurse disagrees and decides not to report. In some states, you are required to make the report yourself, without any interference from others in your organization. Also, in some states, you are protected from retaliatory personnel actions if you make a CPS report in disagreement with your superiors. You can check your local CPS or look up the requirements in your state on the Internet to ascertain the specific requirements of your state.

**Q.** I am a recently graduated social worker who just started a job in a day care center. When I asked the person in charge about the center's CPS procedure, she told me that one was not available and that, in fact, one of my jobs was to develop one. I am not sure how to begin this task. Isn't this a job for an attorney?

**A.** Although it is a good idea to have the finished product checked by an attorney, this sort of task is appropriate to a social worker's professional duties. It does not need to be complicated, and there is absolutely no need to employ legal jargon in assembling it. Language should be simple and clear, and greater importance should be placed on clearly delineating the role and responsibility of each professional involved in the process, time lines, confidentiality requirements, and interviewing protocols for staff, CPS, and the police. Begin by contacting your local CPS and asking for any materials they may be able to provide. Ask similar organizations for copies of their procedures. Go online and read your state's CPS law. Find training sponsored by your state, the local CPS, the local department of social services, or a child advocacy center. A "boilerplate" procedure may even be available. Make sure you keep up with changes in the law. It is entirely appropriate to the role of professional social workers who work with children and families to become involved in serving on CPS advisory boards and child welfare professional action groups. You may testify before legislative bodies and write letters to your elected representatives. Also, if possible, get to know the CPS investigators and supervisors who serve your organization.

**Q.** I am a social worker who has been employed for a long time by a school. I am satisfied that the procedure in my school is effective and legally up to date. I trust my colleagues and my supervisors, and we work well together. However, I recently attended a holiday party at my supervisor's home where there were many people from both within our organization and from other spheres. I was shocked to notice that when the hostess, my supervisor's wife, took my coat in the hallway, there was a pile of CPS reporting forms on the table in the hallway that clearly displayed the names of several children and their families who had been reported to the CPS hotline. I immediately sought out my supervisor and informed him of this. He made a joke about it but immediately removed them to another room. The next week, I asked him about the incident, and he told me that they were unfounded reports he had taken home to check on and then destroy, as required by law. Am I overreacting to be concerned?

**A.** Not at all. While it appears that this incident was entirely unintentional, it is nonetheless a serious breach of law and practice. To begin with, records of this sort should *never* be removed from the location where they are customarily stored, except when they are subpoenaed. It appears that your supervisor's intent was noble in that he was going to work on them on his own time at home, but bringing them home always increases the risk that they will be seen by persons who are not entitled to see them, including family members, guests, or persons working in the home. This rule applies to persons outside the organization, but it also applies to persons inside the organization who have no professional need to see them. It is especially ironic that these were unfounded cases, but the same rule would apply equally to "indicated" cases: persons and their family members referred to CPS have a legal right to privacy, and this means that any official document revealing the existence of a CPS report must be guarded from the view of all persons other than those whose professional duties require them to know. On notification that a CPS report is unfounded, the organization and/or agency must follow its internal procedure for handling unfounded reports while following state law regarding these matters. This lapse in judgment could have placed your supervisor in a position of being sued or having his license suspended.

## REFERENCES

Child Welfare Information Gateway. (2006). *Making and screening reports of child abuse and neglect. Summary of state laws.* Washington, DC: U.S. Department of Health and Human Services, Administration on Children, Youth and Families.

Shusterman, G. R., Hollinshead, D., Fluke, J. D., & Yuan, Y. T. (2005). *Alternative responses to child maltreatment: Findings from NCANDS.* Retrieved September 18, 2006, from http://aspe.hhs.gov/hsp/05/child-maltreat-resp/index.htm

U.S. Department of Health and Human Services, Administration for Children and Families/Children's Bureau and Office of the Assistant Secretary for Planning and Evaluation. (2005). *National study of child protective services systems and reform efforts: Review of state CPS policy.* Washington, DC: U.S. Government Printing Office. This document is also available at http://aspe.hhs.gov/hsp/cps-status03

# 8 After the Report: What Happens Next?

The events that follow a report of suspicion of child abuse or maltreatment that was given in compliance with the requirements by law in your state will depend on numerous factors, including the rules and policies of the jurisdiction in which you practice, the bureaucratic structure of the child protective services (CPS) unit that covers your area, and the type of incident you have reported. Even some important human elements are involved, such as the style of the CPS caseworker assigned to the investigation and, to a significant extent, on your own attitudes, expectations, and experience.

As a professional who is mandated to complete CPS reports, it is important for you to be aware of the procedures involved in a CPS investigation both so that you will be able to maximize your professional influence on the process and so that you will be able to properly counsel (and perhaps even advocate for) clients who have become the subjects of child abuse and neglect investigations. The information in this chapter will help you better understand the process so that you are able to inform and educate your clients.

Stereotypes abound concerning CPS agencies and the professionals who staff them. Many of these stereotypes are propagated by the media or public opinion in the wake of particularly egregious child abuse cases. Often, they are negative stereotypes: The workers are inadequately trained and not responsive to the needs of the client or the community; the agency is too big and bureaucratic to be responsive; the bureaucracy is motivated as much by the need to defend itself as it is by the protection of children; or the field staff are poorly supervised and case hardened, and either do nothing or, on the other hand, take legal action on nearly every case just to be safe rather than to provide effective services.

Of course, reality is a mix. CPS agencies differ widely in the quality of the services they provide. Their actions in response to a CPS report are determined by several factors, including the laws of the jurisdiction in which they exist, budget realities that dictate the numbers of staff, the staff training, the size of their caseloads, and the amount of supervision they receive. In addition, the quality of their practice will be somewhat determined by the nature of the community they serve, including its culture and the policies of its schools, police, hospitals, courts, and mandated reporting community.

## WHAT DOES A CHILD PROTECTIVE SERVICES INVESTIGATION ENTAIL?

Although deadlines and timeline requirements in various jurisdictions will differ, there are certain basic elements that comprise the activities of all CPS investigations. These include the following:

- Contact with the reporting source
- Contact with collateral sources
- Face-to-face contact with subjects of the report
- Face-to-face contact with other persons named in the report
- A home visit
- An interview or observation of the children

Each of these elements will be discussed in the following sections.

## CONTACT WITH THE REPORTING SOURCE

Social workers and other professionals who are mandated to report their suspicions of child abuse and neglect will have provided their names to CPS, but in many cases where nonmandated reporters call in reports, they will have done so anonymously, and it will be impossible for CPS to contact the person who made the report. One of the great trade-offs in CPS is the fact that permitting anonymous reports increases the likelihood of someone reporting because he or she feels safe from revenge, retribution, and embarrassment. However, the impossibility of communicating with the person who made the report places considerable limits on the ability of the CPS investigator to gather information.

Since social workers acting in their professional capacity are mandated reporters, your name will be on record (although in most localities, it will be held confidential during the investigation unless you permit its release). Most mandated reporters have more knowledge about the situation they have reported than the few words that will be used to form the narrative in the report. Therefore, one of the CPS investigator's first activities will be to contact you, usually by telephone. For this reason, it is critical that you provide a phone number where you can be reached.

The person who makes this call varies with each jurisdiction. The call may be placed by the person who is responsible for the entire CPS investigation (he or she is variously called a *caseworker, investigator, CPS worker,* etc.). However, in some jurisdictions, various parts of the investigation may be parceled out to specialists. One person may make the initial phone calls for all investigations, writing brief reports, or "dictation," for the case record. Sometimes, the investigator's supervisor may make this call to assess the seriousness of the case. For the purposes of this chapter, we will refer to the person making the call as a "caseworker."

The caseworker will want to know all the facts you can provide about the family, such as dates of birth, the location of various family members, the identities and locations of other witnesses, other services being provided to the family, and special conditions or circumstances of various family members. The caseworker may ask about the possibility of weapons in the home or the presence of potentially dangerous animals or other risks. Questions may be posed about the overall condition of the home and the children. You may be asked if anyone in the family has a history of violence or making threats. The investigator will ask about any injuries or history of injuries to any children in the family, whether there is a history of arrests, drug or alcohol use, or domestic violence. The investigator will also ask questions that will help to establish the level of urgency of a response.

Because of increasing specialization within organizations that employ many mandated reporters, CPS agencies often differentiate between "the person making the report" and the "source" of the report. For example, it is common for schools to set up a system whereby one person (such as the school social worker or the school nurse) makes all the actual phone calls to the hotline, while various persons employed within the school (such as teachers, aides, or administrators) may be the actual person who encountered the suspicion of neglect or abuse. If you are a person so designated within your organization, you might make this clear early in the investigation, especially if you find yourself unable to supply some of the information that is being requested.

This call is your chance to offer any additional information you may think is worth evaluating and to ask questions and express concerns. It is a good idea to make a few notes for yourself in preparation for the call at the time you make the report. It also is probably a good idea to record a few notes of your own about the call.

Be sure to jot down the name and telephone numbers of the case-worker and his or her supervisor. If you later recall an important fact or something further occurs after this conversation, you should call back to provide additional information. However, if and when you make such calls, be prepared for a somewhat guarded tone. CPS staff are thoroughly indoctrinated in the principle of confidentiality and expect communication to be a one-way affair: Facts flow from you to them, not in the opposite direction. It is best not to take this too personally and not to ascribe it to defensiveness or to an attempt to hide anything. The best approach is to convey your information and your concerns clearly without creating a sense that you expect information in return. In fact, if you make a habit of such calls, you will eventually get to know the persons who are responsible for your area and may be thought of as part of a joint effort.

On the other hand, if you feel that genuinely important information concerning child safety is being overlooked or not taken seriously, do not hesitate to ask to speak to the caseworker's supervisor or even the supervisor's supervisor or manager. If you find it necessary to make such calls, avoid being argumentative, accusatory, or threatening. No matter how busy they are, most people employed in CPS will display a responsive attitude to someone who is sincerely concerned about a child's safety.

If due either to your particular assignment or your individual sense of conscience you find yourself making many reports, you might consider becoming involved with CPS and the larger issue of child welfare in a more general way than individual cases. Child protective and child welfare agencies have advisory boards, public hearings, and open forums with which you may volunteer to become involved. You can also write letters to administrators, commissioners, legislators, and elected executives. You can become familiar with the bureaucratic structure of both public and private child welfare organizations in your area as well as their funding streams and budgetary processes. You may be able to volunteer your time or services or become involved in a program that benefits clients or foster children. Citizen participation is vital to a responsive, high-functioning child welfare program.

## CONTACT WITH COLLATERAL SOURCES

When the CPS investigator calls the person who made the report, he or she will almost always learn of others who have been involved in some way with the child or the child's family. These "others" may be professionals, such as doctors, therapists, teachers, probation officers, or police, or persons who have some connection with the family, such as landlords, friends, relatives, boarders, or ex-spouses. Other times, the caseworker might learn from the initial contact with the person who made the report the names of witnesses to specific events.

The caseworker will make a list of such persons, their role, and their phone numbers. Interviewing each person will help the caseworker put together a fairly complete picture of the child's family, its problems, and how it functions. Equally important, it will help the caseworker assess the level and immediacy of the risks to the child's safety, and possibly even the caseworker. It may also provide insight into strengths in the child's family, and in some cases, it may even give the CPS worker an idea of who might serve to care for the child if the case goes that far.

It should be realized that contacting collateral sources has its limits and that the subjects of the investigation have a right to privacy. Only in the most rare incidents, for example, would CPS investigators contact a neighbor or an employer whose name had *not* been provided to them on the off chance that they might have useful information. In most jurisdictions, actions like this would be undertaken only with supervisory or administrative approval.

Some collateral contacts will be developed during the interview with the family. In most CPS investigations, as a matter of routine, the subjects are asked to sign releases permitting contact with their physicians, schools, and, if applicable, therapists and other service providers.

## FACE-TO-FACE CONTACT WITH SUBJECTS OF THE REPORT

A "subject of the report," or some such wording, refers to the persons who are alleged to have abused or neglected a child. Most often, this is the child's parent or guardian, but depending on the jurisdiction, it could be a wide variety of other persons as well, including a stepparent, paramour, older sibling, boarder in the home, other relative, day care provider, foster parent, babysitter, or family friend. Other persons who might be involved with the child in clearly noncustodial relationships, such as teachers, tutors, coaches, bus drivers, scout leaders, religious instructors, and the like, are not ordinarily counted as "subjects," although if such a person has caused harm to a child, criminal charges might be appropriate.

This contact is widely considered to be one of the core activities of the investigation (the other being the interview with the child or children). Most jurisdictions require that this contact occur early in the investigation. It is the point at which the subjects are first presented with the allegations that have been made against them in the CPS hotline report; are provided with some formal, written notice that a report legally exists; and are notified that they have certain rights as a result of the report. Commonly, this contact occurs in the subject's home.

This is an investigatory activity that calls for well-developed interpersonal skills on the part of the CPS caseworker. The subject is often angry and highly agitated on hearing the allegations. Vehement denials, threats of lawsuits, and righteous indignation are commonly followed by insistent demands that the caseworker provide the name of the person who made the report. The subject is advised that such information cannot be shared, but it must be realized that in some cases, the subject of the report can readily deduce the source of the report based on the allegations. Sometimes, the caseworker is immediately asked to leave; in extreme situations, the caseworker may be threatened or actually assaulted. According to a 1998 national study of child protective caseworkers, more than 70% had been victims of violence or threats of violence in the line of duty (American Federation of State, County, and Municipal Employees, 1998). Ultimately, although emotions are often volatile, most subjects take the opportunity at this moment to "tell their side of the story."

Statutes and policies vary concerning whether the subject of the report is notified of the existence of the CPS report prior to this meeting. In many instances, the contact is unannounced, based on the assumption that knowing of the report in advance of the meeting will result in some risk to the child or cause the subject to pressure the child into keeping quiet, denying the allegations or participating in an invented explanation for the allegations. It is also worth noting that many experts in CPS and law enforcement believe that, if at all possible, the child should be interviewed prior to the contact with the subjects of the report (see the An Interview or Observation of the Children section below), an approach that is permitted without parental permission in most jurisdictions.

CPS laws do not require subjects to meet with the CPS caseworker or to permit the CPS caseworker to enter their home. The subject is free to refuse such a meeting, although, in fact, this rarely occurs. In the event of such a refusal, there is a provision in the law that permits or requires CPS to seek a court order requiring the subjects to meet with the caseworker, to permit the caseworker to inspect the home, or to allow the caseworker access to see or interview the children. Such an order will stipulate the conditions of such contact (whether the subjects will meet the investigator in their home or the CPS office, whether the children will be interviewed alone or in the presence of the subject, who will be present, etc.). The conditions stipulated will largely depend on the strength of the evidence that CPS is able to present to the court– and often, that will depend on information the mandated reporter is able to convey to CPS. Under these circumstances, it is likely that the court will permit the subject to have an attorney present during the interview.

## FACE-TO-FACE CONTACT WITH OTHER PERSONS NAMED IN THE REPORT

When a report is made to CPS, the person making the report will be asked to identify all persons who reside in the home. This will not always be possible, as the caller may not know these details about the child's household. Other persons who are named in the report are adults who reside in the household but are not considered to be involved in caring for the child or culpable in the abuse or neglect of the child. Included would be relatives who reside in the home, such as grandparents, adult siblings, aunts, or uncles, as well as boarders, paramours, or employees.

CPS caseworkers are trained not to assume that the household composition reported to the hotline is correct. One of the important tasks for the caseworker is to discover the identities (names, dates of birth, relationship) of all persons who reside in the home. In most jurisdictions, the caseworker is required not only to list such persons but also to meet with them in person (even if only very briefly). There are several reasons for this provision of the law. First, of course, is that such persons may be important witnesses to the abuse or neglect of the child. However, they may also be directly or indirectly involved in the abuse or neglect.

Last, the caseworker will usually conduct a criminal records check on all persons who reside in the household to determine whether such a person might be deemed a potential risk to the child.

As in the case of the subjects of the report, other persons named in the report are not required to meet with the caseworker. Again, the caseworker may seek a court order directing that such a meeting take place, but the courts may be more reluctant to provide an order for a person who has not been named as a subject and for whom no evidence that they have contributed to the abuse or neglect of the child can be generated.

The contact with such persons can be tricky for the caseworker. Usually, such persons are required to be informed that they have been named in the report, yet the nature of the allegations and the source of the report are confidential information that they do not have an automatic right to have (assuming that they are not named as subjects). If they are witnesses, or can reasonably be regarded as witnesses, they inevitably will have awareness about the nature of the allegations. Furthermore, it can be difficult for the caseworker to interview persons named in the report privately, and this may compromise their willingness to share what they know. A well-trained caseworker will make sure that each such person interviewed knows how to reach him or her if further discussion is desired.

## A HOME VISIT

One of the most important elements of a CPS investigation is for the CPS investigator to see the child's home. This is an activity that will usually occur simultaneously with the interview of the subject of the report and the advisement of his or her rights. And, as in the initial interview with the subject of the report, the visit to the home may occur with or without prior notice. It can be assumed that the investigation will have more valid results if this visit occurs without prior notice, as there is a better possibility that the caseworker will be able to record the child's home environment with the knowledge that no preparation was undertaken for his or her visit.

During the visit to the home, the CPS caseworker will observe the obvious (if the home is reasonably clean and organized, free of hazards, adequately and safely heated and ventilated, with adequate space for the number of inhabitants) but will also ask permission to view areas of the home that are ordinarily less accessible, such as the children's rooms and other areas like garages and basements, especially if they are mentioned in the narrative of the report or if the investigation has turned up allegations related to those areas of the home. The caseworker will try to learn where the child sleeps, plays, and does homework; the degree of privacy the child is permitted; and the extent to which the child participates in family life.

As in most aspects of the investigation, the subject is not required by law to permit such a visit or, even if the visit is permitted, the inspection that is described. And, again, CPS must assess the value of approaching a court to obtain an order to inspect the home or less accessible areas of it. Before granting such an order, which is tantamount to a search warrant, a judge will want to be convinced by evidence that the investigator's failing to see the home could reasonably result in harm to the child.

As in the face-to-face contact with the subjects of the report, the home visit is usually not resisted by the subjects. An important variable here is the level of skill demonstrated by the investigator in his or her use of authority. A subject who has admitted an investigator into the home after being informed at the front door of the existence of CPS allegations does not ordinarily focus attention on the fact that the investigator is in the home but rather on the allegations and the response to the investigator. A skilled investigator (well trained and experienced) will not immediately demand to see the entire house and the children's rooms; later, after perhaps a half hour of conversation in which the subject has had time to vent anger and then calm down, the caseworker will bring up the subject, usually with much deference and respect. Approached in this way, few subjects will refuse the request.

Occasionally, the caseworker will be confronted with a thorny forensic problem: the chain of evidence. When an object has been used in the course of abusing or neglecting a child, that object is potentially useful as physical evidence. However, if the item is presented as evidence at a hearing or a trial, the subject's attorney may object to its admittance unless it can be clearly established that the evidence has not been unaccounted for during a period of time after it can be placed at the scene. The longer the period of time, the weaker its value as evidence (i.e., the more likely it is that the judge will refuse to allow it as evidence). The caseworker may not take the object without the subject's permission.

The problem may be even more difficult if a case goes to criminal trial. The standards of evidence are usually much stricter in a criminal trial compared with the civil trial or hearing that will be conducted in the family court. Now, if a caseworker has attempted to preserve the chain of evidence by asking the subject's permission to take the item when leaving the home, the defense attorney will most likely argue, usually successfully, that the evidence is invalid because the subject was not advised of the right to counsel when this permission was granted.

The police are experts in this area, and this is one of the reasons why, when it is suspected that the child abuse or neglect being investigated is criminal in nature, the police should be involved as early in the investigation as possible. In many jurisdictions, the police or the district attorney will provide caseworkers with training in forensics.

As a mandated reporter, you need to be aware of this aspect of a CPS investigation if it happens that you have *any* item that might be thought of as evidence in your possession. For example, in a counseling session, a child might give you a rope that the child claims was used to tie him or her to a bed. When you make your CPS report, you must be sure to bring this fact to the attention of the hotline interviewer. If the person who calls you back from CPS does not mention the object, bring it up again.

## AN INTERVIEW OR OBSERVATION OF THE CHILDREN

While a competent CPS investigation results from the proper use of several elements, in most CPS reports, there is no single element more important than contact with the child or children who are alleged to have been abused or neglected. This is not only because the child is the primary client of CPS but also because the child is better able, voluntarily or not, to inform the investigator of his or her circumstances than anyone else.

Even where only one child in a household has been reported to the hotline, a matter of central importance for the CPS caseworker is to learn the identities of *all* children in the household and to observe and interview each of them, even if there are no stated or apparent allegations of abuse or neglect involving them. There are several reasons for this. Even if the other children have not been abused or neglected, they are quite likely to have witnessed neglect or abuse of the child mentioned in the report. Furthermore, while it is not out of the question for parents to focus their abuse and neglect on one scapegoated child in the family, more often if one child has been maltreated, so have others in the household–sometimes to greater detriment than the child who was actually reported. Finally, much less likely, a CPS investigation may turn up a child who, although part of the household, is not part of the family, such as a harbored runaway, an illegal custody, or a child who has otherwise been reported as missing.

## Parental Permission

The parental permission step of the investigation introduces some potential controversial issues. The first is the important question of parental permission for a child to be interviewed. In some instances, the way the case is reported offers the opportunity for the caseworker to interview the child before contacting any other family member, such as when a school social worker calls in a report on a child while the child is present in the school building. Under that circumstance, school officials will usually allow the CPS caseworker to visit and interview the child in school as the first step in the investigation. In some states, such cooperation between schools and CPS is mandated by law or suggested by policy. However, in states where this is not so, some schools may be reluctant to permit such access without first informing the parents, especially if the report did not originate from the school.

The face of this issue may change somewhat if the child is presenting with injuries. While this might occur in a school setting, it may also occur in a hospital or other medical setting or sometimes even in the home of a private person, such as the home of a friend. In this situation, the child is more clearly a victim, and quite often, law enforcement personnel may respond with the CPS caseworker. A common principle of the law enforcement interview is that the police usually do not need permission to interview a person who can reasonably be believed to be the victim of a crime.

More often than not, observable injuries are not present, and the practical aspects of the child's situation do not lend themselves to an interview prior to visiting the home and meeting the child's parents, guardians, or custodians. However, the CPS caseworker is nevertheless required to "observe" the child. Such observation will ordinarily include actually seeing the child; observing the nature of the interaction between the child and other family members, including the subjects of the report; viewing the child's room; and interviewing the child. Caseworkers, if not required by statute to attempt to interview the child out of the subjects' earshot, are certainly trained to ask permission for such an interview. However, even where parents permit the child to be interviewed alone in the home, the interview may be hindered and of questionable validity because the child may be extremely nervous and there is no real assurance that parts of the interview have not been overheard, either because of inadequate privacy or because of eavesdropping. The trained and experienced CPS worker is sensitive to these aspects of the in-home interview and will usually not burden the child with an interview that is too probing, especially if there is reason to believe that privacy is compromised. In these circumstances, the caseworker will try to convey concern for the child and let him or her know how to get in touch. The caseworker will assess whether the child is fearful or strongly desires to be removed from the home. Above all, he or she will be quietly assessing the amount of evidence that may be present that will be taken to the courts to request an order to interview the child outside of the presence of the subjects.

## Interviewing Siblings

Another consideration when parents permit children to be interviewed in the home is the question of interviewing siblings. As discussed, the investigation requires that all children in the home be assessed, even if they are not reported with allegations. Ideally, each child should be interviewed privately. However, CPS investigators may interview siblings together privately from the parents, although this would be less than ideal. It should not be assumed that siblings will maintain each other's privacy, and the subject child may be very reluctant to provide information in a group interview.

## Interviewing in the Presence of an Adult

It is possible that the child's parents or guardians will not permit the child to be interviewed out of their presence. This can present a problem, especially if there is no other evidence that the child is at sufficient risk of harm that a court order to interview out of the parents' presence is warranted. Sometimes, CPS jurisdictions will require that the caseworker attempt to interview the child at school after the parents have refused to permit the child to be interviewed at home, but this may be legally dubious, particularly if the parent expressly forbade such an interview when asked for one. A parent's specific statement that CPS is not to interview the child under *any* circumstances usually does not carry enough legal weight in most jurisdictions to prevent it from occurring, but it can often provide a practical obstacle in that others involved with the child (schools, neighbors, relatives) will often refuse to cooperate, and sometimes even CPS will not press the issue unless it is an emergency for fear of legal complications. In situations like these, CPS will usually approach the family or juvenile court for support, and the courts will often require the use of a child advocacy center (CAC).

## Physical Examination

Another controversial issue concerning the child interview is the degree to which the CPS caseworker will conduct a physical examination of the child, and if such an examination is undertaken, the methods used to document it. Sometimes, the child's injuries are obvious to all observers, such as bruises or abrasions on the hands, arms, legs, feet, or head, or when the child is in a cast or bandaged. Other times, the child will provide information verbally about injuries under his or her clothing or in private areas of the body, such as the buttocks, lower abdomen, genitals, or, in the case of girls, the breast area.

Aside from the location of the injury on the body, some of the limits of such observation will be determined by the child's age, the difference in gender between the CPS caseworker and the child, whether the parents have given permission for the observation, and the child's emotional state. Generally, the CPS caseworker will be extremely guarded about observing injuries or wounds that are not located in commonly observable areas of the body. Even when the parents have given permission for a caseworker to observe a child's "private" body areas in their own home while the parent is present, the caseworker may be reluctant, particularly if such an observation is obviously distressing to the child.

A more common approach is to enlist medical professionals to observe and document injuries and marks. This will likely be automatic if it is a medical professional who is making the CPS report. However, other institutions, schools especially, might have a nurse or other medical professional who can document these injuries and perhaps even be recorded as the "person making the report" to the CPS hotline. Another approach is to request that the parents take the child for an immediate medical assessment, sometimes even to a facility already "on call" to CPS, such as a CAC or designated hospital. In the end, the CPS investigator still has recourse to the courts where an immediate court order can be sought requiring the parents to permit a physical or medical examination.

Injuries found or observed during the investigation need to be documented. Anyone who observes injuries, including the person making the report, should accurately and objectively provide a narrative description of the injuries. Unless the person providing the description is a medical professional, medical terminology must be carefully avoided. To a great extent, the value of such narrative descriptions will vary depending on the level of expertise of the person recording the observation, the length of time that has elapsed between the observation and the recording, and the objectivity of the description.

Another method of recording injuries is to provide a technical drawing of them. A general method of accomplishing this is to record the type of injuries observed on a body chart, complete with measurements and descriptions. A more specific method is to make sketches of the injuries, again including measurements. Usually, the body chart is preferable for persons who do not have medical expertise, and sketches should be completed by those who have experience in this field.

Photography can be an excellent method of recording injuries, but it should not be assumed to be infallible. The type of equipment used, the photographic media (film or digital), the expertise of the photographer, the quality of the lighting, and even the ethnic characteristics of the child are all variables that may affect the quality of the picture and the validity of the information it portrays. Errors can be in either direction: The injuries may show up very poorly or not at all, or they may appear more dramatic than they actually are. If photos are taken, they should include not only picture of the injuries but also of the total child in order to confirm identity and other environmental data, such as the date, the size of the injuries, and perhaps even the implement that caused them.

Aside from the fact that the descriptions of an injury produced by a physician will carry more weight than those provided by anyone else, documentation available exclusively to the physician, such as x-rays, various types of scans, a colposcope, and other analyses, are the very best sources of documentation of injuries.

## The Use of Witnesses

Whether an interview with a child is going to be attended by a witness is another source of some controversy. Generally, best practice requires that a witness be present when the CPS investigator conducts a formal interview of a child. Often, the child will have no familiarity with the CPS investigator who is conducting the interview and may be quite anxious about it. Sometimes, it is a good idea to permit someone the child knows, likes, and trusts to sit in on the interview. However, this can also present problems. First, it is extremely important that the person selected does not have a vital stake in the outcome of the interview. Second, the witness must not in any way coach the child, answer questions on his or her behalf, or add details to the child's story, even if such efforts are well intended. Third, issues of confidentiality need to be carefully assessed. Last, in fairness, the witness needs to understand that there is a possibility that he or she may be later required to testify in court. Most of these problems can be avoided if the witness is a professional (fellow CPS investigator, police officer, medical professional, social worker, or teacher), but this may have no value in helping the child feel supported during the interview.

## Interviewer Skills

The last area of controversy in child interviewing is the competency of the CPS interviewer. Training in interviewing is provided to all CPS investigators, but the skill levels of individual investigators will inevitably vary. As many psychological experiments of the past couple of decades have amply demonstrated, children can be very suggestible, and investigators who interview them, not only from CPS but also from the district attorney's office, the police, and mental health professionals ("validators"), must be meticulously objective and nonleading while simultaneously establishing rapport with the child subject. It also is critical for caseworkers to be open to alternative explanations for the allegations during the interview (and throughout the investigation) and to explore alternative explanations when the interview presents them.

The interviewing skill of the CPS caseworker is important in other ways. An interview in which the child feels intimidated, and/or in which he or she perceives disinterest or impatience on the part of an interviewer, may not result in false information but rather *no* information because the child keeps it private. It is important for the interviewer to take time to establish some level of rapport with the child, in order to let the child develop trust and a degree of comfort. Good interviewers will offer the child support without leading them. They will begin the interview in relaxed conversation with the child and gradually move to the focus of the interview. Along the way, they will establish, in the child's language, who they are and the purpose of the interview. They will assess the child's perception of the difference between truth and falsity and the consequences for not telling the truth. They will provide reassurance that they will listen to whatever the child has to say, and they instruct the child to stop them if they use a word that the child does not understand.

## Interview Validity

The majority of child protective interviews will be documented in a narrative report submitted for the case record by the CPS caseworker (this is commonly called *dictation*). While this may not be the most reliable and forensically solid method of documenting an interview, it is the most practical and suitable for most CPS investigations. In some circumstances, especially those involving serious physical injuries or sexual abuse, interviews will need to be backed up by an affidavit—a brief sworn statement drawn up by the CPS investigator that records, in the child's words, a summary of what the child told the investigator. This method is more likely to be employed where the child has verified serious allegations that are virtually certain to come up as evidence in a court of law. Ordinarily, an affidavit must be witnessed and/or notarized, and often they are utilized during multidisciplinary investigations, (often in a CAC) in which the CPS caseworker has interviewed the child jointly with either a police officer or a member of the district attorney's staff. In many jurisdictions, video and/or audio taping of interviews has become common practice.

An important question concerning any interview of a child is the validity of the child's statement. The interview is only as good as the skills of the interviewer, and this aspect of an interview can be difficult to assess. When reading the report of an interview in a case record, there is no way of knowing if the caseworker has asked pertinent questions and correctly understood and recorded the child's responses. Worse, there is no way to be certain that the interviewer has not influenced the child's statement through the use of leading questions or subtle body language that plays into the child's suggestibility. To be clear, while it is not impossible that a caseworker would purposely misrepresent a child's statement, it is rather unlikely. Researchers such as Elizabeth Loftus (2003) have demonstrated that the most well-meaning interviewer may inadvertently coax the child to offer false information that the child believes to be true. This has led to the use of the electronic recording of child interviews in many areas of the country, particularly when the allegations are criminal (e. g., serious assault and sexual abuse).

## CONCLUDING THE INVESTIGATION

A CPS investigation is not permitted to continue indefinitely. They are time limited by statute. The limits vary from state to state but are generally somewhere between 30 and 90 days. Within the overall time limit for the investigation, there are usually various deadlines for the caseworker to achieve the activities listed previously.

While most states require little more than "some credible evidence" (the lowest legal standard of evidence) to list the case in the CPS register as "indicated," the investigation is more than a mere decision as to the believability of the allegations. The important underlying decision involves assessing the current and ongoing safety of the child. This is a decision usually made through a combination of assessing the facts gathered in the investigation; applying them to some sort of guide or decision tree; and, in combination with the investigator's supervisor, arriving at a final decision in the case. While the conclusion of these activities must occur before the expiration of the time limit, it should be understood that the time limit refers to the last possible permissible date that a decision must be reached; the final decision in the case may be reached at any earlier point—in rare cases, even on the first day of the investigation.

No later than the conclusion of the required time limit, the CPS investigator and his or her supervisor will assess the information gathered in the investigation and reach a decision as to the veracity of the allegations and, more important, the safety of the child or children reported.

Specific procedures may vary somewhat from state to state. In the broadest sense, a decision will be made as to the findings, or determination, of the investigation. If the investigation has developed no evidence that the allegations are true or that the children are at risk of harm, the case will be closed "unfounded." Some states require that unfounded cases be expunged (thoroughly erased with no trace remaining), while others may require that the record of the investigation remains on file for reference in the event of future report. In this case, a procedure is established that maintains confidentiality for the record but provides for the retrieval of some or all the information contained in the earlier report for inclusion in the current investigation.

Some states may deem a case to be "unfounded but in need of services," meaning that the investigation discovered a situation in which there was not significant risk to the child but in which the family would benefit from the provision of services and volunteer to receive them, often from a private community agency not operated by the state or county. Usually, it is assumed that the provision of such services reduces the likelihood of future risk of harm to the child.

On the other hand, if the investigation does discover a risk of harm to children in the family, the case will be determined to be "indicated."

The indication of a case will usually signal a new round of evaluation and decision making. In some cases, it may be decided that the risk to the child is mild or no longer evident, and the case may be closed, especially if the family is not interested in receiving services.

However, if the level of risk is higher, the provision of services may be regarded as a necessity to protect the child from future harm. State and local policies vary on this point. If the approach to the provision of services is conservative, CPS may, as a matter of course, refer all such cases to the courts for judicial intervention. In a more open approach, CPS will advise the family of their assessment and offer services; if the parents voluntarily accept services, a case will be opened without court intervention. On the other hand, if they refuse services, the case will be evaluated with legal counsel for the possibility of a petition seeking court supervision that will require the family to accept services for a period of time.

More than one court may be involved with the family. If the parents or caretakers have inflicted serious harm on children in the family, the district attorney may pursue charges in the criminal courts. Or, the family may be in the midst of a divorce with a court attempting to sort out issues of custody, visitation, child support, and–with issues of domestic violence– orders of protection. At the point a case enters the court system, it is usually required that relatives, especially grandparents of the children, be assessed as to their suitability and willingness to provide care for the children. In any event, the goals of the various court systems may be at odds or at least difficult to coordinate. In the simplest sense, the role of the criminal courts is to determine if a crime has been committed and, if this is true, to establish and administer proper punishment; the role of the family or juvenile courts is to provide services to maintain family life while assuring the safety of the child. The services offered are likely to be focused on rehabilitation.

The services provided may not always be thought of by those not involved with the system as "services." For example, when the courts remove children from the custody of their parent or caretaker and place them in foster care (or other "substitute care" facilities), it may seem punitive, especially to the parent, but it is considered to be a service. Certainly, one purpose of the service is to increase child safety by removing the child from a caretaker who is either unable to provide care or whose behavior may reasonably be thought to place the child at risk of harm, but a parallel purpose is to provide the caretaker with services that will permit the child to be safely restored to the caretaker.

## SUBSTITUTE CARE

In recent years, there has been an energetic effort on the part of child welfare organizations around the country to devise service systems that rely less on substitute care (family foster care and institutional foster care or residential placement). While most foster families are very well meaning and extremely dedicated to their role in the system, some provide less than optimal care for children placed in their custody. It can be extremely difficult for child caring agencies to sort out. However, even where the families and institutions that provide custodial care are well intentioned and competently trained, child placement introduces difficulties that can be challenging to overcome. Very often, children who are removed from their homes due to abuse and neglect become depressed and pine for their parents, even when they are able to recognize that their parents have not provided them with sufficient care (Bogolub, 2008).

While experiencing this ambivalence, many children feel that they are betraying their parents when they begin to form a positive attachment to their temporary caretakers. This may intensify a sense of loyalty to their parents. A disturbing and destructive vicious cycle may follow: "Acting out" (running away, stealing, disobedience, destruction of property, self-mutilation, sexual inappropriateness, truancy) often results from these feelings; foster parents then insist on removal; removal reinforces the child's feelings of worthlessness; this intensifies acting out; more restrictive forms of placement, such as institutional care, are then utilized; and the child then learns how to survive in an "institution."

As a result, many intensive, in-home service programs have been developed. In these programs, it is often recognized that having the child remain in the home is not resulting in the best possible care, but the risk of serious deterioration of the child in substitute care is beginning to be understood as not only damaging to the child's future well-being but also perpetuating a generational cycle of abuse and neglect (Davidson-Arad, Englechin-Segal, & Wozner, 2003).

It must be noted that foster parents and institutional residential programs may also be the subject of CPS reports. Persons who are mandated reporters are equally responsible to report suspected child abuse or neglect that occurs in these settings. (Some states are set up to investigate child abuse and neglect somewhat differently in these settings.)

When such a CPS case is indicated, certain events are set in motion that may well involve the mandated reporter. First, even if the case is not taken to the courts by CPS, subjects of the report (parents or other caretakers) have due process rights: They have a right to know all information on file about them (usually not including information about the identity of persons who have provided information during the investigation); they have right to contest the accuracy of that information; they have the right to request that the case be overturned from its indicated status to an unfounded status; and they have a right to some sort of hearing to contest the state's decision if it declines to provide the remedy requested. This process is usually administrative in nature and is called a *fair hearing*.

While the fair hearing is conducted in informal circumstances, it is a legal proceeding subject to rules of evidence, the appearance of witnesses, and formal recording. These hearings are ordinarily held in a conference room rather than a courtroom and are conducted by an administrative law judge (who usually does not sit at a bench or wear robes). It is common for clients to represent themselves, although in some areas, they may more commonly be represented by an attorney. Nevertheless, witnesses may be subpoenaed to appear, will be sworn, and are required by law to provide truthful testimony.

Whether or not a family receives services (court ordered or voluntarily), when a case is indicated, the case remains on file and as a matter of record. Usually, these are not open records, but the states have devised various methods and categories of releasing information concerning their CPS files. Most often, it is possible for organizations that employ persons who will have direct contact with children to check if applicants for employment have been the subject of an indicated CPS case.

## FREQUENTLY ASKED QUESTIONS

**Q.** I called the state child abuse hotline, and they accepted the case for investigation. But so far, I have not heard from anyone even though I gave my name and phone number.

**A.** You should usually hear from CPS within a few days. The more serious the allegations, the more quickly you should expect to hear. There are several other factors to consider: Was another person involved in making the report? If so, ascertain if that person has been contacted. If there is something you wish to add, obtain the contact number from that person, and call CPS yourself. As well, be certain that the hotline did indeed list the report for investigation and that your name and contact information were correctly recorded.

If simple problems such as these are ruled out, contact CPS directly and explain your concerns. Of course, have at hand all the identifying information you have about the case. If you do not have a central contact number for CPS, find the number in the telephone directory or online. You will probably be speaking with someone in "Intake," "Hotline," "Response," or the like. If you have worked with someone from CPS before and know how to reach that person, call and explain your concerns.

**Q.** I made a CPS report, but the person who called me back from CPS seemed hurried and disinterested. I felt I had a lot more to say, but I was sort of cut off.

**A.** As a general practice, when CPS calls back to follow up on the report, it is a good idea to take the name and phone number of the person who is calling as well as the person's title and supervisor's name. At the beginning of the conversation, you should be firm (although polite) about asking your own questions, probably before the person begins to ask you questions. Ask if this is the person who will perform the investigation. If not, ask for the name of the investigator who will be assigned *and* the supervisor. If the name is not provided, ask for the unit number. If your role causes you to be in touch with CPS more than occasionally, ask to be provided with an internal phone list for the organization.

After you have been asked questions about the case you reported, if you feel that there is information that is important that has not been covered, say clearly, "There is something else I need to add." If you believe that the information you are providing or attempting to provide is not being taken into serious consideration, ask to be permitted to speak with either the actual person assigned to investigate. Or, if you are already speaking to that person, then you may ask to speak to his or her supervisor.

**Q.** I made a CPS report and received a call back from a person who seemed very concerned and asked all the right questions. However, when I did not hear anything else, I called again, but that person is usually unavailable or seems unwilling to talk to me.

**A.** As in the response to the last situation, always be sure to take all the identifying information you can gather when you receive a call from anyone.

In this scenario, there are a couple possibilities. First, CPS usually sees itself as a gatherer of information rather than a provider of it. If you are calling to provide additional information, someone will usually listen. However, if you are calling to inquire about the investigation, you may encounter a lot of reluctance to share information. CPS usually tries to avoid forming a decision before a case is determined to be either indicated or unfounded, so they will avoid discussing an "investigation" as if it were already a "case."

The second consideration concerns your legal right to know the information for which you are calling. In many states, mandated reporters do not necessarily have the right to information that has been discovered by CPS, and the staff in CPS are reluctant to discuss a case because they are concerned that they may, perhaps even inadvertently, give away or hint at information that may violate the client's right to privacy. Often, CPS staff will inform you of this quite directly. However, in some states, mandated reporters who have a "need to know" may have a right to some limited information about the investigation. If the communication you seek is blocked by a disagreement about what you sincerely believe is your need to know, always ask to take this issue up with someone higher than the person who is speaking with you.

A third possibility is that the person assigned to the case is quite busy. It is common for CPS investigators to have high caseloads. If you are calling out of curiosity or simply to discuss new developments on the case that do not impact child safety, calling you back may have become "deprioritized" to the bottom of the to-do list. If you believe what you need to discuss is important, ask to speak with the unit supervisor.

A fourth possibility is that you are calling too often about a case that is not a high priority. If you think this might be the situation, ask directly if it is so. Again, if you believe important information is being ignored, call someone higher in the bureaucracy. Certainly, if a caseworker or a supervisor cannot diplomatically articulate this position, an administrator should be able to assist.

**Q.** I made a CPS report and specifically told the person I spoke to that I did not want my name used at all. However, a few days later, the child's parent called me in a very angry state accusing me of making the report. When I was not willing to admit this, the parent told me that the caseworker confirmed that I made the report. Now, the parents are threatening me with a lawsuit.

**A.** This is a very common event and may be the most often-heard complaint of persons who are mandated reporters of child abuse and neglect, and the most common focus of the subject of a report on learning that a report to the hotline has been made is the matter of "Who said this about me?" For a high percentage of subjects, it is a matter of passionate concern, so much so that it is often a large part of the case-worker's task in the initial interview to guide the person to a discussion of the allegations. Most CPS workers are trained to avoid discussion of the source of the report, and maintaining the confidentiality of those with legal protection from the release of their names is perhaps one the CPS worker's most important ethical concerns. It is *extremely* unlikely that your name has actually been provided by the CPS caseworker.

There are very few situations reported by mandated reporters that do not, by their nature, provide a clue as to the source of the report. It usually is a fairly easy guess for the subject. Some subjects are so piqued by this that they get in touch with the mandated reporter and, usually in the midst of a heated discussion, blurt out that "the caseworker *told* me it was *you*" to provide emphasis and power to the claim.

Even though very unlikely to be true, this claim does not in any way require you to admit that you made the report. In most states, your right to remain confidential is absolute until you are a sworn witness. You may deny you made the report, refuse to discuss if you made it, refuse contact with the subject entirely, or admit you made it. The choice is yours. However, for social workers, a more common choice is to discuss his or her role in the report with tactful honesty, a statement of their legal responsibilities in the matter, the priority of concerns for child and the family, and a summary of the possible benefits of the involvement of CPS. An additional option for many social workers is to function as an advocate for the family with the CPS bureaucracy, even though he or she made the initial report.

As for the threat of lawsuits, mandated reporters of suspected child abuse are virtually always immune from prosecution for making a "false" report if this report was made in connection with the dis-charge of their professional duties. A mandated reporter of suspected child abuse or maltreatment faces far more risk for a willful failure to report suspicions than for reporting suspicions that later turn out to be misplaced.

Confrontations or events such as these should be reported to the caseworker or the caseworker's supervisor, even if they do not appear to impact the safety of the child.

Last, it must be stated that there is a remote possibility that the subject's claim that the caseworker informed him or her of the source of the report is true. If you believe it is, and especially if you have some corroboration, it is imperative that this be reported to the case-worker's supervisor or some higher level of management. This sort of breach of CPS ethics and even state law will not be tolerated by a CPS organization.

**Q.** I reported a situation that I discovered only because the child in question developed a lot of trust in me and told me about things that I truly believe placed the child at risk of harm. However, I later learned that CPS determined that the case was "unfounded," and now the child seems angry with me and wants nothing to do with me.

**A.** There are really two elements here: first, your disagreement with the findings of CPS, and second, your sense of frustration concerning the damage done to your relationship with the child.

Each case is described by its own, very individual, details, and these may not be evident to you. CPS usually requires only the smallest evidence to "indicate" a case but will need substantially more evidence if the court system is needed to require a family to accept services. However, if you truly believe that evidence or circumstances were overlooked, you may either contact CPS to request an explanation, or, especially if conditions that you believe to be potentially or actually harmful to the child continue to exist, you may make another report to the child abuse hotline. In addition, you may write a letter to the CPS agency, the agency's head (commissioner or administrator), or your elected officials, in which you list your specific concerns.

As for the disruption of your relationship with the child, this, of course, is a more subtle problem. Frequently, a CPS investigation is very embarrassing for a family. The parents will usually be able to figure out the origin of the report and that the report was based on information provided by their child. Sometimes, they chide the child for "telling tales" or "airing dirty laundry." The child may be hurt or feeling betrayed, angry, or embarrassed and therefore avoiding you.

Depending on the age and maturity of the child, the severity of the allegations, and the urgency of the child's safety, it is sometimes a good idea to let the child understand that you are contemplating a CPS report. However, this requires careful judgment on your part. In less severe circumstances where there is a low level of physical risk to the child, such a discussion may help to alleviate the alienation of the child later. Sometimes, children are taken by surprise when they have assumed they were speaking to someone in confidence and the result is a CPS investigation. Abused and/or neglected children often do not recognize that they are being abused or neglected, and the child may view your making a report as an overreaction or as an unwarranted invasion of privacy even though, in the end, it served to protect him or her.

**Q.** I reported a situation in which a child repeatedly appears to be undernourished, unsupervised, exposed to chaotic family interactions, and living in squalor. CPS indicated the case, but other than that, they haven't done a thing, and the child is still living in the same circumstances.

**A.** Squalid circumstances are sometimes a thorny problem for CPS agencies. Conditions that most of us would find horrifying for ourselves or our own children, while offensive, may not be sufficiently dangerous for the children involved to be removed from the family. Often, CPS will offer the family services in an attempt to bring the household to minimally accepted levels of habitation. Some levels of dirt, dust, and disorder may not be entertained by a court as sufficient cause to remove the children. Conditions that would be considered unsafe include those that are potentially injurious, such as broken glass, open electrical circuits, broken stairs, weakened flooring, open flame heating or cooking, dangerous methods of fuel storage, indoor barbeques, or space heaters. Organic filth, such as animal or human feces, rotting food, vermin infestation, or standing water would likely be considered actionable. Action may also be taken if the ordinary activities of life are severely curtailed—there are no clean dishes in the household, bathing and toilet facilities are inoperable, or no clean clothing is ever available. Other very dangerous circumstances that are less often encountered might include home methamphetamine labs, unsecured firearms or explosive materials, poisonous substances, or ferocious animals (real cases have involved large boa constrictors or "big" cats kept in a family home).

Again, if you believe a circumstance that presents a clear and identifiable danger to a child has been overlooked, do not seethe in silence. Call CPS and explain, in detail, your concerns. Ask for a general description of CPS policies in these kinds of cases (they will be unable to discuss the individual case with you). If you continue to be unsatisfied, write a letter to the head of the agency or one of your elected representatives. Attend public hearings, or volunteer for the CPS advisory board.

**Q.** I reported a case that CPS indicated and then took the parents to court. I was subpoenaed to testify, but when I did, one of the attorneys asked me if I made the report, and I said that I do not have to answer that question. The judge got angry and told me to answer it. I was upset because I thought I was right.

**A.** Your right to remain confidential, as the source of the report, even if the law requires you to make the report, is only assured during the investigation. This protection is not extended to any evidentiary hearing (fair hearing, administrative hearing, or trial). You should be advised of this at the time you are called to appear as a witness.

**Q.** I reported a case that CPS indicated and then took the parents to court. I was subpoenaed to testify, and I did, but it was a horrible experience. The parents' attorney not only made me admit that I made the report but also went on questioning me in a tone that I thought was accusatory and humiliating. The CPS attorney objected several times, but it kept happening. The judge did not seem to notice. I am a dedicated professional with a good record who was only doing my job. I feel disgusted by the whole process.

**A.** This can indeed be an awful experience for anyone who is subjected to it. However, if possible, try not to take it too personally. Yes, that is very much easier said than done, but one of the tactics used by some attorneys (actually not that many) is to try to get you to lose your temper or react emotionally on the stand. If you do, they hope that the judge or jury may get a glimpse of you as a person who made the report, at least partially, for personal and emotional reasons rather than professional reasons. The best approach is to remain calm, pause before answering questions, request clarification of any question you do not understand, and honestly say you do not know the answer if that is the case.

**Q.** A case I reported to CPS was indicated and then brought to court, and the family was ordered to accept services. However, I have observed that the child seems worse off than before, and it appears that the services they are receiving do not seem to be making any difference at all.

**A.** This problem should be brought to the attention of CPS, preferably in writing by mail. In many jurisdictions, the person or organization providing services may not be the same as the person who investigated the original allegations. If the problems you are seeing are different from those originally reported, call the hotline and make a new report. If the family is being dishonest in some way (e. g., participating in drug counseling but continuing to use drugs), report this to the caseworker or agency that is working with the family. Some CPS jurisdictions will require you to create a new report to the CPS hotline.

If you have taken these steps and continue to feel that the child is at risk of harm, write to the head of the agency or to your elected representatives. You might also become active as a volunteer in CPS issues in your community.

**Q.** A case I reported to CPS was indicated, and the children were ordered into foster care some time ago. Recently, I have begun to receive phone calls from one of the children. From what this child is telling me, I think the children may be more badly mistreated in the foster home than they were at their own home. I am very concerned, but the child does not want me to say anything, and I am worried that even if I do, the children will only be sent to yet another foster home.

**A.** Foster parents are responsible for the safety and well-being of the children who are placed in their care. Foster parents can be the subject of a CPS report just as readily as any other caretaker. As a mandated reporter, you are equally responsible to report child abuse or neglect that is occurring in a foster home, just as you would report it if it were occurring in any other custodial situation. Your reluctance based on the child's perceiving the report as a violation of trust is certainly understandable. That is why you need to do all you can to help the child understand your obligations in the matter as well as the child's right not to be mistreated *wherever he or she lives.*

**Q.** I have made many reports to CPS, and I know many in my profession who have also made reports. When we discuss our experiences, we all have the same opinion. Most of the workers seem well intentioned but poorly trained and overwhelmed. Even when cases are indicated, no changes seem to result. Reports are made over and over on the same families with no results. Calls to supervisors and administrators are rebuffed or produce the usual rhetoric. We are very worried about the safety of some of the children we have reported.

**A.** The CPS system is, sadly, far from perfect. While some jurisdictions have evolved into first-class operations staffed by highly trained, well-equipped professionals with controlled caseloads who often work in a well-coordinated, multidiscipline environment, it must be stated that just as many are understaffed, poorly trained, professionally isolated, overworked, and burned out. It is a sad fact that reform of such agencies often remains unchanged until a scandal, often involving a child fatality, moves the public to insist on changes.

As a mandated reporter you are an important part of this system. If you believe that your local CPS is inadequate, then there is room for your involvement. Show up and speak up consistently at various public meetings that CPS is required to conduct. Contact the administrator in charge or the commissioner, and clearly express your concerns in writing. Be in touch repeatedly. Keep up contact with the field supervisor who covers your area. Join committees, task forces, and other bodies who have input into the system or seek to reform it. Be in touch with your elected representatives at all governmental levels, including your elected executives. Ask to be appointed to the CPS advisory panel.

## REFERENCES

American Federation of State, County, and Municipal Employees. (1998). *Double jeopardy: Caseworkers at risk helping at-risk children. A report on the working conditions facing child welfare workers*. Washington, DC: Author.

Bogolub, E. (2008). Child protective services investigations and the transition to foster care: Children's views. *Families in Society*, 89, 90–99.

Davidson-Arad, B., Englechin-Segal, D., & Wozner, Y. (2003). Short-term follow-up of children at risk: Comparison of the quality of life of children removed from home and children remaining at home. *Child Abuse and Neglect*, 27(7), 733–750.

Loftus, E. F. (2003). Our changeable memories: Legal and practical implications. *Nature Reviews Neuroscience*, 4, 231–234.

# 9

# Legal and Ethical Issues in Mandated Reporting

Social workers may find the responsibility of being a mandated reporter in conflict with other legal and ethical responsibilities they have toward their clients. Whether working in social service administration, case management, as a clinician, or even a researcher, social workers are expected to maintain client confidences and keep case information private. Mandated reporters of child abuse and neglect, on the other hand, are required by law to reveal client confidences that suggest child abuse or neglect has occurred or is imminent. How can social workers do both at once?

In communities where family involvement in child protective services (CPS) is prevalent, social workers are often not trusted because they are mandated reporters. As a result, those in greatest need of social work services may choose not to seek such services for fear of being reported to CPS.

This chapter examines the legal and ethical guidelines for the negotiation of the social worker's dual roles of confidante and mandated reporter. This chapter also provides suggestions for social workers to negotiate these conflicting roles so that clients feel more comfortable seeking the services of social workers and social workers feel comfortable in their role as professional reporters of child abuse and neglect.

## CLIENT CONFIDENTIALITY

There are many laws that require mental health professionals to keep client information confidential. Many jurisdictions also recognize that information passed between client and clinical social worker during a therapy session is privileged. Confidentiality and privilege are related, although not synonymous, concepts.

Confidentiality means that information will not be shared beyond the relationship. Confidentiality in the social worker—client relationship means that what the client tells the social worker, the social worker will not reveal to others. Confidentiality encourages clients to be honest and open; when they feel comfortable that what they say will not be shared with others, they are more likely to share information that they would otherwise keep to themselves. Confidentiality thus encourages clients to share information that is not only potentially embarrassing but also may be self-incriminating. The social workers' obligation to keep client confidences is supported through state and federal law.

Information about children and their families received through a CPS investigation is generally considered confidential. CPS can use relevant information in subsequent court actions involving the family, such as abuse and neglect proceedings. However, CPS is limited in their ability to share information about families with others, including the professional who made the report of suspected child abuse and neglect. For more information on this subject, refer to chapter 8.

The social work profession holds strongly to the importance of client confidentiality. Social work practice classes, at both the bachelor and master's levels, include many discussions about the topic of confidentiality. Social work students learn early in their professional careers about keeping client confidences and pride themselves on adhering to the concept.

Client confidentiality is further supported through workplace norms and rules. Social work agencies have internal policies on client confidentiality and design systems that maximize the protection of client information.

## Client Confidentiality in the National Association of Social Workers Code of Ethics

Confidentiality is a major tenet of the Code of Ethics for the National Association of Social Workers (NASW). The NASW Code outlines the goals of the social work profession, as prescribed by NASW. The Code also provides guidance for the ethical behavior of social workers.

It is important to note that the NASW Code itself is not law. The NASW is the premier national association of professional social workers but is not a governmental entity. Not all social workers in the United States are members of NASW. The NASW Code was written by NASW to provide guidance on ethical behavior for its membership and all social workers. However, the NASW Code was not written by the government and therefore is not in and of itself law.

The NASW Code has been translated into law in some jurisdictions. Some state social work licensing boards have adopted the Code (part or parcel) as regulations for the professional conduct of licensed social workers. In those jurisdictions where the Code is adopted into regulation, it is considered law. Failure to follow the NASW Code in such jurisdictions can make a social worker subject to malpractice lawsuits and actions against his or her professional license. When the Code has not been adopted as law in a particular jurisdiction, failing to follow it does not meet the same penalties as failing to follow the law.

Failing to follow the NASW Code, regardless of its application to the law, can lead to sanction, censure, or suggested corrective action for social workers who are members of the NASW. Since the NASW is neither a legal nor governmental entity, it does not have the authority to rescind professional licenses or order damages be paid. Corrective action ordered by the NASW as a result of failing to follow the NASW Code can only be administered to their own members. Social workers who are not members of the NASW are not subject to their disciplinary procedures.

However, the NASW Code can be used as evidence in legal proceedings, regardless of whether it has been adopted into law. For instance, the Code can be used as a model of professional standards in a malpractice case against a social worker in any jurisdiction. If a social worker is accused of malpractice, the person who sues can claim that the social worker failed to meet the minimum standards of the profession by comparing the social worker's actions to those suggested by the NASW Code. On the other hand, the social worker being sued can also use the Code to his or her advantage. The social worker can show how guidelines of the NASW Code were followed as a defense to malpractice.

Section 1.07 of the NASW Code outlines the social worker's obligation to keep client information private and confidential. This section provides that "social workers should respect clients' right to privacy" (NASW Code, 1.07[a]). The NASW Code provides that this right to privacy extends to clients even after death (NASW Code, 1.07[r]). Social workers should also take reasonable precautions to protect client confidentiality in the event of their own termination of practice, incapacitation, or death (NASW Code 1.07[o]).

To protect client confidences, the NASW Code provides that "social workers should not discuss confidential information in any setting unless privacy can be ensured." For instance, "social workers should not discuss confidential information in public or semipublic areas such as hallways, waiting rooms, elevators, and restaurants" (NASW Code, 1.07[i]). The NASW Code also provides that "social workers should protect the confidentiality of clients' written and electronic records and other sensitive information." To fulfill this responsibility, "social workers should take reasonable steps to ensure that clients' records are stored in a secure location and that clients' records are not available to others who are not authorized to have access" (NASW Code, 1.07[l]). At the end of their relationship with a client, the NASW Code provides that "social workers should transfer or dispose of clients' records in a manner that protects clients' confidentiality and is consistent with state statutes governing records and social work licensure." (NASW Code, 1.07[n]).

## Exceptions to Client Confidentiality

There are, of course, exceptions to the ethical rule and applicable law on client confidentiality. Clients often know some of these exceptions without them being listed by the social worker. For instance, social workers are often expected to share client confidences within their agencies in order to receive professional supervision or seek advice from colleagues (e.g., the staff psychiatrist).

Clients often ask social workers to share confidential information with others. For instance, clients will "release" social workers to share information with other service providers. The NASW Code recognizes this and suggests disclosure is appropriate when the social worker has "valid consent from the client or a person legally authorized to consent on behalf of the client" (NASW Code, 1.07[b]).

In these instances, social workers should be careful to receive such releases in writing. In these written releases, the client should specify what content the social worker is allowed to share with the other party as well as what information the client specifically does not want the social worker to share.

Oftentimes during an investigation, CPS will request documents or information from a social worker, whether the social worker was the source of the report or simply a service provider to the family. CPS may provide a release to a social worker that is signed by a client. It is good practice for the social worker to reach out to the client to discuss the release and the information that the social worker intends to share as a result of the release before sharing any information.

The law in all states, and even the NASW Code, acknowledges that there are instances in which client confidences must be broken to protect the greater good, such as in the mandated reporting of child abuse and neglect. The NASW Code provides that "social workers should protect the confidentiality of all information obtained in the course of professional service, except for compelling professional reasons" (NASW Code, 1.07[a]). The Code further provides that "the general expectation that social workers will keep information confidential does not apply when disclosure is necessary to prevent serious, foreseeable, and imminent harm to a client or other identifiable person" (NASW Code, 1.07[c]).

The duty of social workers to protect their clients, and other persons, from harm can be derived from relevant case law. The duty to protect others from harm at the hands of client originated in a California Supreme Court decision, *Tarasoff v. Regents of the University of California* (1976). (For case details, see chapter 10). In the *Tarasoff* case, the court found that mental health professionals have a duty to protect a potential victim of impending harm, which trumps the responsibility to keep client confidences private. Social workers join psychologists, psychiatrists, and other mental health professionals in carrying this duty. Mandated reporting of child abuse and neglect is considered one such situation that falls within the duty found in the *Tarasoff* case.

In all instances in which a social worker breaks client confidentiality to meet another purpose, the social worker should disclose the least amount of confidential information necessary to achieve the desired purpose. Only information that is directly relevant to the purpose for which the disclosure is made should be revealed (NASW Code, 1.07[c]). For instance, just because a social worker breaks confidentiality to make a report does not mean that all that was said in confidence with the social worker should be shared with CPS. Some states (such as New York Social Services Law sec. 413) have provisions that specify that only information necessary for the determination of the allegations be shared.

## Consequences for Breaking Client Confidentiality

The law in most states provides that when information that is deemed confidential is shared without client permission or without other legal authority to do so (i.e., mandated reporting, order of the court), the professional can be sued and found liable in a civil court. Social workers who breach client confidentiality without an exception to their legal obligations can also have their licenses revoked or receive professional censure. Client confidentiality is a serious and important concept.

Even when breaking client confidentiality to meet a higher legal burden, such as mandated reporting of child abuse and neglect, social workers should be careful not to release more information than necessary to satisfy their obligations as mandated reporters. Sharing more information than necessary can also make them subject to civil liability. They can be successfully sued for sharing too much information.

## PRIVILEGED COMMUNICATIONS

Privilege is a separate concept from, but related to, confidentiality. Privilege protects confidential client information from being brought to light in a legal proceeding. When information is considered privileged, it cannot be submitted as evidence in a legal proceeding, such as a court case.

Privilege generally derives from a relationship in which there is an expectation that information passed within the relationship will remain confidential. The information shared in confidence is protected in court through privilege in recognition of the importance of these relationships in society. For example, if patients did not share their medical information with doctors because they feared that doctors would share that information with others, then doctors would not have enough information to help or cure their patients. For this reason, the information between a doctor and patients is privileged, and when testifying in a court case, a doctor will be limited in what information he or she is allowed to share with the court because of the doctor–patient privilege.

There are many such privileges found in American law. These privileges include the aforementioned doctor–patient privilege, marital testimonial privilege, and therapist–client privilege. Marital testimonial privilege was created to protect the marital relationship. If one spouse were forced to testify against the other, sharing negative information, the marriage might suffer. It is important to note that the spouse that can assert marital testimonial privilege is the spouse who is called to testify. The spouse who is called to testify is the one who "holds" this privilege. If the spouse chooses to testify, the court will allow the spouse to do so. He or she cannot, however, be forced to testify.

An exception to privilege for most professional relationships includes when the professional is being sued by the client. In that situation, the professional can share privileged information with the court as necessary as a defense against the client's accusations (e.g., a doctor in a malpractice lawsuit).

## Social Workers and Privilege

Social workers are often served subpoenas (requests for evidence for a court proceeding) that ask for client information. In some circumstances, government agencies serve subpoenas before a court proceeding has commenced. Subpoenas served on social workers usually call for client information in the form of testimony from the social worker or for case records.

The subpoena will specify the information being sought. It is the social worker's responsibility to prepare the information in response to the subpoena. It is important for the social worker to read the subpoena carefully and only provide information that is specifically called for. If the information being sought is confidential, the social worker needs to be careful not to share too much information.

The social worker should speak to his or her supervisor too before responding to a subpoena. The supervisor can provide assistance in collecting case record information as well as help the social worker prepare for a courtroom experience.

If the social worker feels like the subpoena is too broad (i.e., asking for the complete case record when the issue of the legal proceeding is limitedly discussed in the client file), he or she can assert privilege. The social worker would go to court on the specified date to provide testimony or records and to tell the judge why he or she believes the subpoena is overbroad. It is then up to the judge to determine if the scope of the subpoena should be more limited. Information that a social worker believes should not be shared with the court may be successfully protected from inclusion in a court proceeding if privilege is asserted.

## Social Worker–Client Privilege?

A U.S. Supreme Court case, *Jaffee v. Redmond* (1996), addressed this question: "Is the psychotherapist–patient relationship privileged?" In *Jaffee*, a police officer, Mary Lu Redmond, was sued in civil court for wrongfully killing a man when she responded to a fight in progress. The man, Ricky Allen, was allegedly brandishing a butcher knife and refused to drop the weapon when ordered to do so by Officer Redmond. At issue in this case was whether discussions with a clinical social worker who counseled Officer Redmond after the incident could be admissible as evidence in this case. Officer Redmond asserted that the content of those sessions should be protected by privilege.

At the time, the existence of a psychotherapist–patient privilege was not uniform across federal court districts. However, most state courts are bound by such a privilege through their own rules of evidence or statute. The Supreme Court ultimately agreed with Officer Redmond and found in the *Jaffee* case that such a privilege should exist in *all* federal courts.

An important component of the *Jaffee* decision is the clarification that the psychotherapist–patient privilege is not a "social worker–client" privilege. In the decision for the court, it is made clear that there was no hesitation on the part of the Court on extending a privilege to psychologists and psychiatrists. The court, after consideration, found good reason to extend the psychotherapist–patient privilege to "licensed social workers in the course of psychotherapy." The court reasoned (referencing an amicus brief from NASW) that social workers provide a significant amount of the mental health treatment in the United States. Additionally, often clients with limited financial means are not able to afford the services of psychologists and psychiatrists and instead receive psychotherapy from social workers. Therefore, the Court explicitly includes social workers in the psychotherapist–patient privilege. However, the privilege established in *Jaffee* did not result in a privilege intended for all social workers and their clients.

Therefore, not all forms of social work are covered by this privilege in federal courts. As long as the social worker meets the criteria of being licensed, and the relationship with the client is in the form of psychotherapy, this privilege can be asserted in federal courts. Social workers who are not licensed and/or not practicing psychotherapy with their client cannot.

In his dissenting opinion in the *Jaffee* case, Justice Antonin Scalia explained his displeasure with the majority decision to include social workers in the psychotherapist–patient privilege. Justice Scalia argued against the extension of privilege to social workers by noting the differences between psychologists, psychiatrists, and social workers. For instance, he found it clear that a "licensed psychiatrist or psychologist is an expert in psychotherapy." However, he presumed "that a social worker does *not* bring this greatly heightened degree of skill to bear, which is alone a reason for not encouraging" consultation with a social worker "as generously" as with a psychiatrist or psychologist. He questioned, "Does a social worker bring to bear at least a significantly heightened degree of skill—more than a minister or rabbi, for example?" He admitted that he did not have an answer to that question. He argued that the main purpose of psychologists and psychiatrists is to provide psychotherapy, and therefore their professions deserve universal privilege. However, he noted that social workers are more diverse in their training and skills and less specialized in psychotherapy. He suggested in the alternative that privilege for social workers only be provided when it is clear that the communications are in the course of psychotherapy instead of providing a blanket privilege for licensed social workers who provide psychotherapy.

Even though the Court in *Jaffee* refused to find a global "social worker–client" privilege in federal courts, and Justice Scalia's dissent suggested that even less privilege should be afforded to social workers, many state courts adopted such a privilege even before the *Jaffee* decision. Some states limit the privilege to the practice of clinical social work, specifically in the role of psychotherapist, as does the *Jaffee* decision. Other states limit the privilege to licensed social workers, regardless of their practice area. The reservation of privilege for social workers as psychotherapists, and not the inclusion of all types of social workers, continues a great divide currently found in profession regarding the relative status of clinical social workers to other areas of professional social work, including administration and case management.

## How Does Privilege Work?

When someone seeks to enter information into evidence in a legal proceeding that could be considered privileged due to the relationship of the witness to the information, permission is needed from the protected party; alternatively, the court must order the release of the information. The court can determine, after weighing the costs and benefits of forcing disclosure, that privileged information is necessary for the proceeding and order the information to be shared. Often, the judge, alone, will look over the information that is being sought (called an *in-camera review*) or speak to the parties of the privileged relationship before making such a ruling.

Judges in family court are ultimately charged with determining the best interests of a child. Therefore, judges often order the release of privileged information in child protective proceedings because they deem the information more important for deciding the safety of the child than preserving a privilege. For this reason, when social workers who have confidential relationships with victims or perpetrators of abuse or neglect are called to testify in child abuse and neglect hearings, the court often orders that information be shared, overruling claims that such information is privileged.

If the court orders the release of privileged information, the social worker should work with the court to provide only the information necessary to the case at hand and nothing more. The NASW Code provides guidance for the practice of social workers in this situation. The code says that social workers should protect their client's confidentiality during legal proceedings to the extent permitted by the law (NASW Code, 1.07[j]).

However, if the court, or other legally authorized body, orders a social worker to disclose confidential or privileged information without a client's consent and such disclosure could cause harm to the client, the social worker should request that the court withdraw the order or limit the order as narrowly as possible or maintain the records under seal, unavailable for public inspection (NASW Code, 1.07[j]). To contest the disclosure of confidential client information, the social worker should appear at a court date on the case and ask to be heard on the issue. The social worker does not need to hire private legal counsel but can choose to if that would make him or her comfortable.

## NEGOTIATING CLIENT CONFIDENTIALITY WITH MANDATED REPORTING

Social workers are required by law and professional ethics to keep client secrets, while being simultaneously required to protect children by sharing client confidences. The question remains as to how can social workers reconcile their confidential relationships with clients with their mandated reporting obligations. Defining these issues at the outset of the professional relationship between the social worker and client can help to mediate the conflict between professional and reporter. The NASW Code suggests that social workers use informed consent to negotiate the boundaries of their relationships with clients (NASW Code, 1.03).

Informed consent involves the use of clear and understandable language to inform clients of the purpose of the services (NASW Code, 1.03[a]). Through informed consent, social workers should discuss with clients and other interested parties the nature of confidentiality and limitations of clients' right to confidentiality (NASW Code, 1.03[a]). Essentially, informed consent involves talking to clients about what they can expect from you as their social worker as well as what you will seek from them. During this process, "social workers should provide clients with an opportunity to ask questions" (NASW Code, 1.03[a]).

The process of informed consent is considered one element of the contracting process a social worker should conduct with the client. Contracting involves outlining the responsibilities of the practitioner and the expectations from the client. Informed consent and the contracting process make the process involved in the relationship between social worker and client transparent. Informed consent and contracting help clients take responsibility for their part of the professional relationship and encourage them to be honest and committed.

## Guidance on the Process of Informed Consent

Informed consent should include a discussion of what the relationship between the social worker and client will involve. This is the time to discuss basic protocols, such as appointment scheduling and canceling, as well as theories of practice that the social worker ascribes to in his or her practice. This discussion should also involve what services the social worker can provide and what information the client can expect the social worker to keep confidential.

When possible and appropriate, the social worker can provide informed consent in writing. In an agency setting, such a document may already exist. Social workers working in private practice may seek to create their own informed consent document. In that case, the social worker may choose to have an attorney review this document. However, a written statement of informed consent alone may not be sufficient (i.e., in the case of illiterate clients). The social worker should discuss with the client the details of informed consent, using layman's terms whenever possible. The social worker should then solicit questions and concerns from the client in an effort to determine whether the client understands the concept of informed consent and how it defines their relationship.

## Timing of Informed Consent

The informed consent discussion should occur as soon as possible in the social worker–client relationship and as needed throughout the course of the relationship (NASW Code, 1.03[e]). Informed consent should occur at the outset of the professional relationship for a variety of reasons. Through informed consent, clients can make an educated decision as to whether they want to continue with the social work services and/or how they want to participate in the services. Early discussion of the potential for breaking client confidences in the future can help to ease future tensions if the potential turns into reality.

Informed consent is not just a one-time discussion. The process of informed consent can take place over a series of meetings. It is important for professional social workers to continue to reinforce informed consent throughout their relationship with their client. The concept can be revisited at regular intervals and/or when the need arises.

## Is Informed Consent Necessary With *All* Clients?

All clients are entitled to informed consent. Special attention should be paid to the informed consent process with clients of limited capacity, including children. Professionals who otherwise have confidential relationships with clients often assume that when they are working with children or adults with limited mental capacity, the social worker does not have the same professional obligations. This is untrue.

Social workers should make extra effort when working with such clients to ensure that the client understands the bounds of the relationship. The NASW Code provides that social workers should take reasonable steps to enhance such clients' ability to give informed consent (NASW Code, 1.03[c]).

Whereas competent adults may understand what "abuse" or "neglect" entail without explanation, children and adults with limited mental capacity may need further explanation. Instead of describing what behaviors the social worker has to report to the authorities, the social worker can explain that part of the job is to keep children safe. The social worker can explain to the client that if he or she is concerned that a child is not safe, someone must be told about it so that the child can be kept safe.

## Informed Consent and the Mandated Client

Due to the nature of the relationship of the social work profession with governmental institutions, such as the penal and court systems, social workers are often involved in providing treatment or services to clients who are mandated to participate. The relationship between a social worker and a client mandated to services ("mandated client") requires special attention, especially when considering the informed consent process. The NASW Code provides that "when clients are receiving services involuntarily, social workers should provide information about the nature and extent of services and about the extent of clients' right to refuse service" (NASW Code 1.07[d]). Mandated clients are entitled to the same level of informed consent as other clients, especially regarding the social worker's role as mandated reporter.

## Informed Consent and Nonclinical Social Workers

Informed consent is an applicable concept for all social workers with clients. The responsibility of social workers to provide informed consent, including maintaining a confidential relationship with clients, is not limited to clinical social workers. Social workers involved in other positions, including school social workers and case managers, should provide informed consent to their clients, including a discussion of their responsibilities as mandated reporters.

## Informing the Client About Mandated Reporting

More important than discussing what information the social worker will keep confidential is informing the client when the social worker will have to release otherwise confidential information, such as in the instance of mandated reporting of child abuse and neglect. In essence, the social worker should inform the client that although the client should feel safe to share information because the social worker will keep it a secret, the social worker cannot keep *all* information secret.

   The social worker should explain that the law requires that instances of suspected child abuse or neglect must be reported. Even if the social worker is sure that the client knows that he or she is a mandated reporter, the client should still be reminded of the social worker's role and responsibility. The social worker should also explain to the client that if confidentiality must be broken to make a report to CPS, everything in his or her power will be done to minimize the amount of confidential information that is shared.

When discussing your responsibilities as a mandated reporter, you can advise your clients that you may or may not tell them when you are going to make a report. You are *not* required by law to tell your client that you made a report. The NASW Code also does not require you to inform your client that you made a report to CPS.

When deciding whether to inform the client about your decision to report suspected child abuse or neglect, consideration should be made as to your safety, the safety of any children involved, forensic integrity, and the impact of such disclosure on your professional relationship with the client. For instance, it is generally not recommended that parents be informed of the decision to report allegations of sexual abuse or extreme physical abuse against them, as the child may be subjected to retaliatory abuse. Additionally, some clients, when informed of a report being made against them, will make efforts to cover up or eliminate evidence, thereby impacting the integrity of forensic evidence that CPS seeks in their investigation. They may also attempt to coach the child to lie about events that took place.

In the event that the social worker chooses not to inform the client that he or she is the source of the report, the social worker may be confronted by the client, who questions if he or she made the report. Before responding, the social worker should consider the reasons that the client was not informed of the report in the first place. If necessary, the social worker can lie to the client and deny making the report, especially if such an assertion will protect the safety of the social worker and/or others.

The NASW Code suggests that social workers should inform clients, to the extent possible, about the disclosure of confidential information and the potential consequences, when feasible, before the disclosure is made. This applies whether social workers disclose confidential information on the basis of a legal requirement or client consent (NASW Code, 1.07[d]).

Many social workers choose to speak with their clients about their decision to make a report. Some social workers tell the client before the report is made; others do so after. Some social workers have the client sit with them when a report is made so that the client hears what the social worker tells CPS and understands the process. It is up to the social worker as an individual professional to make the decision about whether the client will be informed.

The law differs from state to state regarding whether the mandated reporter's identification can be known to the subject of the report and at what point this information is available to the subject (see appendix A for specific information on the policy in your state). As discussed in chapter 8, some states allow for anonymous reporting by mandated reporters. In those states, if the mandated reporter chooses not to share identifying information when making a report, there is no way that the subject of the report will be able to confirm the source of the report. In other states, mandated reporters are not allowed to make anonymous reports, and as a result, the identifying information becomes part of the record of that report.

In states where the mandated reporter's identification is part of the report, there is usually a procedure that enables his or her identity to be withheld from the client by the child protective investigator. However, many clients have a good idea about who made the report because of the nature of the report (i.e., if it contains allegations or details that only one particular person would know).

In some states where the identification of the mandated reporter is part of the CPS report (such as New York State), protection of identity is only provided through the investigation phase. In those jurisdictions, if the case goes to court, identifying information of the mandated reporter will become part of the court file. When the client appears in court, he or she will have the opportunity to find out who made the report.

The social worker's obligation to a client does not end when the confidential relationship is challenged by making a report. Social workers should continue to do all they can to ensure that their working relationship will continue with the client after the report or, alternately, the client is availed of other social work services. The social worker can help to educate the client about the CPS system. Social workers should, where appropriate, assure the client of their loyalty to their client and their commitment to advocate for their best interests. It is often helpful for the client to know that the social worker will be supportive through the CPS process.

## Costs and Benefits of Informed Consent

Informing clients of your responsibilities as a mandated reporter of child abuse and neglect during the informed consent process may discourage clients from sharing information with you that they believe may necessitate you to make such a report. However, using informed consent in a contracting process with clients encourages clients to be honest and accepting of the consequences.

The benefits of informed consent are lost when the professional does not acknowledge the importance of the process. Often, social workers are wary of broaching informed consent. They may be uncomfortable with the potential for disruption. New social workers may be especially afraid that clients will not want to continue services if they know that the social worker is a mandated reporter. Other social workers want to forego informed consent so that they can get "right to business." Skipping the informed consent process can start the social worker–client relationship on the wrong foot. Additionally, failing to provide informed consent can come back to "bite" the social worker in the future.

## CONFIDENTIALITY, MANDATED REPORTING, AND THE HEALTH INSURANCE PORTABILITY AND ACCOUNTABILITY ACT OF 1996

In recent years, developments in federal confidentiality law have renewed concern that mandated reporting violates other legal mandates of professionals, including social workers. The federal Health Insurance Portability and Accountability Act of 1996 (HIPAA) was passed by Congress and signed into law by President Bill Clinton in an attempt to safeguard patient/client information when transferred electronically (Davidson, 2003). Most relevant for this discussion are the portions of HIPAA that provide new protections for the security and privacy of patient information (Davidson). HIPAA reinforces other forms of law that require patient information to be safeguarded and only released when legally appropriate.

The NASW responded to HIPAA by amending the NASW Code to advise social workers to take "precautions to ensure and maintain the confidentiality of information transmitted to other parties through the use of computers, electronic mail, facsimile machines, telephones and telephone answering machines, and other electronic or computer technology" (NASW 1.07[m]). Further, the NASW Code provides that "disclosure of identifying information should be avoided whenever possible" (NASW 1.07[m]).

Under HIPAA, clients can expect more sensitivity of practitioners when sharing private information. For instance, after HIPAA, practitioners are more likely to seek written permission to release client files. However, HIPAA does not require mandated reporters to get such permission from clients before making a report of suspected child abuse or neglect.

Confusion arose when mandated reporters covered by HIPAA began to claim that they could no longer report child abuse or neglect without patient/client authorization, because such unauthorized disclosure was a violation of their legal obligations under HIPAA. However, this assertion is incorrect. In fact, HIPAA specifically permits the disclosure of otherwise protected patient information without patient authorization to further specific public health interests (Disclosures for Public Health Activities, 2003). The identification of suspected child abuse and neglect is one such public health interest.

HIPAA provides that protected health information can specifically be disclosed to report suspected child abuse or neglect. To meet the HIPAA exception, the report must be made to a public health authority or other appropriate government authority authorized by law to receive such reports. For instance, in most jurisdictions, mandated reporters are required to report to a department of the state or local government, with the legal authority to receive reports of child abuse or neglect. Reports to these entities would be permitted under HIPAA (Disclosures for Public Health Activities, 2003). Therefore, compliance with HIPAA does not conflict with the mandated reporter's legal requirement to report suspected child abuse and neglect.

## MANDATED REPORTING IN THE CONTEXT OF SUBSTANCE ABUSE TREATMENT

In the 1970s, the federal government recognized that the fear of stigma related to substance abuse deterred people from seeking necessary services (Substance Abuse and Mental Health Services Administration, 2004). Since then, federal confidentiality regulations have protected the privacy of millions of people seeking substance abuse treatment (Confidentiality of Alcohol and Drug Abuse Patient Records, 2002). The question then remains that if there is special protection provided to those in substance abuse treatment through federal law, can substance abuse treatment providers be mandated reporters of child abuse? For instance, if social workers are employed in a substance abuse treatment program, how do they negotiate their duty as mandated reporters of child abuse with the special federal confidentiality regulations afforded to those in substance abuse treatment?

The privacy protections required by most substance abuse treatment providers are currently governed by HIPAA. The few treatment programs that are not required to be HIPAA compliant still follow the federal confidentiality regulations found under the Confidentiality of Alcohol and Drug Abuse Patient Records section of federal regulations (2002) . Both HIPAA and this section of the federal regulations find an exception to holding client information confidential for the purposes of child abuse reporting. Therefore, social workers who are substance abuse treatment providers continue to be mandated reporters of child abuse.

However, the important thing to note is that not all parents seeking substance abuse treatment should be reported for suspected child abuse or neglect. Those substance abuse treatment providers who are mandated to report suspected child abuse or neglect should be knowledgeable about the law in their particular state regarding substance abuse and child abuse reporting. For instance, in New York State, the law does not define substance abuse itself as a form of abuse or neglect. Instead, the mandated reporter must consider the impact of the substance abuse on the parents' ability to care for their children, in combination with the effect of the drug use on the children, and the willingness on the part of the parents to participate in treatment services. However, mandated reporters can always call the appropriate CPS hotline to discuss their concerns about substance abusing parents to determine if a report needs to be made.

## MANDATED REPORTING OF CLIENTS ALREADY INVOLVED WITH CHILD PROTECTIVE SERVICES

Some social workers provide services for families who are already involved with CPS either because they have voluntarily applied for services or because they have been mandated by a court to participate in a service plan. In these instances, the social worker is still a mandated reporter. The family has already been the subject of a CPS report and investigation, which may have resulted in the family seeking services from the social worker. The social worker is still required to report suspected abuse or neglect that is beyond the original allegations. If the social worker learns of additional details or episodes of abuse or neglect that were previously unknown to CPS, the social worker has the legal obligation to report such information to CPS. CPS may choose to file this new information in the open file or open another investigation, depending on the details of the new information.

## FREQUENTLY ASKED QUESTIONS

**Q.** Isn't it breaking client confidentiality to make a child abuse report?

**A.** Although confidentiality is an important part of the social worker— client relationship, the law in all states, as well as the NASW Code, allows for client confidences to be shared to report suspected child abuse. In fact, you cannot claim client confidentiality as a defense to failure to report child abuse.

**Q.** How do I tell my client, who is a child, about my obligation as a mandated reporter?

**A.** When explaining to a child client the boundaries of your relationship, you can tell the child that you will keep secret most of what is told to you but that there are some times when you cannot keep things secret. You can tell the child, for instance, that if you are worried that he or she is being hurt, or in danger, you have to tell someone about it because it is your job to help keep them safe. You can provide the child with examples of when you would not be able to keep a secret. As is good practice, you can ask the child to explain back to you what you have said to see if it is understood. Be sure to use language that is appropriate for the age and maturity of the child client.

**Q.** How can I report child abuse when HIPAA protects patient privacy?

**A.** HIPAA provides exceptions to protection of patient privacy. One such exception is for reporting of suspicions of child abuse. Therefore, fol- lowing HIPAA is not an excuse for failing to report suspected child abuse.

**Q.** As a substance abuse treatment provider, doesn't the federal govern- ment require me to take extra precautions to protect client privacy?

**A.** Although federal protections for client privacy in substance abuse treatment are long-standing, they have always included an exception for the reporting of suspicions of child abuse. It is important to note that substance abuse itself may not be enough to require a report of suspected child abuse or neglect. Consult the laws in your particular state to determine when substance abuse meets the definition of child abuse or neglect.

**Q.** I'm working with a client who has already been reported to CPS. The client just shared a story with me that I think suggests abuse, but I think it may have already been investigated in the prior report. Do I have to make another report?

**A.** If you have not already made a report on these suspicions, then yes, it is your mandate to make a report with this information. CPS will then make a determination if this new information necessitates a new investigation or if these allegations have already been investigated.

**Q.** I have been subpoenaed to testify in court. I want to protect my client's confidences and share only the amount of information that is necessary. How can I do that?

**A.** Thank you for your commitment to protecting your client's confidences. Talk to your client's attorney, if possible, before the court appearance to explain your concerns, and seek the attorney's assistance in protecting your client's confidential information. It is also important to explain to the judge your concerns about sharing client confidences. Whenever a question is asked of you that you are uncomfortable with answering, you can turn to the judge and explain your concerns. Do you think the information is irrelevant to the current case? If so, then say so. Can you offer limited details to answer the question? If you can, then do so. When case files are requested for evidence in a court case, you can ask the judge to limit the request to sections of the case file that are relevant to the issue at hand. It is important to note that social workers may be subpoenaed to testify because they were the source of the report or otherwise were a past or current service provider for the family. Either way, this guidance is applicable. A courtroom may be an intimidating environment to you, and your requests for limited intrusion of your client's privacy may be seen by the judge and/or lawyers as a waste of their time, but be confident that you are serving a very important function in discussing your concerns. Your client is fortunate to have such a thoughtful social worker. Remember, however, that whenever the judge orders you to answer the question you must do so, or you will be subject to the charge of contempt of court.

## REFERENCES

Confidentiality of drug and alcohol abuse patient records, 42 C.F.R. 2 (2002).

Davidson, H. (2003). *The impact of HIPAA on child abuse and neglect cases*. Washington, DC: American Bar Association, Center on Children and the Law.

Disclosures for public health activities, 45 C.F.R 164.512(b) (2003).

Jaffee v. Redmond, 518 U.S. 1 (1996).

National Association of Social Workers. (1999). *Code of ethics of the National Association of Social Workers*. Washington, DC: Author.

United States Substance Abuse and Mental Health Services Administration. (2004). *The confidentiality of alcohol and drug abuse patient records regulation and the HIPAA privacy rule: Implications for alcohol and substance abuse programs*. Rockville, MD: Author.

Tarasoff v. Regents of the University of California, 17 Cal. 3d 425 (1976).

# 10 Legal Protections and Consequences for Mandated Reporters

The drafters of the original mandated reporting legislation were aware that unless they provided legal incentives and protections, reporters would be hesitant to make reports of suspected child abuse and neglect, especially when the reporters were not confident in their suspicions. To address these concerns, states adopted legislation along with mandated reporting legislation that provided a certain level of protection for those who make a report, while simultaneously providing legal consequences for those who fail to make a report when required by law. This chapter will provide guidance on when a mandated reporter is protected from legal action for making a report as well as when a mandated reporter is at risk of legal action for not making a report.

## LEGAL IMMUNITY FOR REPORTS MADE IN "GOOD FAITH"

Mandated reporters who make a report of suspected child abuse or neglect contemplate their decision before they make the report. Many reporters wonder, "What if I'm wrong?" "Can I be sued?" "Can I lose my license?" These are all important questions. The law in each state provides an answer. Federal law (Child Abuse Prevention and Treatment Act of 1974 [CAPTA], described in chapter 1) requires the states to provide provisions in their law that protect reporters from legal action when fulfilling their legal obligation to report. States must include such an immunity provision in their laws in order to receive federal grants for their child protective system (CAPTA, 1974).

If the resulting investigation does, in fact, substantiate the allegations raised by the reporter, there is no cause of action against the reporter. If the resulting investigation does not substantiate the allegations raised by the reporter, a reporter (whether mandated to report or not) is protected from legal retaliation *if the report was made in "good faith."* This protection from legal retaliation is called *immunity*. Without immunity, a reporter could potentially be held liable for defamation, infliction of emotional distress, and other offenses if the report is not substantiated.

The "good faith" immunity provisions were included in the law to address hesitancy in making reports and encourage reports to be made, even when the reporter is unsure that abuse or neglect has occurred (Kalichman, 1999). Making a report in good faith means that the reporter has reason to believe that the allegation made is true to the best of his or her knowledge. The reporter does not have to be sure that the allegations are true. The reporter is not supposed to investigate suspicions before making the report. As long as the reporter has reason to believe that the child in question is being abused or neglected, a resulting report will be considered made in good faith.

In a few states, including California, the mandated reporter benefits from absolute immunity (see appendix A for specific details about immunity in your particular state). Absolute immunity means that immunity is provided to mandated reporters regardless of whether or not the report is made in good faith. In these states, however, absolute immunity is not provided for nonmandated reporters.

Legal immunity does not mean that the mandated reporter cannot or will not be sued for making the report, although such lawsuits are very rare. However, mandated reporters should be able to successfully defend themselves if they are sued by asserting immunity. In some states, such as California, there are provisions in which mandated reporters can be reimbursed for expenses made to defend themselves in such suits.

To successfully defend a legal challenge by asserting immunity, the report must have been made in good faith. In more than 15 states (and the District of Columbia), there is a "presumption of good faith" for reports made by all persons, not just mandated reporters. This means that in these states, the burden is on the person accusing the reporter to prove that the report was not made in good faith. The reporter does not have to show evidence to prove that the report was made in good faith unless the accuser has convinced the court otherwise beyond a preponderance of the evidence. In that case, the reporter will then have the opportunity to rebut the case. A presumption of good faith does not mean that the accuser cannot sue the reporter. A presumption should be seen as a legal advantage for the reporter.

In all states (regardless of whether there is a legal "presumption" of good faith), the burden is on the person filing the claim to prove that the report was *not* made in good faith. This is a difficult legal burden to meet.

It is important to note that behaviors outside the reporting of the suspected child abuse or neglect are not protected through statutory immunity, even in absolute immunity states such as California. For instance, if a mandated reporter not only shares the report with CPS but also broadcasts the allegations over the Internet and the allegations are found to be untrue, the mandated reporter may be liable for the damage caused by the Internet broadcast but not damage caused by the report to CPS.

## PENALTIES FOR FILING A FALSE REPORT

Contrary to protections for making reports in good faith, the law provides punishment for reporters who make reports in "bad faith." The law in almost all states provides civil and/or criminal liability for knowingly filing a false report. The reporter must have "willfully" or "intentionally" made a false report of child abuse or neglect. This means that the reporter knew that the report was false or knew that it was likely that the report was false. Cases of false reporting by mandated reporters are few and far between, although there are many such cases of false reporting by non-mandated reporters seeking to disrupt and intentionally injure a family, like disgruntled neighbors and ex-lovers. In states with absolute immunity for reporting by mandated reporters, there is no legal repercussion to a mandated reporter who makes a false report, but a false report filed by a nonmandated reporter would still be subject to criminal and civil action.

### Criminal Liability

Most states classify false reporting as a crime at the low level of a misdemeanor. In a handful of states, the offense of filing a false child abuse report is a higher-level crime—a felony. Criminal penalties include fines ranging from $100 to $5,000 or from 90 days to 5 years in jail or prison. In a few states, reporters who are found to have filed more than one false report are subject to even harsher penalties (see appendix A for details for your particular state).

## Civil Liability

Besides the criminality of making a knowingly false report of suspected child abuse or neglect, reporters who make false reports can also be subject to civil liability. Mandated reporters who knowingly make false reports may be subject to civil liability for compensatory and/or punitive damages.

Compensatory damages are meant to address any losses that were caused by the false report. The losses need not be financial, but the damage award will generally be monetary. Such compensatory damages can include damage to reputation, disruption caused by the investigative process, and even assault and battery for unwarranted physical examinations of children in response to a false report.

Reporters who make false reports of suspected child abuse or neglect may not only have to pay compensatory damages but may also be subject to punitive damages. Punitive damages are meant to "punish" bad behavior. Punitive damages generally involve a large monetary award that is above and beyond the actual damages caused by the report.

## CONSEQUENCES FOR FAILURE TO REPORT

Even though millions of reports of suspected child abuse and neglect are made every year in the United States, research has shown that there are many cases that never are reported (Delaronde, King, Bendel, & Reece, 2000). The law in all states is designed to encourage reports through the provision of immunity for reporters but also through punishment for failure to report suspected child abuse or neglect (see appendix A for details on your particular state).

Penalties for failure to report child abuse or neglect only attach when it can be shown that the mandated reporter knew or should have known that he or she was legally obligated to report particular suspicions. This standard can be further classified as a "willful failure" of the mandated reporter to fulfill the legal duty to report suspected child abuse or neglect. Some mandated reporters may fail to make a report because they feel they do not have the time to make the report or be involved in an investigation. Other mandated reporters may fail to make a report because their previous experiences with CPS were troubling, and they do not want to go through a similar experience. Willful failure can even include situations where the mandated reporter simply delays making the report.

## Criminal Liability

The law is specifically designed to provide strong penalties for failing to make a report. In 48 states (not including Maryland or Wyoming), there are criminal penalties for mandated reporters who fail to make a report when required by law.

In most states, failure to report is a misdemeanor. Misdemeanor offenses are usually punishable by fine. In some states, misdemeanor offenses can carry a sentence of jail time or probation. In some states, such as Arizona, failure to report serious allegations (such as physical and sexual abuse) carries stronger penalties, such as being classified a felony offense. In some states, when a reporter fails to report child abuse or neglect more than once, harsher criminal penalties can be expected. In states where there is not a specific provision for criminal liability for failure to report, such an offense may be considered a crime under general criminal law (Besharov, 1990). Contrary to the case of civil liability (described below), further harm to the child does not need to occur for the failure to report to incur criminal sanction.

## Civil Liability

In a handful of states, a mandated reporter who fails to make a report when required by law can also be subject to civil liability through specific provisions of the reporting laws. Through action in a civil case, a mandated reporter who fails to make a report when required by law to do so can be held responsible to pay damages to the child and/or his or her family incurred after the report should have been made (Besharov, 1990). For instance, the mandated reporter will not be held responsible for the damage of the abuse or neglect that occurred before the reporter should have made a report. However, the mandated reporter will be held responsible for any damage as a result of abuse or neglect that occurs *after* the reporter should have made a report.

In states that do not have specific civil liability provisions for a mandated reporter's failure to report suspected child abuse or neglect, failure to report may be considered negligence under general civil law. Negligence is a civil action most often used against professionals, such as social workers, who are bound by ethical responsibilities to protect others in addition to their legal responsibilities as a mandated reporter (see discussion below). To be held liable for negligence, a mandated reporter must be shown to have a duty that he or she failed to fulfill. The failure of such duty must have caused damage. The mandated reporter would then be liable for any damage caused by failure to fulfill his or her duty.

One duty that may be implicated by a failure to report child abuse or neglect is the duty of mental health professionals to protect persons from likely harm, regardless of any duty to protect the confidentiality of their client. This duty to protect was first determined by the California Supreme Court in the case of *Tarasoff v. Regents of the University of California* (1976). In this case, a psychologist, Dr. Lawrence Moore, was held responsible for failing to protect Tatiana Tarasoff of impending danger by one of Dr. Moore's clients. The client, Prosenjit Poddar, told Dr. Moore during a therapy session at the University of California Mental Health Clinic that he intended to kill Ms. Tarasoff because she rejected his romantic advances. Although Dr. Moore reported these statements to the campus police, and Mr. Poddar was briefly held in their custody, Dr. Moore did not contact the local police department, nor did he warn Ms. Tarasoff herself. The court found fault in Dr. Moore for these failures and coined the responsibility of mental health professionals to protect a potential victim of impending harm.

Although the *Tarasoff* duty was a result of case law in California, and therefore the court's holding would be limited in coverage to California, subsequent changes to the statutory law, as well as similar court cases, in other states has generally codified this duty across the country. Therefore, social workers generally have a legal duty to warn known potential victims of impending harm. The *Tarasoff* duty can be considered relevant to child abuse and neglect reporting in that a report to CPS is made to protect children from future harm.

## ETHICAL CONSIDERATIONS

Regardless of the legal consequences for failing to report a case of suspected child abuse or neglect, there are ethical considerations to be made by professional social workers. Guidance on ethical decision making for social workers can be found in the Code of Ethics for the National Association of Social Workers (NASW, 1999). The latest version of the Code was revised in 1999. The Code provides that "social workers' primary goal is to help people in need and to address social problems" (NASW Code, Ethical Principle). By not reporting a case of suspected child abuse or neglect, the social worker is failing to fulfill this ethical principle because such failure may subject that child to harm from abuse or neglect.

Social workers familiar with the Code are aware of the strength of the sections on keeping client confidences (see chapter 9). Therefore, social workers are concerned that breaking the confidentiality of their relationship with their client to report suspected child abuse or neglect is in defiance of the Code. However, the Code specifically provides that "social workers should protect the confidentiality of all information obtained in the course of professional service, *except for compelling professional reasons* [italics added]" (NASW Code, 1.07[c]). For instance, the expectation that social workers "keep information confidential does not apply when disclosure is necessary to prevent serious, foreseeable, an imminent harm to a client or other identifiable person" (NASW Code, 1.07[c]). This exception would include suspicions of child abuse or neglect.

Even though the Code provides for an exception to confidentiality for instances such as mandated reporting of child abuse and neglect, the Code highlights the importance of "disclosing the least amount of confidential information necessary to achieve the desire purpose" (NASW Code, 1.07[c]). For instance, social workers should only provide information to CPS that is "directly relevant" to the suspicions and subsequent investigation. Sharing of information that is not relevant to the CPS report and investigation would constitute a failure to maintain client confidentiality as prescribed by the Code and could subject the social worker to civil liability.

## Case Examples of Failure to Report

Although research shows that mandated reporters fail to report almost half of their suspicions to CPS (Delaronde, King, Bendel, & Reece, 2000), prosecution of mandated reporters for failure to report is very rare. Even though such cases are few and far between, they are often followed with high-profile media coverage (Kalichman, 1999). A case involving teachers in New York State is representative of the national experience.

In Bedford Hills, New York, a northern suburb of New York City, school officials' failure to report suspicions of sexual abuse of a young female student failed to protect a girl from further abuse and threatened the jobs of teachers and administrators alike. In late 2005, the mother of an elementary school student reported to a teacher in charge of the school that her daughter told her that one of her 9-year-old classmates had sex with an adult (Saunders, 2007). The school responded by performing an internal investigation. The alleged victim's teachers were asked if they noticed anything wrong with the student that would suggest sexual abuse. When none of the student's teachers reported any behavior out of the ordinary, the school did not report the suspicions to CPS. When the mother of the alleged victim pursued criminal action against her paramour for raping her daughter, it became known that the school was aware of the allegations and failed to report them to CPS. Criminal charges were filed against the principal. The charges were later dismissed after the principal agreed to share her story in a number of trainings to mandated reporters across New York State. Civil charges filed by the alleged victim's mother against the principal and involved teachers are still pending (Whitaker, 2006). The jobs of the principal and involved teachers were threatened, but with support of their union, they were able to retain employment through the school district (Saunders, 2007). The principal lost her position and title but was rehired by the school district in another capacity.

In response to this case, the state increased its training efforts in the schools for mandated reporters. It is important to note that the mother of the classmate also failed to make a report to CPS, but since she was not a mandated reporter, she could not be held liable. This case highlights an important point for consideration by mandated reporters. Mandated reporters should not be asking themselves "Can I prove child abuse occurred in this instance?" but instead, "Does it make reasonable sense that I am suspicious that abuse might have occurred?" In this case, it was reasonable to believe that sexual abuse might have occurred merely by the fact that the child shared such information with her classmates, even if there were no behavioral indicators to note, and even if she denied the abuse when asked.

## Professional Consequences

As experienced in the Bedford Hills case, mandated reporters' employment is in jeopardy when they fail to fulfill their duties as mandated reporters. Failing to fulfill their duties as mandated reporters can serve as "cause" to lose even the most "secure" job.

Also in jeopardy when a mandated reporter fails to report suspected child maltreatment is any professional license he or she might hold. In states where social workers are licensed professionals, the law generally requires them to follow all applicable federal, state, and local laws. Failure to report child abuse when mandated to do so would be a failure to follow state law. Therefore, social workers could be subject to state license board intervention in the form of fine, suspension, or even revocation of their license.

Professional associations, such as the NASW, may sanction (including expulsion from the professional organization), censure, or suggest corrective action for social workers who are found to have failed in the legal and ethical obligation to report suspected child abuse. It is important to note that professional organizations for social workers are neither legal nor governmental authorities and do not have the authority to rescind professional licenses or order damages be paid. Additionally, professional associations only have the ability to impact their own members. Social workers who are not members of a given professional association are not subject to their disciplinary procedures.

## LEGAL OBLIGATIONS WHEN REPORTING FROM WITHIN AN AGENCY

Although many social workers work in private practice, where they are the ultimate authority on decisions regarding their own work, many more social workers work in agencies in which their work and responsibilities are further prescribed by agency policy. The decision to report suspected child abuse or neglect is often a point of contention in agency settings.

### Responsibility to Report Lies With Individual, Not Agency

Often, an individual social worker in an agency setting is found to be at odds with the decisions of superiors. In some situations, the social worker feels that suspicions of child abuse or neglect rise to the level in which a report to CPS is required, but the supervisor does not agree with the assessment. It is important to point out here that the obligation to report the suspected child abuse or neglect sits with the person who has the suspicion, not the agency from which the case is drawn. If the social worker believes that there is reason for a report to be made, and there is legal obligation to do so by mandated reporting law, then the social worker must insure that the report is made. He or she cannot hide behind the opinions or assessment of the supervisors.

However, it is important to note that if the social worker seeks guidance from the supervisor (or peers) before making such a report and through such counsel the original social worker no longer suspects child abuse or neglect,·then he or she is not required by law to make the report. In essence, if by seeking guidance about the decision to report the social worker has a change of mind, he or she is not hiding behind the opinions of their supervisors, or peers, but is resting on professional judgment when the decision is made not to make a report.

Discussion of circumstances that may require a report should be just that—a discussion between professionals who are both required to report suspicions of child abuse, not a debate. If the discussion leads to a sincere change of mind for the one who felt that his or her suspicions might be reasonable, no report needs to be made. But if the discussion does not lead to a sincere change of mind, then regardless of any difference of opinion, the burden to report remains.

In the case where a subordinate wants to make the report but is prevented from doing so by a direct order from his or her superior, the legal obligation of the individual mandated reporter remains. If the supervisor threatens, or actuates, retaliation against a social worker who makes a report against the guidance of the supervisor, the employee social worker is covered by certain legal protections. At least 18 states provide specific legal provisions to protect reporters from retaliation at their workplace for making a report of suspected child abuse or neglect. In other states, employees may be protected by general provisions of the law.

## Agency-Designated Reporters

In some places of employment, there is a particular person who is designated to make all reports to CPS for the agency. This person is often times referred to as the "designated reporter." Designated reporters are used by agencies to centralize reporting responsibilities and provide structure to the agency's relationship with CPS.

In agencies where someone else other than the individual social worker is responsible for making the report to CPS, the social worker's obligation to report suspected child abuse or neglect is generally not satisfied by reporting to the designated reporter. It is important for the social worker to follow-up with the designated reporter, and his or her supervisor and CPS if necessary, to prove that the report was filed in a timely manner. If the designated reporter fails to make the report on behalf of the social worker's suspicions, the social worker does not have a defense against liability for failure to report unless the social worker is falsely told that the report was made (Besharov, 1990). So, to ensure that the report was made timely by the designated reporter, the social worker should follow-up to ensure such a report was made.

In 2007, New York State amended its law on the issue of designated reporters and no longer allows mandated reporters to report their allegations through a designated reporter. Each mandated reporter is required to report his or her own allegations to CPS immediately (New York State Social Services Law). This change in the law was designed to address concerns of information in the official report coming from second- and thirdhand sources instead of from the person with firsthand knowledge.

## FREQUENTLY ASKED QUESTIONS

**Q.** I suspect that one of my child clients is being abused at home. I spoke to my supervisor about my suspicions, and she doesn't think there is abuse happening. She told me not to make a report. What should I do?

**A.** You are legally required to make a report when you suspect abuse or neglect. You can seek the counsel of other professionals, including your supervisor, to help you consider your concerns. If you do not agree, ultimately it is *your* obligation to make the report if you still have reasonable cause to suspect abuse or neglect has occurred or is imminent. You can remind your supervisor of your responsibilities as a mandated reporter and inform him or her of your decision to make the report. You can also call the child abuse hotline to inquire in the hypothetical if your suspicions necessitate a report.

When you choose to make a report in opposition to the opinion of your supervisor, you do not have to flagrantly disobey your superior. You can instead make the report in privacy or even outside your place of employment. However, it is still your obligation to make the report immediately.

**Q.** Families in the neighborhood where I work don't seek services from social service agencies because they are afraid they'll be called in to

CPS. To encourage families to come to our agency and stay with our agency, my director tells the staff that we don't make reports to CPS. I suspect neglect in one of my cases, but my supervisor told me not to call CPS. What should I do?

**A.** You are legally required to make a report when you suspect abuse or neglect. You can seek the counsel of other professionals, including your supervisor, to help you consider your concerns. If you do not agree, ultimately it is *your* obligation to make the report if you still have suspicions. You can choose to remind your supervisor of your responsibilities as a mandated reporter and inform him or her of your decision to make the report. Alternately, you can choose to not flagrantly disobey your superior and instead make the report in privacy or even outside your place of employment. However, it is still your obligation to make the report immediately.

**Q.** One of my colleagues made a physical abuse report against a parent she's been working with. My colleague told me that she didn't have any reason to believe there was abuse happening, but she wanted to scare the parent into shaping up and being a better parent. Did she do something wrong?

**A.** Yes, she did something wrong. Knowingly making a false report is punishable by civil and criminal law. Besides adding to the already overwhelmed caseload of CPS and costing the government money for a needless investigation, your colleague subjected that family to unnecessary intrusion and could have negatively impacted their well-being.

**Q.** I made a report because I suspected that one of my child clients was being sexually abused. The investigation ended without being substantiated. The parents are furious and told my supervisor that they are going to sue me and the agency. What should I do?

**A.** You are protected by the law, which provides immunity from liability for reports made by mandated reporters if made in good faith. Even if your suspicions were not substantiated, you are protected from liability. Although being protected by legal immunity does not mean that you cannot be sued, historically, the outcome of the case should be that you are not found liable. The family would have to prove by a fair preponderance of the evidence that you had made a frivolous report. Under the "fair preponderance" standard, the family would have to show that it is more likely than not that your report was made in bad faith. This is a high burden to meet.

The potential for being sued in your professional capacity necessitates being covered by malpractice insurance. If you are self-employed, get coverage. If you work for an agency or other type of organization, check with your employer to make sure that you are covered by the company's malpractice insurance.

## REFERENCES

Besharov, D. J. (1990). *Recognizing child abuse: A guide for the concerned.* New York: The Free Press.

Child Abuse Prevention and Treatment Act, 42 U.S.C.A. sec. 51106a(b)(2)(A)(iv) (1974).

Delaronde, S., King, G., Bendel, R., & Reece, R. (2000). Opinions among mandated reporters toward child maltreatment reporting policies. *Child Abuse and Neglect, 24*(7), 901.

Kalichman, S. C. (1999). *Mandated reporting of suspected child abuse: Ethics, law & policy.* Washington: American Psychological Association.

National Association of Social Workers. (1999). *Code of ethics of the National Association of Social Workers.* Washington, DC: Author.

New York State Social Services Law sec. 413.

Saunders, S. (2007). What you need to know about child abuse: A cautionary tale from Bedford Hills. *New York Teacher.* Latham, NY: NYSUT.

Tarasoff v. Regents of the University of California, 17 Cal. 3d 425 (1976).

Whitaker, B. (2006, December 10). Bedford Hills principal will have charge dropped. *New York Times*, 14WC, Column 6, p. 2.

county welfare or probation department every known or suspected instance of child abuse or neglect reported to it that is alleged to have occurred as a result of the action of a person responsible for the child's welfare, or as the result of the failure of a person responsible for the child's welfare to adequately protect the minor from abuse when the person responsible for the child's welfare knew or reasonably should have known that the minor was in danger of abuse. A law enforcement agency also shall send, fax, or electronically transmit a written report thereof within 36 hours of receiving the information concerning the incident to any agency to which it makes a telephone report under this subdivision. (U.S. Department of Health and Human Services, 2007b)

Per New York Social Services Law sec. 423(1)(e),

Except as provided by law, the child protective service shall be the sole public agency responsible for receiving and investigating or arranging with the appropriate Society for the Prevention of Cruelty to Children to investigate all reports of child abuse or maltreatment made pursuant to law for the purpose of providing protective services to prevent further abuses or maltreatment to children and to coordinate, provide or arrange for, or monitor the provision of those services necessary to safeguard and ensure the child's well-being and development and to preserve and stabilize family life wherever appropriate. (U.S. Department of Health and Human Services, 2007b)

New York Social Services Law sec. 423(6) further states,

A social services district may establish a multidisciplinary investigative team or teams . . . at a local or regional level, for the purpose of investigating reports of suspected child abuse or maltreatment. The social services district shall have discretion with regard to the category or categories of suspected child abuse or maltreatment such team or teams may investigate, provided, however, the social services district shall place particular emphasis on cases involving the serious abuse of children. . . . A multidisciplinary investigative team may include, but is not limited to, representatives from the child protective service and the office of the district attorney or local law enforcement. Additional team members may include the medical profession, public health agencies, mental health agencies, schools and medical facilities, including hospitals or other appropriate agencies or institutions, and personnel of any existing child advocacy centers. Notwithstanding any other provision of law to the contrary, members of a multidisciplinary investigative team or a child advocacy center may share client-identifiable information concerning the

<br>

## 11 | The Role of Law Enforcement in the Protection of Children

When an incident of child abuse or neglect requires investigation, as discussed in previous chapters, a local law enforcement agency is often called in. In many communities, this involves a parallel investigation where child protective services (CPS) and law enforcement must work closely together on the same case. At times, this can be difficult, as law enforcement investigators often do not view child abuse and neglect in the same ways as CPS.

### DIFFERENCES BETWEEN LAW ENFORCEMENT AND CHILD PROTECTIVE SERVICES

Unless they have been trained in the philosophy of child protection, law enforcement investigators will generally see little importance in family preservation. They may believe that a parent or caretaker who abuses or neglects a child does not deserve to care for the child. Many law enforcement investigators may want to make an arrest and see the parent or caretaker prosecuted. Based on the evidence available, if there is probable cause to arrest an alleged perpetrator, then the investigator will be expected to take him or her into custody.

CPS caseworkers approach the job from a different perspective. CPS is obligated to attempt to keep the family together or, once separated, to work toward family reunification. In fact, under federal law (Public Law 96–272) and many state laws, the juvenile or family court requires CPS agencies to demonstrate that they attempted reasonable efforts to prevent out-of-home placement. It is this role that may become a major source of conflict between CPS and law enforcement, particularly in neglect cases. While neglect allegations are the most common form of child maltreatment reported to child protection agencies, criminal investigation and prosecution occurs in only a small minority of these cases. Unless law enforcement investigators find a clear and present danger to the child that requires immediate action, they will rarely act independently in child neglect cases. Criminal prosecution of physical and sexual child abuse, or child fatality, is more common than prosecution of neglect, and there the role of law enforcement becomes clearer. Law enforcement may not understand the CPS philosophy that if a child's safety can be assured, the child's own family is the preferred place for him or her.

Some communities have many options for avoiding foster care placement in neglect cases. These include intensive family preservation programs, day care, teaching homemakers, parenting classes, and traditional counseling. For some neglectful parents, the answer is financial aid, with CPS referring them to income maintenance and job search programs. Law enforcement officers generally lack access to those services and consequently are handicapped in neglect investigations unless CPS is involved. The decision-making processes of the two systems also differ in many ways. Law enforcement officers are accustomed to making rapid life and death decisions in the field without supervisory consultation or approval. On the other hand, many CPS agencies have procedures that involve "shared decision making" on critical issues such as the emergency removal of a child. Police find the CPS's need to consult with supervisors to be frustrating, time-consuming, and an example of bureaucracy at its worst. CPS caseworkers find that consultation reduces inappropriate actions based on the emotions of the moment (Pence & Wilson, 1992).

Child abuse cases also represent a departure from most other criminal cases that law enforcement will have to investigate. Most crime reports can be accepted as generally factual. That is, if Mr. Shaw reports that he has been assaulted, the responding police officers can enter the case with the presumption that a crime has occurred and set out to find the person responsible. In CPS cases, however, the detectives must first establish that a crime has actually occurred. They cannot assume, in the absence

of other evidence, that a physical or sexual assault reported and that the child's condition is the result of an individua willful inactions. In fact, about 60% of cases of child abu reported to CPS do not present adequate evidence to be substantiated (U.S. Department of Health and Human Ser The role of the law enforcement officer (and the CPS casew to determine if abuse or neglect has occurred and if so who i and then to decide what actions, if any, are necessary to prot Only then can the law enforcement really focus on collecting necessary for a criminal prosecution.

It is hoped that as law enforcement investigators gain cases of child maltreatment, they will begin to appreciate th tion alternatives that CPS offers, the value of casework inte the need for efforts to protect children without resorting to placement.

## HOW AND WHEN LAW ENFORCEMENT IS NOTIFIED II AND MALTREATMENT CASES

The Child Abuse Prevention and Treatment Act, as amende 5106a), requires states to make provision for the cooperati forcement officials and human service agencies in the inve sessment, prosecution, and treatment of child abuse or Department of Health and Human Services, 2007b). All District of Columbia, and the U.S. territories have statut procedures that state agencies must follow in handling re pected child abuse or neglect. In most states, these procedur quirements for cross-system reporting and/or information s professional entities. Typically, reports are shared among s agencies, law enforcement departments, and prosecutor Department of Health and Human Services).

Per the California Penal Code sec. 11166(k), for examp

A law enforcement agency shall immediately, or as soon as pr ble, report by telephone, fax, or electronic transmission to the responsibility for investigation of cases . . . and to the district a every known or suspected instance of child abuse or neglect except acts or omissions . . . which shall be reported only to th fare or probation department. A law enforcement agency sha

child or the child's family with other team members to facilitate the investigation of suspected child abuse or maltreatment. (U.S. Department of Health and Human Services, 2007b)

Mandated reporters should note that law enforcement is often able to react to emergency situations faster than CPS. If the mandated reporter learns that a child is being seriously abused or the alleged perpetrator is trying to flee the jurisdiction with the child, law enforcement can generally get to the scene much faster than CPS and stabilize the situation until CPS can arrive.

As stated previously, in cases where there is an allegation of child sexual abuse, serious physical abuse, or a child fatality, states have developed protocols for CPS to notify the law enforcement jurisdiction where the crime took place. Of note, the jurisdiction that is assigned the primary investigation for CPS is determined by where the child permanently resides. On the other hand, law enforcement jurisdiction is determined by where the crime took place. For example, say a child is abused by her father during visitation to his home in one state and then returns home to her mother who lives in another state, making an allegation to her teacher that her father abused her. The teacher would be mandated to make a report to CPS in the state where the child resides (mom's home). At that point, CPS would notify the law enforcement in the jurisdiction where the abuse took place (dad's home).

Some states have established guidelines limiting who can be the subject (the person who is alleged to have abused the child) of the report and have developed protocols as to how to handle reports where a potential crime has taken place but has not fallen under CPS jurisdiction. For example, if a social worker reports that a child was sexually molested by a teacher or a coach, the guidelines in some states would be to obtain the information from the mandated reporter and pass such information on to local law enforcement where the alleged crime may have taken place. It would be up to law enforcement to follow up on the allegation, not CPS.

## HOW CHILD PROTECTIVE SERVICES AND LAW ENFORCEMENT WORK TOGETHER

The conflicts inherent in the relationship between CPS and law enforcement do not have to present roadblocks to working together effectively.

Communicating and formalizing the relationship, where possible, can break down barriers to effective teamwork. A team approach with CPS and law enforcement working collaboratively is desirable and can improve investigative outcomes.

Investigators involved in child abuse and neglect cases recognize the need to eliminate unnecessary duplication of effort, promote proper and expeditious collection and preservation of evidence, and develop a coordinated system for identifying and investigating appropriate calls. This is best accomplished through a multidisciplinary team approach where both CPS and law enforcement share information, assign investigative tasks, and participate in a shared decision-making process. As a result of a team effort, the victim is less likely to be further traumatized by the investigation, and a positive outcome for all investigative parties is enhanced.

Initially, when notified by CPS, the law enforcement investigators must determine if a crime has occurred. If a crime has occurred, the investigators must determine who is responsible, if any actions on law enforcement's part are necessary to protect the child, and if criminal prosecution is warranted.

It is important that the CPS and law enforcement investigators have certain information prior to initiating the investigation. Normally, the CPS caseworker should have already obtained the necessary information from the mandated reporter prior to contacting the law enforcement investigator (as described in chapter 7). The more comprehensive the information provided by the mandated reporter, the better investigators are able to determine the appropriateness of the report for law enforcement and/or CPS intervention, the level of risk to the child, and the urgency of the response needed.

Information gathering should focus on demographic information about the child and family; details regarding the alleged maltreatment; and biographical information about the child, the parents, caretakers, and the family as a whole. CPS should have obtained information about the nature and severity of the abuse. As mentioned previously, it is also important to determine where the abuse took place. The CPS worker should also obtain information from the mandated reporter about the nature of the abuse and who is alleged to have abused the child (e.g., if there were any serious injuries or what type of sexual abuse was perpetrated on the child). It is also helpful for the investigators to know if there have been prior reported incidents.

Based on the information obtained, law enforcement will make a determination whether to actively participate in the CPS investigation. If they do, it is called a *joint response investigation*. The benefit for CPS and law enforcement investigators to make an early decision to work together on an investigation is that they can continue to actively share information and reduce the number of interviews involving the child victim.

It is critical that CPS and law enforcement investigators feel comfortable and confident with each other throughout the investigation. It is also critical that they understand each other's purpose and goals related to completing an investigation. Unfortunately, in jurisdictions where the investigators from CPS and law enforcement are not cross trained, conflicts often develop between the agencies, and additional frustrations and trauma may be experienced by the victim and the victim's family.

An area that at times causes some conflict between the agencies is the time frame related to when to begin an investigation and interview the parties involved. As described in chapter 7, all states have requirements for CPS to initiate an investigation within a short period of time after the report is made. Law enforcement does not have such time frames and can hold off interviewing alleged victims and perpetrators while they attempt to locate additional information.

For example, if a child tells her school social worker that her father, who is residing in the home, has been sexually abusing her, the social worker as a mandated reporter would need to call in the report immediately. After the report is made and accepted, it would be assigned to a CPS investigator. In many jurisdictions, the expectation would be for the CPS investigator to notify local law enforcement and share information gathered from the mandated reporter with the law enforcement investigator. Since the issue of the child's safety would be of immediate concern, the CPS and law enforcement investigator would need to make an immediate investigative intervention plan. Each agency would have its own protocol on how to implement the plan.

## WHAT LAW ENFORCEMENT WILL ASK OF THE MANDATED REPORTER

In the scenario described above, law enforcement would likely begin the interview process as soon as possible. Typically, appropriate protocol would require the investigator to be in contact with the mandated reporter prior to initiating the interviews. The purpose is to gather any additional information about the allegation from the mandated reporter. The mandated reporter must share any additional information related to the allegation with the investigators and cooperate with them throughout the investigative process. As discussed in chapter 10, mandated reporters are protected from criminal and civil liabilities as long as they make the report in good faith.

To effectively evaluate the level of risk to the child and determine the urgency of the response, investigators should request detailed information from the mandated reporters. Some of the information may have already been provided in the initial report (as discussed in chapter 7).

With regard to the victim, the following information should be obtained: the age and sex of the child, the child's physical and emotional condition, any ongoing learning problems and disabilities, and any history of behavioral problems or history of prior physical and/or sexual abuse. In families where more than one language is spoken, it is important for the investigators to know the child's primary language. If the child has made a disclosure of the abuse directly to the social worker, it is critical to share all information that the child disclosed. It is also important to say if the child previously told anyone else about the abuse.

With regard to the parents/caretakers, the following information should be obtained: any knowledge about their emotional and physical condition and their behavior, history, view of the child, child-rearing practices, and quality of their relationships outside the family. This data may help to determine the level of risk to the child. Information regarding suspected substance abuse, physical or mental illness, or incapacity is also helpful. Additional information, such as if there is a history of abuse or neglect of other children and if there is a history of their own trauma or victimization would also be helpful. Additionally, let the investigator know if you are aware of anyone else who resides in the family and/or what outside resources and supports they have.

Concern for the safety of the investigators should also be taken into consideration. Is the alleged perpetrator violent? Does he or she have a history of problems with the law or a history of engaging in bizarre or irrational behavior?

Gathering this in-depth information is essential because it helps to determine how quickly an investigation must begin. It enables investigators to identify other potential victims, the alleged perpetrator, and how to locate them so that the initial investigation can be conducted. It also identifies other possible sources of information about the family that will help evaluate the possibility of past, current, or future abuse or neglect. Finally, it will assist the investigator in accurately and effectively planning the approach to the investigation.

## THE INTERVIEW OF THE CHILD

After all background information available has been gathered, the CPS and law enforcement investigators will plan out the investigative process. The first interviewee is often the child (dependent on the access the investigation team has to the child). If the child is of school age, there may be an arrangement to interview the child in school, especially if the mandated reporter is a school employee. Otherwise, it could be possible to interview the child in a neutral child-friendly environment like a local child advocacy center.

If the child has disclosed the abuse directly to the mandated reporter, the mandated reporter should prepare the child for the investigation process—but, as mentioned previously, the mandated reporter should not try to do an investigative interview on his or her own. The investigators will need to obtain as much information as possible directly from the child, and it is best if professionals specifically trained in forensic investigative interviewing talk with the child.

When CPS and law enforcement conduct a joint investigation, they will need to interview the child together. The mandated reporter may also want to participate in this interview, but investigators will often encourage the mandated reporter not to participate, as this may contaminate the information or evidence gathered. In some situations—particularly with very young or disabled children—the child may want the mandated reporter to participate in the interview. In such a case, the investigators will need to consider the impact of that person's presence on the interview.

On occasion, it is necessary for individuals not directly involved in the investigative interview to be present during the child's interview. This situation often arises when a child is interviewed at a school or hospital and the institution policy requires that a nonparticipatory adult be present.

Experience has shown that children often do not disclose accurate information when the mandated reporter is present because he or she feels embarrassed or ashamed, may fear the mandated reporter's reaction, or may want to protect the mandated reporter from the information. Furthermore, to outside eyes, the mandated reporter's presence in the interview may be perceived as coaching or an indicator that the child has been coached. In addition, mandated reporters need to understand that any individual who is present during the interview is subject to being called at a later date as a witness in a legal or civil proceeding. If called as a witness, that person will not be available to support the child during the legal proceeding. The individual will need to determine at which phase of the investigation and subsequent prosecution he or she wants to be able to support the child.

If at any point during the investigative interview it appears that the child has become comfortable talking with the investigators, it is often best for the mandated reporter to excuse him or herself from the interview (after letting the child know that he or she is still available if the child needs him or her).

If the mandated reporter is going to be present for the whole interview, he or she needs to be very careful not to interfere with the investigators and not try to answer questions for the child. If at any point the child looks to the mandated reporter for guidance, the mandated reporter should simply remind the child of the importance of telling the truth. Once the investigators have begun to establish a rapport with the child, the mandated reporter should sit out of the child's visual range, if at all possible, so that it cannot be said that the mandated reporter influenced the child's disclosure. The mandated reporter should not speak or take notes during the interview. It is critical for the social worker to focus their attention on the child so that the child feels what he/she is saying is important. Additionally, the mandated reporter should avoid any reaction to a disclosure. This is especially true for audible reactions, facial expressions, and body posture.

If a child does not disclose everything that she may have told the mandated reporter, or if the disclosure is different, it is important to bring this to the interviewer's attention at a prearranged time prior to the end of the interview. This should be done privately rather than correcting the child or pointing out the discrepancy in the presence of the child. It is also important to remember that whatever is discussed in the interview process is confidential and should not be shared with anyone unless legally mandated. The mandated reporter should remember that the interview and case should not be discussed with the suspect or anyone else, as doing so can jeopardize the case.

Whether or not the mandated reporter is present in the investigative interview, it is important to understand the process of investigative forensic interviewing. Although both the CPS and law enforcement investigators are conducting a joint interview, often only one of the investigators should be the lead interviewer. This is often determined prior to initiating the interview, but it may change after the interview starts if it is apparent that the child is more comfortable talking with the other investigator.

At the beginning of the interview, one of the investigating team members should explain, if the child is old enough to understand, why he or she is there and what will be going on during the interview. Depending on the allegations and/or the child's age, the investigator may need to visually examine the child for signs of obvious trauma. Investigators will need to document any injuries noted and, if possible, photograph areas of injury or of questionable physical findings. Especially in child sexual abuse cases, it will also be necessary for the investigators to interview the child in depth about the alleged sexual abuse, as often there is no physical or medical signs of the abuse.

The investigators will spend some time establishing a relationship with the child and determining the child's developmental level and memory capabilities. Also depending on the age of the child and the local laws related to children's testimonial capacity, they will assess the child's ability to understand the need to tell the truth and the consequences for lying. It will be critical that the child be able to share with the investigators in his or her own words what happened, where and when it happened, and identify the abuser. CPS and law enforcement will also be interested in who else may have been abused and who else knew about the abuse. If the investigator finds that the child has sustained life-threatening or severe injuries, the first priority is securing emergency medical attention for the child.

Once the interview is finished and the investigators believe that the child is safe, the investigation will continue. If the child is not safe, the CPS investigator will need to take action to provide needed protection for the child.

## INTERVIEWS WITH OTHER WITNESSES

After interviewing the child, the investigators should plan to interview other potential victims and/or witnesses to the abuse. The period between the initial interview of the child and the subsequent interviews of other potential victims and/or witnesses is often a critical one for the investigators. Especially in cases where the only evidence apparently available is the child's statement, investigators must gather information from other sources as soon as possible.

If they can obtain immediate access to the parent/caretaker, the investigators will compare the information provided by the child with that of the parent/caretaker. During this phase, CPS will be exploring safety concerns, and law enforcement will be looking to gather additional potential evidence related to the allegation. A parent/caretaker who is not alleged to have abused the child is interviewed as soon as possible after the child, since that parent may be willing to provide critical information about the alleged perpetrator that will corroborate the child's allegations. Such information can often be helpful when the investigators interview the alleged perpetrator.

If the investigators can obtain an admission from the alleged perpetrator that the child indeed was abused, it will often result in quicker legal action to protect the child and prosecute the alleged perpetrator. The admission of abuse often will help to reduce the trauma that the child may have experienced if he or she is required to testify in court.

## THE ROLES OF OTHER PROFESSIONALS IN CHILD ABUSE AND MALTREATMENT

Child abuse and neglect is a complex issue, and many communities have developed multidisciplinary teams to address the problem. After the initial response of CPS and law enforcement, there potentially will be a number of agencies and professionals involved in the investigation, prosecution, and supervision of the child victim and his or her family. By pooling expertise, professionals can be more effective in protecting child victims, rehabilitating families, and prosecuting—when appropriate—the alleged perpetrators. A multidisciplinary team may include medical personnel, the district attorney's office, victim advocates, mental health professionals, community service agencies, probation, and social service workers. These professionals are by written agreement able to coordinate their work on a particular case, sharing all necessary information in order to produce a more thorough and coordinated investigation, prosecution, supervision, and treatment in cases of child abuse and neglect.

Depending on the initial reason the mandated reporter was involved with the child and his or her family, the mandated reporter may continue to play an important role throughout the case. For example, if the mandated reporter is a school social worker or a mental health worker, he or she may continue working with the child throughout the investigation.

After the investigation has been completed, it may be necessary for the mandated reporter to obtain a release from the parent/caregiver before further information can be shared with other members of the multidisciplinary team. If there is future prosecution of the case in family/juvenile or criminal court, the child and the family will often need ongoing support. In this situation, it is critical for the mandated reporter to understand the legal process and work closely as needed with the other professionals involved. If at any point the mandated reporter learns of a new abuse or neglect situation, he or she will again be mandated to report such information to CPS. If a situation like this occurs, the social worker—if appropriate—should continue to be supportive to the child and the family. If as a result of legal action the child and family are placed under the supervision of the court, the social worker should continue to try to work closely with the other agencies involved. It is important to remember that the protection of children is the responsibility of all those involved in the social work profession.

## REFERENCES

Pence, D., & Wilson, C. (1992). *The role of law enforcement in the response to child abuse and neglect user manual series* (Public Law 96–272). Washington, DC: U.S Department of Health and Human Services.

U.S. Department of Health and Human Services, Administration on Children, Youth and Families. (2007a). *Child maltreatment 2006.* Washington, DC: U.S. Government Printing Office.

U.S. Department of Health and Human Services, Administration on Children, Youth and Families. (2007b). *Cross-reporting among responders to child abuse and neglect: Summary of state laws.* Washington, DC: U.S. Government Printing Office.

| | |
|---|---|
| When to Report | A report must be made when the mandated reporter reasonably believes that a minor is a victim of abuse or neglect. |
| Confidentiality of Mandated Reporters | Inclusion of the reporter's name in the report is not required by statute. Disclosure of the reporter's identity is not discussed in statute. |
| How Do Mandated Reporters Make a Report? | Mandated reporters would contact the Child Abuse State Hotline number @ (888) SOS-CHILD. |
| Immunity Provisions | Any person making a complaint or providing information or otherwise participating in the program authorized by Arizona State law shall be immune from any civil or criminal liability by reason of such action, unless such person acted with malice or unless such person has been charged with or is suspected of abusing, abandoning, or neglecting the child or children in question. |
| Penalties for False Reporting | A person acting with malice who knowingly and intentionally makes a false report of child abuse or neglect, or a person acting with malice who coerces another person to make a false report of child abuse or neglect, is guilty of a Class 1 misdemeanor. A person who knowingly and intentionally makes a false report that another person made a false report is guilty of a Class 1 misdemeanor. |
| Penalties for Failure to Report | A person who violates Arizona law requiring the reporting of child abuse or neglect is guilty of a Class 1 misdemeanor, except if the failure to report involves a reportable offense, in which case the person is guilty of a Class 6 felony. |
| Relevant Internet Resources | *Web site for Statutes:* http://www.azleg.state.az.us/ArizonaRevisedStatutes.asp |
| | *Citations:* Child Protection: Title 8, Chapter 10, Articles 1 and 2 Child Welfare: Title 8, Chapter 5; Chapter 10, Articles 3–7; Chapter 11 |
| | *Web site for Administrative Code:* http://www.azsos.gov/public_services/Table_of_Contents.htm See Title 6, Chapter 5, Articles 55, 56, 58–60, 65–67, 69, 70, 74, 75, and 80. |
| | Department of Economic Security, Division of Children, Youth and Families Protect Our Children—Child Protective Services https://www.azdes.gov/ASPNew/default.asp |

(*continued*)

## ARKANSAS

| | |
|---|---|
| Who Are Mandated Reporters? | Physicians, surgeons, osteopaths, resident interns, coroners, dentists, nurses, or medical personnel; teachers, school officials or counselors, day care center workers; child care workers, foster care workers; social workers, foster parents, or department employees; mental health professionals; domestic violence shelter employees or volunteers; law enforcement personnel, peace officers, prosecuting attorneys, domestic abuse advocates, judges; Court Appointed Special Advocate (CASA) program staff or volunteers; juvenile intake or probation officers; any members of clergy, including ministers, priests, rabbis, accredited Christian Science practitioners, or other similar functionary of a religious organization |
| When to Report | A report must be made when the mandated reporter has reasonable cause to suspect child maltreatment or when the mandated reporter has observed the child being subjected to conditions or circumstances that would reasonably result in child maltreatment. |
| Confidentiality of Mandated Reporters | Inclusion of the reporter's name in the report is not required by statute. The identity of the reporter shall not be disclosed unless a court determines that the reporter knowingly made a false report. |
| How Do Mandated Reporters Make a Report? | Mandated reporters would contact the Child Abuse State Hotline number @ (800) 482-5964. |
| Immunity Provisions | Any person or agency required to participate and acting in good faith in making notification, the taking of photographs or radiological tests or the removal of a child while exercising protective services shall be immune to suit and to liability, both civil and criminal. If acting in good faith, all other persons making notification shall be immune from liability. Any publicly supported school, facility, or institution acting in good faith pursuant to § 12-12-510(a)(1)(2) shall be immune from liability. |
| Penalties for False Reporting | Any person, official, or institution willfully making false notification pursuant to the reporting laws, knowing such allegations to be false, shall be guilty of a Class A misdemeanor. Any person, official, or institution willfully making false notification pursuant to the reporting laws, knowing such allegations to be false, and who has been previously convicted of making willful false allegations shall be guilty of a Class D felony. |

| | |
|---|---|
| Penalties for Failure to Report | Any person, official, or institution negligently or willfully failing to make notification when required by the reporting laws shall be guilty of a Class C misdemeanor. Any person, official, or institution required to make notification of suspected child maltreatment who willfully fails to do so shall be civilly liable for damages proximately caused by that failure. |
| Relevant Internet Resources | *Web site for Statutes:* http://www.arkleg.state.ar.us/NXT/gateway.dll?f= templates&fn=default.htm&vid=blr:code |
| | *Citations:* Child Protection: Title 9, Subtitle 3, Chapter 30 Child Welfare: Title 9, Subtitle 2, Chapter 16; Subtitle 3, Chapters 27, 28, 29, 32, and 34 Department of Human Services, Division of Children and Family Services |
| | Reference Center http://www.state.ar.us/dhs/chilnfam/referencecenter.htm |

## CALIFORNIA

| | |
|---|---|
| Who Are Mandated Reporters? | Teachers, teacher's assistants, administrative officers, certificated pupil personnel employees of any public or private school; administrators and employees of public or private day camps, youth centers, youth recreation programs, or youth organizations; employees of child care institutions, including, but not limited to, foster parents, group home personnel, and personnel of residential care facilities; social workers, probation officers, or parole officers; any person who is an administrator or a counselor in a child abuse prevention program in any public or private school; district attorney investigators, peace officers, firefighters, except for volunteer firefighters; physicians, surgeons, psychiatrists, psychologists, dentists, licensed nurses, dental hygienists, optometrists, marriage counselors, family and child counselors, clinical social workers; emergency medical technicians I or II or paramedics; state or county public health employees; coroners or medical examiners; commercial film and photographic print processors; child visitation monitors; animal control officers or humane society officers; clergy members, which includes priests, ministers, rabbis, religious practitioners, or similar functionary of a church, temple, or recognized denomination or organization; any custodian of records of a clergy member; employees or volunteers of Court Appointed Special Advocate (CASA) programs |

(*continued*)

| | |
|---|---|
| When to Report | A mandated reporter must make a report when in his or her professional capacity, he or she has knowledge of or observes a child whom the reporter knows or reasonably suspects is the victim of abuse or neglect; commercial film and photographic print processors must report when they have knowledge of or observe any film, photograph, videotape, negative, or slide depicting a child under the age of 16 years engaged in an act of sexual conduct. |
| Confidentiality of Mandated Reporters | Reports made by mandated reporters shall include the name, business address, and telephone number of the mandated reporter and the capacity that makes the person a mandated reporter. The identity of the reporter shall be confidential and shall be disclosed only (1) to agencies investigating the report, (2) when the reporter waives confidentiality, and (3) by court order. |
| How Do Mandated Reporters Make a Report? | Mandated reporters would contact the Child Abuse State Hotline number @ (800) 4-A-CHILD. |
| Immunity Provisions | No mandated reporter shall be civilly or criminally liable for any report required or authorized by this article, and this immunity shall apply even if the mandated reporter acquired the knowledge or reasonable suspicion of child abuse or neglect outside of his or her professional capacity or outside the scope of his or her employment. Any other person reporting a known or suspected instance of child abuse or neglect shall not incur civil or criminal liability as a result of any report authorized by law, unless it can be proven that a false report was made and the person knew that the report was false or was made with reckless disregard of the truth or falsity of the report, and any person who makes a report of child abuse or neglect known to be false or with reckless disregard of the truth or falsity of the report is liable for any damages caused. No mandatory reporter, nor any person taking photographs at his or her direction, shall incur any civil or criminal liability for taking photographs of a suspected victim of child abuse or neglect without parental consent, or for disseminating the photographs with the reports required by law. However, California law does not grant immunity from liability with respect to any other use of the photographs. Any person who, pursuant to a request from a government agency investigating a report of suspected child abuse or neglect, provides the requesting agency with access to the victim of known or suspected instance of child abuse or neglect shall not incur civil or criminal liability as a result of providing that access. |

| Penalties for False Reporting | Any person reporting a known or suspected instance of child abuse or neglect shall not incur civil or criminal liability as a result of any report unless it can be proven that a false report was made and the person knew that the report was false or was made with reckless disregard of the truth or falsity of the report. |
|---|---|
| | Any person who makes a report of child abuse or neglect known to be false or with reckless disregard of the truth or falsity of the report is liable for any damages caused. |
| Penalties for Failure to Report | Any mandated reporter who fails to report an incident of known or reasonably suspected child abuse or neglect is guilty of a misdemeanor punishable by up to 6 months in a county jail, by a fine of $1000, or both. If a mandated reporter intentionally conceals his or her failure to report an incident known by the mandated reporter to be abuse or severe neglect, the failure to report is a continuing offense until an agency specified in § 11165.9 discovers the offense. |
| | Any supervisor or administrator who violates § 11166(1) (that prohibits impeding others from making a report), shall be punished by not more than 6 months in a county jail, by a fine of not more than $1000, or both. |
| | Any mandated reporter who willfully fails to report abuse or neglect, or any person who impedes or inhibits a report of abuse or neglect, where that abuse or neglect results in death or great bodily injury, shall be punished by not more than 1 year in a county jail, by a fine of not more than $5000, or both. |
| Relevant Internet Resources | *Web site for Statutes:* http://www.leginfo.ca.gov/calaw.html |
| | *Citations:* Child Protection: Penal Code, Part 1, Title 9, Chapters 1, 2; Welfare and Institutions Code, Division 9, Part 6, Chapters 11, 12, and 12.5 |
| | Child Welfare: Family Code, Division 12, Part 3, Chapter 5; Part 5; Part 6; Welfare and Institutions Code, Division 2, Part 1, Chapter 2, Articles 6–13.5; Division 2; Chapter 4; Division 9, Part 4, Chapters 1, 2.5, 3, and 5; Part 4.4; Division 9, Part 6, Chapters 4, 4.5, and 6.2 |
| | *Note:* See Division 11: Foster Care, and Division 31: Child Welfare Services Manual |

*(continued)*

## COLORADO

| | |
|---|---|
| Who Are Mandated Reporters? | Physicians, surgeons, physicians in training, child health associates, medical examiners, coroners, dentists, osteopaths, optometrists, chiropractors, podiatrists, nurses, hospital personnel, dental hygienists, physical therapists, pharmacists, registered dieticians; public or private school officials or employees; social workers, Christian Science practitioners, mental health professionals, psychologists, professional counselors, marriage and family therapists; veterinarians, peace officers, firefighters, or victim's advocates; commercial film and photographic print processors; counselors, marriage and family therapists, or psychotherapists; clergy members, including priests, rabbis, duly ordained, commissioned, or licensed ministers of a church, members of religious orders, or recognized leaders of any religious bodies; workers in the State Department of Human Services |
| When to Report | Mandated reporters must make a report when they have reasonable cause to know or suspect child abuse or neglect or when they have observed a child being subjected to circumstances or conditions that would reasonably result in abuse or neglect. Commercial film and photographic print processors must make a report when they have knowledge of or observe any film, photograph, videotape, negative, or slide depicting a child engaged in an act of sexual conduct. |
| Confidentiality of Mandated Reporters | The report made by mandated reporters shall include the name, address, and occupation of the person making the report. Statute provides that the identity of the reporter shall be protected but without specificity. |
| How Do Mandated Reporters Make a Report? | Mandated reporters would contact the Child Abuse State Hotline number @ (800) 4-A-CHILD. |
| Immunity Provisions | Any person, other than the perpetrator, complicitor, coconspirator, or accessory, participating in good faith in the making of a report pursuant to the reporting laws, the facilitation of the investigation of such a report, a judicial proceeding resulting therefrom, the taking of photographs or x-rays, the placing in temporary protective custody of a child, or otherwise performing his duties or acting pursuant to law shall be immune from any civil or criminal liability or termination of employment that otherwise might result by reason of such acts of participation, unless a court of competent jurisdiction determines that such person's behavior was willful, wanton, and malicious. |

For the purpose of any civil or criminal proceedings, the good faith of any such person reporting child abuse, any such person taking photographs or x-rays, and any such person who has legal authority to place a child in protective custody shall be presumed.

**Penalties for False Reporting**

No person, including a mandatory reporter, shall knowingly make a false report of abuse or neglect to a county department or local law enforcement agency.
Any person who violates this provision:
- Commits a Class 3 misdemeanor and shall be punished as provided by law
- Shall be liable for damages proximately caused

**Penalties for Failure to Report**

Any mandatory reporter who willfully fails to report as required by § 19.3.304(1):
- Commits a Class 3 misdemeanor and shall be punished as provided by law
- Shall be liable for damages proximately caused

**Relevant Internet Resources**

*Web site for Statutes:*
http://www.michie.com/colorado/lpext.dll?f=templates&fn=main-h.htm&cp=

*Citations:*
Child Protection: Title 19, Article 3, Part 3
Child Welfare: Title 19, Article 3

*Web site for Agency Policies:*
http://www.sos.state.co.us/CCR/Welcome.do

## CONNECTICUT

**Who Are Mandated Reporters?**

Physicians or surgeons, nurses, medical examiners, dentists, dental hygienists, physician assistants, pharmacists, or physical therapists; psychologists or other mental health professionals; school teachers, principals, guidance counselors, or coaches; social workers; police officers, juvenile or adult probation officers, or parole officers; members of the clergy; alcohol and drug counselors, marital and family therapists, professional counselors, sexual assault counselors, or battered women's counselors; emergency medical services providers; any person paid to care for a child in any public or private facility, child day care center, group day care home, or family day care home that is licensed by the state; employees of the Department of Children and Families and the Department of Public Health who are responsible for the licensing of child day care center, group day care homes, family day care homes, or youth camps; the child advocate and any employee of the Office of Child Advocate

(*continued*)

| When to Report | Mandated reporters must make a report when, in the ordinary course of their employment or profession, they have reasonable cause to suspect or believe that a child has been abused or neglected. |
| --- | --- |
| Confidentiality of Mandated Reporters | The reporter is not specifically required by statute to include his or her name in the report; however, the commissioner shall use his or her best efforts to obtain the name and address of the reporter. The identity of the reporter shall not be released to the subject of the report unless there is reasonable cause to believe that the reporter knowingly made a false report. |
| How Do Mandated Reporters Make a Report? | Mandated reporters would contact the Child Abuse State Hotline number @ (800) 842-2288. |
| Immunity Provisions | Any person, institution, or agency that, in good faith, makes or, in good faith, does not make a report shall be immune from any liability, civil or criminal, that might otherwise be incurred or imposed and shall have the same immunity with respect to any judicial proceeding that results from such report provided such person did not perpetrate or cause such abuse or neglect. |
| Penalties for False Reporting | Any person who knowingly makes a false report of child abuse or neglect shall be punished by one or both of the following:<br>■ A fine of not more than $2000<br>■ Imprisonment of not more than 1 year |
| Penalties for Failure to Report | Any person required to report, who fails to make such report shall be:<br>■ Fined not more than $500<br>■ Required to participate in an educational and training program pursuant to § 97a.101(d) |
| Relevant Internet Resources | *Web site for Statutes:*<br>http://www.cga.ct.gov/2005/pub/titles.htm<br><br>*Citations:*<br>Child Protection: Title 46b, Chapter 815t<br>Child Welfare: Title 17a, Chapters 319 and 319a<br><br>*Web site for Agency Policies:*<br>http://www.state.ct.us/dcf/pol_regs.htm |

## DELAWARE

| Who Are Mandated Reporters? | Physicians, dentists, interns, residents, osteopaths, nurses, or medical examiners; school employees; social workers or psychologists |
| --- | --- |

| When to Report | Mandated reporters must make a report when they know or in good faith suspect child abuse or neglect. |
|---|---|
| Confidentiality of Mandated Reporters | Although reports may be made anonymously, the division shall request the name and address of any person making a report. Disclosure of the reporter's identity is not prescribed by statute. |
| How Do Mandated Reporters Make a Report? | Mandated reporters would contact the Child Abuse State Hotline number @ (800) 292-9582 or (302) 577-6550. |
| Immunity Provisions | Anyone participating in good faith in the making of a report or notifying police officers, performing a medical examination without the consent of those responsible for the care, custody, and control of the child, or exercising emergency protective custody in compliance with provisions of this chapter shall have immunity from any liability, civil or criminal, that might otherwise exist, and such immunity shall extend to participation in any judicial proceedings resulting from the above actions taken in good faith.<br>Delaware law shall not limit the liability of any health care provider for personal injury claims due to medical negligence that occurs as a result of any examination performed pursuant to statute. |
| Penalties for False Reporting | This issue is not addressed in the statutes reviewed. |
| Penalties for Failure to Report | Any mandatory reporter who knowingly and willfully violates the requirement to report shall be punished by one or both of the following:<br>■ A fine of not more than $1000<br>■ Imprisonment of not more than 15 days |
| Relevant Internet Resources | *Web site for Statutes:*<br>http://delcode.delaware.gov/index.shtml<br><br>*Citations:*<br>Child Protection: Title 16, Chapter 9<br>Child Welfare: Title 31, Chapters 3 and 38<br><br>*Web site for Agency Policies:*<br>http://www.state.de.us/kids/information/policy.shtml |

## DISTRICT OF COLUMBIA

| Who Are Mandated Reporters? | Physicians, medical examiners, dentists, chiropractors, or nurses; school officials, teachers, or day care workers; psychologists or other mental health professionals; law enforcement officers (except an undercover officer whose identity or investigation might be jeopardized); social service workers |

*(continued)*

| | |
|---|---|
| When to Report | Mandated reporters must make a report when they know or have reasonable cause to suspect that a child known to them in their official capacity has been or is in danger of being abused or neglected or when they have reasonable cause to believe that a child is abused as a result of inadequate care, control, or subsistence in the home environment due to exposure to drug-related activity. |
| Confidentiality of Mandated Reporters | Mandated reporters are required to provide their name, occupation, and contact information when making a report. The central register shall not release the identity of the reporter without first obtaining the permission of the reporter. |
| How Do Mandated Reporters Make a Report? | Mandated reporters would contact the Child Abuse State Hotline number @ (877) 671-SAFE or (202) 671-7233. |
| Immunity Provisions | Any person, hospital, or institution participating in good faith in the making of a report pursuant to the reporting laws shall have immunity from liability, civil or criminal, that might otherwise be incurred or imposed with respect to the making of the report. Any such participation shall have the same immunity with respect to participation in any judicial proceeding involving the report.<br>In all civil or criminal proceedings concerning the child or resulting from the report, good faith shall be presumed unless rebutted. |
| Penalties for False Reporting | This issue is not addressed in the statutes reviewed. |
| Penalties for Failure to Report | Any person required to make a report under the reporting laws who willfully fails to make such a report shall be subject to one or both of the following:<br>■ Fined not more than $300<br>■ Imprisoned for not more than 90 days |
| Relevant Internet Resources | *Web site for Statutes:*<br>http://michie.lexisnexis.com/dc/lpext.dll?f=templates& fn=main-h.htm&cp=dccode<br>*Citations:*<br>Child Protection: Division I, Title 4, Chapter 13; Division II, Title 16, Chapter 23, Subchapter I<br>Child Welfare: Division I, Title 4, Chapter 14; Division II, Title 16, Chapter 23, Subchapters III, IV, and V; Chapter 48<br>*Web site for Administrative Code:*<br>http://os.dc.gov/os/cwp/view,a,1206,q,522357,osNav, %7C31374%7C.asp<br>Title 29: Public Welfare is not available online. |

## FLORIDA

| | |
|---|---|
| Who Are Mandated Reporters? | Physicians, osteopaths, medical examiners, chiropractors, nurses, or hospital personnel; other health or mental health professionals; practitioners who rely solely on spiritual means for healing; school teachers or other school officials or personnel; social workers, day care center workers, or other professional child care, foster care, residential, or institutional workers; law enforcement officers or judges |
| When to Report | Mandated reporters must make a report when they know or have reasonable cause to suspect that a child is abused, abandoned, or neglected. |
| Confidentiality of Mandated Reporters | The professionals who are mandated reporters are required to provide their names to hotline staff. The names of reporters are held confidential and may be released only (1) to the department, (2) the central abuse hotline, (3) law enforcement, (3) the appropriate state attorney, or (4) if the reporter consents to release in writing. |
| How Do Mandated Reporters Make a Report? | Mandated reporters would contact the Child Abuse State Hotline number @ (800) 96-ABUSE. |
| Immunity Provisions | Any person, official, or institution participating in good faith in any act authorized or required by the reporting laws or reporting in good faith any instance of child abuse, abandonment, or neglect to the department or any law enforcement agency shall be immune from any civil or criminal liability that might otherwise result by reason of such action. Nothing contained in the reporting laws shall be deemed to grant immunity, civil or criminal, to any person suspected of having abused, abandoned, or neglected a child, or committed any illegal act on or against a child. |
| Penalties for False Reporting | A person who knowingly and willfully makes a false report of child abuse, abandonment, or neglect, or who advises another to make a false report, is guilty of a felony of the third degree. On conviction, the person may be: ■ Imprisoned for a term not to exceed 5 years ■ Fined $5000 In addition to any other penalty authorized by this section or other law, the department may impose a fine, not to exceed $10000 for each violation, on a person who knowingly and willfully makes a false report of abuse, abandonment, or neglect of a child, or a person who counsels another to make a false report. |

*(continued)*

| | |
|---|---|
| Penalties for Failure to Report | A person who is required to report known or suspected child abuse or neglect, and who knowingly and willfully fails to do so, or who knowingly and willfully prevents another person from doing so, is guilty of a misdemeanor of the first degree. On conviction, the person may be:<br>■ Imprisoned for a term not to exceed 1 year<br>■ Fined $1000<br>    Unless the court finds that the person is a victim of domestic violence or that other mitigating circumstances exist, a person who is 18 years of age or older and lives in the same house or living unit as a child who is known or suspected to be a victim of child abuse, neglect of a child, or aggravated child abuse, and knowingly and willfully fails to report the child abuse commits a felony of the third degree. On conviction, the person may be:<br>■ Imprisoned for a term not to exceed 5 years<br>■ Fined $5000 |
| Relevant Internet Resources | *Web site for Statutes:*<br>http://www.flsenate.gov/statutes/index.cfm?<br><br>*Citations:*<br>Child Protection: Title V, Chapter 39, Parts I–III<br>Child Welfare: Title V, Chapters 39, Parts IV–XIII<br><br>*Web site for Administrative Code:*<br>http://fac.dos.state.fl.us/<br>See Chapter 65, Sections B-5, B-6, C-7–C-19, and C-24.<br><br>*Web site for Agency Policies:*<br>http://www.dcf.state.fl.us/publications/policies.shtml |

## GEORGIA

| | |
|---|---|
| Who Are Mandated Reporters? | Physicians, hospital and medical personnel, podiatrists, dentists, or nurses; school teachers, administrators, guidance counselors, school social workers, or psychologists; psychologists, counselors, social workers, or marriage and family therapists; child welfare agency personnel (including any child-caring institution, child-placing agency, maternity home, family day care home, group day care home, or day care center), child-counseling personnel, or child service organization personnel; law enforcement personnel; persons who process or produce visual or printed matter |
| When to Report | Mandated reporters must make a report when they have reasonable cause to believe that a child has been abused or when they have reasonable cause to believe that the visual or printed matter submitted for processing or producing depicts a minor engaged in sexually explicit conduct. |

| | |
|---|---|
| Confidentiality of Mandated Reporters | Inclusion of the reporter's name in the report is not required by statute. Any release of records shall protect the identity of any person reporting child abuse. |
| How Do Mandated Reporters Make a Report? | Mandated reporters would contact the Child Abuse State Hotline number @ (800) 4-A-CHILD. |
| Immunity Provisions | Any person or persons, partnership, firm, corporation, association, hospital, or other entity participating in the making of a report or causing a report to be made to a child welfare agency providing protective services or to an appropriate police authority pursuant to the reporting laws or any other law or participating in any judicial proceeding or any other proceeding resulting therefrom shall, in so doing, be immune from any civil or criminal liability that might otherwise be incurred or imposed, provided such participation is made in good faith.<br><br>Any person making a report, whether required by reporting laws or not, shall be immune from liability. |
| Penalties for False Reporting | A person who willfully and knowingly gives or causes a false report of a crime to be given to any law enforcement officer or agency of this state is guilty of a misdemeanor. |
| Penalties for Failure to Report | Any person or official required by law to report a suspected case of child abuse who knowingly and willfully fails to do so shall be guilty of a misdemeanor. |
| Relevant Internet Resources | *Web sites for Statutes:*<br>http://www.lexis-nexis.com/hottopics/gacode/default.asp<br><br>*Citations:*<br>Child Protection: Title 19, Chapters 5, 14, and 15; § 19-7-5<br>Child Welfare: Title 15, Chapter 11, §§ 15-11-58; 15-11-93 to 15-11-106; Title 49, Chapter 5<br><br>*Web site for Administrative Code:*<br>http://rules.sos.state.ga.us/<br>See Department of Human Resources, Chapters 290-2 and 290-9-2.<br><br>*Web site for Agency Policies:*<br>http://www.odis.dhr.state.ga.us/contents.htm<br>See Family and Children.<br><br>*Statewide Model Child Abuse Protocol:*<br>http://dfcs.dhr.georgia.gov/DHR-DFCS/DHR-DFCS_CommonFiles/19906193Abuse_Protocol_Final.pdf |

*(continued)*

| Hawaii | |
|---|---|
| Who Are Mandated Reporters? | Physicians, physicians in training, psychologists, dentists, nurses, osteopathic physicians and surgeons, optometrists, chiropractors, podiatrists, pharmacists, and other health-related professionals; medical examiners or coroners; employees or officers of any public or private school; child care employees; employees or officers of any licensed or registered child care facility, foster home, or similar institution; employees or officers of any public or private agency or institution, or other individuals, providing social, medical, hospital, or mental health services, including financial assistance; employees or officers of any law enforcement agency, including, but not limited to, the courts, police departments, correctional institutions, and parole or probation offices; employees of any public or private agency providing recreational or sports activities |
| When to Report | Mandated reporter must make a report when, in their professional or official capacity, they have reason to believe that child abuse or neglect has occurred or that there exists a substantial risk that child abuse or neglect may occur in the reasonably foreseeable future. |
| Confidentiality of Mandated Reporters | Inclusion of the reporter's name in report is not specifically required in statute. However, every reasonable good faith effort shall be made by the department to maintain the confidentiality of the name of a reporter who requests that his or her name be confidential. |
| How Do Mandated Reporters Make a Report? | Mandated reporters would contact the Child Abuse State Hotline number @ (800) 832-5300 (Oahu); others call (800) 4-A-CHILD. |
| Immunity Provisions | Anyone participating in good faith in the making of a report pursuant to the reporting laws shall have immunity from any civil or criminal liability that might otherwise be incurred or imposed by or as a result of making the report. Any such participant shall have the same immunity with respect to participation in any judicial proceeding resulting from such report. Any individual who assumes a duty or responsibility pursuant to statute shall have immunity from civil liability for acts or omissions performed within the scope of the individual's duty or responsibility. |

| Penalties for False Reporting | A person commits the offense of false reporting to law enforcement authorities if the person intentionally makes a report or causes the transmission of a report to law enforcement authorities relating to a crime or other incident within their concern when he or she knows that the information contained in the report is false. False reporting to law enforcement authorities is a misdemeanor. |
|---|---|
| Penalties for Failure to Report | Any mandatory reporter who knowingly prevents another person from reporting, or who knowingly fails to provide information as required by the reporting laws, shall be guilty of a petty misdemeanor. |
| Relevant Internet Resources | *Web site for Statutes:* <br> http://www.capitol.hawaii.gov/site1/docs/docs.asp? press1=docs <br><br> *Citations:* <br> Child Protection: Volume 7, Chapter 350; Volume 12, Chapter 587, Parts I–III <br> Child Welfare: Volume 12, Chapter 587, Parts III–VIII <br><br> *Web site for Administrative Code:* <br> http://www.hawaii.gov/ltgov/office/adminrules/ <br> See Title 17, Sections 17-804 to 17-893, 17-920.1, and 17-943.1 to 17-945. <br><br> Department of Human Services <br> A Guide to Child Welfare Services <br> http://hawaii.gov/dhs/protection/social_services/ child_welfare/guide_to_cws |

## IDAHO

| Who Are Mandated Reporters? | Physicians, residents on hospital staffs, interns, nurses, or coroners; school teachers or day care personnel; social workers or law enforcement personnel |
|---|---|
| When to Report | Mandated reporter must make a report when they have reason to believe that a child has been abused, abandoned, or neglected or when they observe a child being subjected to conditions or circumstances that would reasonably result in abuse, abandonment, or neglect. |
| Confidentiality of Mandated Reporters | Inclusion of the mandated reporter's name in the report is not addressed in statutes reviewed. Conditions under which the disclosure of the reporter's identity will be made were also not addressed in statutes reviewed. |

*(continued)*

| How Do Mandated Reporters Make a Report? | Mandated reporters would contact the Child Abuse State Hotline number @ (800) 926-2588. |
|---|---|
| Immunity Provisions | Any person who has reason to believe that a child has been abused, abandoned, or neglected and, acting on that belief, makes a report of abuse, abandonment, or neglect as required by the reporting laws shall have immunity from any liability, civil or criminal, that might otherwise be incurred or imposed. Any such participant shall have the same immunity with respect to participation in any judicial proceeding resulting from such report. |
| | Any person who reports in bad faith or with malice shall not be protected by Idaho law. |
| Penalties for False Reporting | Any person who makes a report or allegation of child abuse, abandonment, or neglect knowing the report is false, or who reports or alleges the same in bad faith or with malice, shall be liable to the party or parties against whom the report was made for the amount of actual damages sustained or statutory damages of $2500, whichever is greater, plus attorney's fees and costs of suit. |
| | If the court finds that the defendant acted with malice or oppression, the court may award treble actual damages or treble statutory damages, whichever is greater. |
| Penalties for Failure to Report | Failure to report as required by the reporting laws shall be a misdemeanor. |
| Relevant Internet Resources | *Web site for Statutes:*<br>http://www3.state.id.us/idstat/TOC/idstTOC.html |
| | *Citations:*<br>Child Protection: Title 16, Chapter 16<br>Child Welfare: Title 16, Chapters 16, 20, and 21 |
| | *Web site for Administrative Code:*<br>http://adm.idaho.gov/adminrules/agyindex.htm<br>See Health and Welfare, Department of, Sections 16.05.06, 16.06.01, and 16.06.02. |
| | Department of Health and Welfare<br>Child Protection Manual<br>http://www.isc.idaho.gov/childapx.htm |

## ILLINOIS

| | |
|---|---|
| Who Are Mandated Reporters? | Physicians, hospital administrators and personnel, surgeons, physician assistants, osteopaths, chiropractors, genetic counselors, dentists, coroners, medical examiners, emergency medical technicians, nurses, acupuncturists, respiratory care practitioners, or home health aides; school personnel, directors or staff of nursery schools or child day care centers, recreational program or facility personnel, child care workers, or homemakers; substance abuse treatment personnel, crisis line or hotline personnel, social workers, domestic violence program personnel, psychologists, psychiatrists, or counselors; social services administrators, foster parents, or field personnel of the Illinois Department of Public Aid, Public Health, Human Services, Corrections, Human Rights, or Children and Family Services; truant officers, law enforcement officers, probation officers, funeral home directors or employees; clergy members; commercial film and photographic print processors |
| When to Report | Mandated reporters must make a report when they have reasonable cause to believe that a child known to them in their professional capacity may be abused or neglected. Commercial film and photographic print processors must make a report when they have knowledge of or observe any film, photograph, videotape, negative, or slide that depicts a child engaged in any sexual conduct. |
| Confidentiality of Mandated Reporters | The report shall include the name, occupation, and contact information of the person making the report. Any disclosure of information shall not identify the person making the report. |
| How Do Mandated Reporters Make a Report? | Mandated reporters would contact the Child Abuse State Hotline number @ (800) 252-2873, (217) 785-4020, or (217) 782-6533 (after hours). |
| Immunity Provisions | Any person, institution, or agency, under the reporting laws, participating in good faith in the making of a report or referral, the investigation of such a report or referral, the taking of photographs and x-rays, retaining a child in temporary protective custody, or making a disclosure of information concerning reports of child abuse and neglect in compliance with the reporting laws shall have immunity from any civil, criminal, or other liability that might result by reason of such actions. |

*(continued)*

For the purpose of any civil or criminal proceedings, the good faith of any persons required or permitted to report or refer under the reporting laws or required to disclose information concerning reports of child abuse and neglect or cases of suspected child abuse or neglect shall be presumed.

| | |
|---|---|
| Penalties for False Reporting | Any person who knowingly transmits a false report to the department commits the offense of disorderly conduct. Any person who violates this provision a second or subsequent time shall be guilty of a Class 3 felony. |
| Penalties for Failure to Report | Any physician who willfully fails to report suspected child abuse or neglect shall be referred to the Illinois State Medical Disciplinary Board for action in accordance with the Medical Practice Act of 1987. Any dentist or dental hygienist who willfully fails to report suspected child abuse or neglect shall be referred to the Department of Professional Regulation for action in accordance with the Illinois Dental Practice Act. Any mandatory reporter who willfully fails to report suspected child abuse or neglect shall be guilty of a Class A misdemeanor for a first violation and a Class 4 felony for a second or subsequent violation. If the person acted as part of a plan or scheme having as its object the prevention of discovery of an abused or neglected child by lawful authorities for the purpose of protecting or insulating any person or entity from arrest or prosecution, the person is guilty of a Class 4 felony for a first offense and a Class 3 felony for a second or subsequent offense. |
| Relevant Internet Resources | *Web site for Statutes:* http://www.ilga.gov/legislation/ilcs/ilcs.asp *Citations:* Child Protection: Chapter 325, ILCS 2, 5, and 15 Child Welfare: Chapter 20, ILCS 505 and 520; Chapter 705, ILCS 405, Article II *Web site for Agency Policies:* http://www.state.il.us/dcfs/policy/index.shtml Department of Child and Family Services Manual for Mandated Reporters http://www.state.il.us/DCFS/docs/MANDATED2002.pdf |

## INDIANA

| | |
|---|---|
| Who Are Mandated Reporters? | Any staff member of a medical or other public or private institution, school, facility, or agency; any person who has reason to believe that a child is a victim of abuse or neglect. |

| When to Report | Mandated reporters have reason to believe that a child is a victim of abuse or neglect they must make a report. |
|---|---|
| Confidentiality of Mandated Reporters | The written report must include the name and contact information for the person making the report. The identity of the reporter is protected whenever the report is made available to the subject of the report. |
| How Do Mandated Reporters Make a Report? | Mandated reporters would contact the Child Abuse State Hotline number @ (800) 800-5556 or (317) 542-7002. |
| Immunity Provisions | A person, other than a person accused of child abuse or neglect, who makes or causes to be made a report of a child who may be a victim of child abuse or neglect, is a health care provider and detains a child for purposes of causing photographs, x-rays, or a physical medical examination to be made, makes any other report of a child who may be a victim of child abuse or neglect, or participates in any judicial proceeding or other proceeding resulting from a report that a child may be a victim of child abuse or neglect or relating to the subject matter of the report is immune from any civil or criminal liability that might otherwise be imposed because of such actions. Immunity does not attach for a person who has acted maliciously or in bad faith. A person making a report that a child may be a victim of child abuse or neglect or assisting in any requirement of the reporting laws is presumed to have acted in good faith. |
| Penalties for False Reporting | A person who intentionally communicates to a law enforcement agency or the department a report of child abuse or neglect knowing the report to be false commits a Class A misdemeanor. The offense is a Class D felony if the person has a previous unrelated conviction for making a report of child abuse or neglect knowing the report to be false. A person who intentionally communicates to a law enforcement agency or the department a report of child abuse or neglect knowing the report to be false is liable to the person accused of child abuse or neglect for actual damages. The finder of fact may award punitive damages and attorney's fees in an amount determined by the finder of fact against the person. |

*(continued)*

| Penalties for Failure to Report | A person who knowingly fails to make a report required by law commits a Class B misdemeanor. |
|---|---|
| | A person who, in his capacity as a staff member of a medical or other institution, school, facility, or agency, is required to make a report to the individual in charge of the institution, school, facility, or agency, or his designated agent, and who knowingly fails to make a report commits a Class B misdemeanor. This penalty is imposed in addition to the penalty imposed above. |
| Relevant Internet Resources | *Web site for Statutes:* http://www.in.gov/legislative/ic/code/ |
| | *Citations:* Child Protection: Title 31, Article 33 Child Welfare: Title 31, Articles 34 and 35 |
| | *Web site for Administrative Code:* http://www.in.gov/legislative/iac/ See Title 465, Article 2. |
| | Department of Child Services Protocol for Investigating Institutional Child Abuse/ Neglect Allegations http://www.in.gov/dcs/protection/institutionprotocol.html |

## IOWA

| Who Are Mandated Reporters? | Health practitioners; social workers; school employees, certified paraeducators, coaches, or instructors employed by community colleges; employees or operators of health care facilities, child care centers, Head Start programs, family development and self-sufficiency grant programs, substance abuse programs or facilities, juvenile detention or juvenile shelter care facilities, foster care facilities, or mental health centers; Employees of Department of Human Services institutions; peace officers, counselors, or mental health professionals; commercial film and photographic print processors |
|---|---|
| When to Report | When, in the scope of professional practice or their employment responsibilities, mandated reporters reasonably believe that a child has been abused, they must make a report. A commercial film and photographic print processor who has knowledge of or observes a film, photograph, videotape, negative, or slide that depicts a minor engaged in a prohibited sexual act or in the simulation of a prohibited sexual act must make a report. |
| Confidentiality of Mandated Reporters | The report shall contain the name and address of the person making the report. However, the department shall not reveal the identity of the reporter to the subject of the report. |

| | |
|---|---|
| How Do Mandated Reporters Make a Report? | Mandated reporters would contact the Child Abuse State Hotline number @ (800) 362-2178 or (515) 281-3240. |
| Immunity Provisions | A person participating in good faith in the making of a report, photographs or x-rays or in the performance of a medically relevant test pursuant to the reporting laws, or aiding and assisting in an investigation of a child abuse report pursuant to the reporting laws shall have immunity from any civil or criminal liability that might otherwise be incurred or imposed. The person shall have the same immunity with respect to participation in good faith in any judicial proceeding resulting from the report or relating to the subject matter of the report. "Medically relevant test" means a test that produces reliable results of exposure to cocaine, heroin, amphetamine, methamphetamine, or other illegal drugs or combinations or derivatives of the illegal drugs, including a drug urine screen test. |
| Penalties for False Reporting | A person who reports or causes to be reported to the department false information regarding an alleged act of child abuse, knowing that the information is false or that the act did not occur, commits a simple misdemeanor. |
| Penalties for Failure to Report | Any person, official, agency, or institution required to report a suspected case of child abuse who knowingly and willfully fails to do so is guilty of a simple misdemeanor. Any person, official, agency, or institution, required by § 232.69 to report a suspected case of child abuse who knowingly fails to do so, or who knowingly interferes with the making of such a report in violation of § 232.70, is civilly liable for the damages proximately caused by such failure or interference. |
| Relevant Internet Resources | *Web site for Statutes:* http://www.legis.state.ia.us/IowaLaw.html <br><br> *Citations:* <br> Child Protection: Title VI, Subtitle 5, Chapter 232, Division III; Subtitle 6, Chapter 235A <br> Child Welfare: Title VI, Subtitle 5, Chapters 232, 235, and 237; Title XV, Subtitle 1, Chapter 600A <br><br> *Web site for Administrative Code:* http://www.dhs.state.ia.us/policyanalysis/rulespages/ RulesChap.htm <br> See Chapters 107, 108, 112–114, 117, 142, 155–158, 160, 175, and 200–204. <br><br> *Web sites for Agency Policies:* http://www.dhs.state.ia.us/dhs2005/dhs_homepage/ reports_pubs/program_policy/index.html <br> http://www.dhs.state.ia.us/policyanalysis/ PolicyManualPages/PolManual.htm |

*(continued)*

## KANSAS

| | |
|---|---|
| Who Are Mandated Reporters? | Physicians, dentists, optometrists, nurses, chief administrative officers of medical care facilities, or emergency medical services personnel; teachers, school administrators, or other school employees; licensed child care providers; psychologists, clinical psychotherapists, marriage and family therapists, social workers, clinical marriage and family therapists, professional counselors, or alcohol and drug abuse counselors; firefighters, mediators, law enforcement officers, or juvenile intake and assessment workers |
| When to Report | Mandated reporters must make a report when they have reason to suspect that a child has been injured as a result of maltreatment or when they know of the death of a child. |
| Confidentiality of Mandated Reporters | Inclusion of the reporter's name in the report is not specifically required in statute. However, authorized disclosures of information shall not identify a reporter of a child in need of care. |
| How Do Mandated Reporters Make a Report? | Mandated reporters would contact the Child Abuse State Hotline number @ (800) 922-5330 or (785) 296-0044. |
| Immunity Provisions | Anyone participating without malice in the making of an oral or written report to a law enforcement agency or to the Department of Social and Rehabilitation Services relating to injury inflicted on a child as a result of physical, mental, sexual, or emotional abuse or neglect or in any follow-up activity to or investigation of the report shall have immunity from any civil liability that might otherwise be incurred or imposed. Any such participant shall have the same immunity with respect to participation in any judicial proceedings resulting from the report. |
| Penalties for False Reporting | Any person who willfully and knowingly makes a false report pursuant to Kansas law or makes a report that such person knows lacks factual foundation is guilty of a Class B misdemeanor. |
| Penalties for Failure to Report | Willful and knowing failure to make a report required by Kansas law is a Class B misdemeanor. It is not a defense that another mandatory reporter made a report. Intentionally preventing or interfering with the making of a report required by this section is a Class B misdemeanor. |

| Relevant Internet Resources | *Web site for Statutes:*<br>http://www.kslegislature.org/legsrv-statutes/index.do |
|---|---|
| | *Citations:*<br>Child Protection: Chapter 38, Article 15, §§ 38–1502 and 38–1521 to 38–1530<br>Child Welfare: Chapter 38, Article 15 |
| | *Web site for Agency Policies:*<br>http://www.da.ks.gov/ps/documents/regs/default.htm |

## KENTUCKY

| Who Are Mandated Reporters? | Physicians, osteopathic physicians, nurses, coroners, medical examiners, residents, interns, chiropractors, dentists, optometrists, emergency medical technicians, paramedics, or health professionals; teachers, school personnel, or child-caring personnel; social workers or mental health professionals; peace officers; any other person who knows or has reasonable cause to believe that a child is dependent, neglected, or abused |
|---|---|
| When to Report | Mandated reporters must make a report when they know or have reasonable cause to believe that a child is dependent, neglected, or abused. |
| Confidentiality of Mandated Reporters | Inclusion of the reporter's name in the report is not specifically required in statute. However, the identity of the reporter shall not be disclosed except (1) to law enforcement officials, (2) the agency investigating the report, (3) to a multidisciplinary team, (4) under court order, after a court has found reason to believe the reporter knowingly made a false report. |
| How Do Mandated Reporters Make a Report? | Mandated reporters would contact the Child Abuse State Hotline number @ (800) 752-6200 or (502) 595-4550. |
| Immunity Provisions | Anyone acting on reasonable cause in the making of a report or acting in good faith shall have immunity from any liability, civil or criminal, that might otherwise be incurred or imposed. Any such participant shall have the same immunity with respect to participation in any judicial proceeding resulting from such report or action. |
| Penalties for False Reporting | Any person who knowingly makes a false report and does so with malice shall be guilty of a Class A misdemeanor. |
| Penalties for Failure to Report | Any person intentionally violating the provisions of this chapter shall be guilty of a Class B misdemeanor. |

*(continued)*

| | |
|---|---|
| Relevant Internet Resources | *Web site for Statutes:*<br>http://lrc.ky.gov/Statrev/frontpg.htm<br>*Citations:*<br>Child Protection: Title LI, Chapter 620, §§ 620.020 to 620.180<br>Child Welfare: Title LI, Chapters 620 and 625<br>*Web site for Administrative Code:*<br>http://lrc.ky.gov/KAR/titles.htm<br>See Titles 920–922.<br><br>Cabinet for Health and Family Services, Department for Community Based Services<br>Division of Protection and Permanency Standards of Practice (SOPs)<br>http://manuals.chfs.ky.gov/dcbs_manuals/DPP/index_dpp.asp |

## LOUISIANA

| | |
|---|---|
| Who Are Mandated Reporters? | Physicians, surgeons, physical therapists, dentists, residents, interns, hospital staff members, podiatrists, chiropractors, licensed nurses, nursing aides, dental hygienists, emergency medical technicians, paramedics, optometrists, coroners, or medical examiners; psychiatrists, psychologists, marriage or family counselors, or social workers; members of the clergy, including priest, rabbis, deacons or ministers, Christian Science practitioners, or other similar functionary of a religious organization; teachers, child care providers, school principals, teacher's aides, school staff members, foster home parents, or group home or other child care institutional staff members, personnel of residential home facilities, day care providers, or any individuals who provide such services to children; police officers, law enforcement officials, or probation officers; commercial film or photographic print processors; mediators |
| When to Report | Mandated reporters must make a report when they have cause to believe that a child's health is endangered as a result of abuse or neglect. Commercial film or photographic print processors are required to report when they have knowledge of or observe any film, photograph, videotape, negative, or slide depicting a child that constitutes child pornography. |
| Confidentiality of Mandated Reporters | The report must include the name and address of the reporter. The identity of the reporter shall not be released unless a court finds that the reporter knowingly made a false report. |
| How Do Mandated Reporters Make a Report? | Mandated reporters would contact the Child Abuse State Hotline number @ (225) 342-6832. |

| | |
|---|---|
| Immunity Provisions | No cause of action shall exist against any: |
| | ■ Person who in good faith makes a report, cooperates in any investigation arising as a result of such report, or participates in judicial proceedings authorized under the provisions of Louisiana law. |
| | ■ Caseworker who in good faith conducts an investigation, makes an investigative judgment or disposition, or releases or uses information contained in the central registry for the purpose of protecting a child |
| | Such individuals shall have immunity from civil or criminal liability that otherwise might be incurred or imposed. |
| | This immunity shall not be extended to: |
| | ■ Any alleged principal, conspirator, or accessory to an offense involving the abuse or neglect of the child |
| | ■ Any person who makes a report known to be false or with reckless disregard for the truth of the report |
| Penalties for False Reporting | The filing of a report, known to be false, may subject the offender to criminal prosecution. |
| | Any person who reports a child as abused or neglected or sexually abused to the department or to any law enforcement agency, knowing that such information is false, shall be guilty of a misdemeanor and on conviction shall be subject to one or both of the following: |
| | ■ A fine of not more than $500 |
| | ■ Imprisonment for not more than 6 months |
| Penalties for Failure to Report | Violation of the duties imposed on a mandatory reporter subjects the offender to criminal prosecution. |
| | Any person who is required to report the abuse or neglect or sexual abuse of a child and knowingly and willfully fails to do so shall be guilty of a misdemeanor and on conviction shall be subject to one or both of the following: |
| | ■ A fine of not more than $500 |
| | ■ Imprisonment for not more than 6 months |
| Relevant Internet Resources | *Web site for Statutes:* http://www.legis.state.la.us |
| | *Citations:* Child Protection: Children's Code, Articles 501–526, 601–670 Child Welfare: Children's Code, Articles 671–717 |
| | *Web site for Administrative Code:* http://doa.louisiana.gov/osr/lac/lac.htm See Title 67, Part III, Subpart 13; Part V, Subparts 3, 5, and 6. |
| | *Web site for Agency Policies:* http://stellent.dss.state.la.us/LADSS/index.jsp See OCS (Office of Community Services). |

(*continued*)

| Maine | |
|---|---|
| Who Are Mandated Reporters? | Allopathic and osteopathic physicians, emergency medical services persons, medical examiners, podiatrists, physicians' assistants, dentists, dental hygienists and assistants, chiropractors, nurses, home health aides, medical or social service workers; teachers, guidance counselors, school officials, children's summer camp administrators or counselors, or child care personnel; social workers, psychologists, or mental health professionals; court appointed special advocates, guardians ad litem, homemakers, law enforcement officials, fire inspectors, municipal code enforcement officials, or chairs of licensing boards that have jurisdiction over mandated reporters; commercial film and photographic print processors; clergy members acquiring the information as a result of clerical professional work except for information received during confidential communications; humane agents employed by the Department of Agriculture, Food and Rural Resources |
| When to Report | Mandated reporters must make a report when they know or have reasonable cause to suspect that a child is or is likely to be abused or neglected. |
| Confidentiality of Mandated Reporters | The report shall include the name, occupation, and contact information for the person making the report. The identity of the reporter is protected in any release of information to the subject of the report. |
| How Do Mandated Reporters Make a Report? | Mandated reporters would contact the Child Abuse State Hotline number @ (800) 452-1999 or (207) 287-2983. |
| Immunity Provisions | A person, including an agent of the department, participating in good faith in reporting under the reporting laws or participating in a related child protection investigation or proceeding, including, but not limited to, a multidisciplinary team, out-of-home abuse investigating team, or other investigating or treatment team, is immune from any criminal or civil liability for the act of reporting or participating in the investigation or proceeding. Good faith does not include instances when a false report is made and the person knows the report is false. Nothing in Maine law may be construed to bar criminal or civil action regarding perjury or regarding the abuse or neglect that led to a report, investigation, or proceeding. A person participating in good faith in taking photographs or x-rays pursuant to the reporting laws is immune from civil liability for invasion of privacy that might otherwise result from these actions. In a proceeding regarding immunity from liability, there shall be a rebuttable presumption of good faith. |

| Penalties for False Reporting | Immunity from any criminal or civil liability for the act of reporting or participating in the investigation or proceeding is not extended in instances when a false report is made and the person knows the report is false. Nothing in Maine law may be construed to bar criminal or civil action regarding perjury. |
|---|---|
| Penalties for Failure to Report | This issue is not addressed in the statutes reviewed. |
| Relevant Internet Resources | *Web site for Statutes:* <br> http://janus.state.me.us/legis/statutes/ <br><br> *Citations:* <br> Child Protection: Title 22, Chapter 1071, Subchapters 1–4 and 11-A <br> Child Welfare: Title 22, Chapter 1071, Subchapters 1, 5–7, and 15; Title 22, Chapter 1153 <br><br> *Web site for Administrative Code:* <br> http://www.maine.gov/sos/cec/rules/rules.html <br> See Chapter 10 148. <br><br> *Web sites for Agency Policies:* <br> http://www.maine.gov/dhhs/bcfs/policy/policy.htm |

## MARYLAND

| Who Are Mandated Reporters? | Health practitioners; educators or human service workers; police officers; any other person who has reason to believe that a child has been subjected to abuse or neglect |
|---|---|
| When to Report | Mandated reporters must make a report when, acting in a professional capacity, they have reason to believe that a child has been subjected to abuse or neglect. |
| Confidentiality of Mandated Reporters | Inclusion of the reporter's name in the report is not specifically required in statute. Disclosure of the reporter's identity is not prescribed by statute. |
| How Do Mandated Reporters Make a Report? | Mandated reporters would contact the Child Abuse State Hotline number @ (800) 332-6347. |
| Immunity Provisions | Any person who makes or participates in making a report of abuse or neglect under §§ 5-704, 5-705, or 5-705.1 or participates in an investigation or a resulting judicial proceeding shall have immunity from civil liability or criminal penalty. |

*(continued)*

| | |
|---|---|
| Penalties for False Reporting | A person may not make, or cause to be made, a statement, report, or complaint that the person knows to be false as a whole or in material part, to a law enforcement officer with intent to deceive and to cause an investigation or other action to be taken as a result of the statement, report, or complaint.<br>A person who violates this section is guilty of a misdemeanor and on conviction is subject to one or both of the following:<br>■  Imprisonment not exceeding 6 months<br>■  A fine not exceeding $500 |
| Penalties for Failure to Report | This issue is not addressed in the statutes reviewed. |
| Relevant Internet Resources | *Web site for Statutes:*<br>http://www.michie.com/maryland/lpext.dll?f=templates&<br>  fn=main-h.htm&2.0<br><br>*Citations:*<br>Child Protection: Family Law, Title 5, Subtitles 7, 7A, and 9<br>Child Welfare: Family Law, Title 5, Subtitles 5, 6, and 12<br><br>*Web site for Administrative Code:*<br>http://www.dsd.state.md.us/comar/title_search/<br>  Title_List.htm<br>See Title 07, Subtitles 02 05. |

## MASSACHUSETTS

| | |
|---|---|
| Who Are Mandated Reporters? | Physicians, hospital personnel, medical examiners, emergency medical technicians, dentists, nurses, chiropractors, optometrists, or psychiatrists; teachers, educational administrators, day care workers or persons paid to care for or work with children in facilities that provide day care or residential services, family day care systems and child care food programs, or school attendance officers; psychologists, social workers, licensed allied mental health and human services professionals, drug and alcoholism counselors, clinical social workers, or guidance or family counselors; probation officers, clerk or magistrates of district courts, parole officers, foster parents, firefighters or police officers; priests, rabbis, clergy members, ministers, leaders of any church or religious body, accredited Christian Science practitioners, persons performing official duties on behalf of a church or religious body, leader of any church or religious body, or persons employed by a church or religious body to supervise, educate, coach, train, or counsel a child on a regular basis |
| When to Report | Mandated reporters must make a report when, in their professional capacity, they have reasonable cause to believe that a child is suffering injury from abuse or neglect that inflicts harm or a substantial risk of harm. |

| Confidentiality of Mandated Reporters | Reports shall include the name of the reporter. Disclosure of the reporter's identity was not prescribed by reviewed statute. |

How Do Mandated Reporters Make a Report?

Mandated reporters would contact the Child Abuse State Hotline number @ (800) 792-5200 or (617) 232-4882.

Immunity Provisions

No person required to report shall be liable in any civil or criminal action by reason of such report. No other person making a report shall be liable in any civil or criminal action by reason of such report if it was made in good faith, provided, however, that such person did not perpetrate or inflict the abuse or cause the neglect. Any person making such report who, in the determination of the department or the district attorney, may have perpetrated or inflicted the abuse or caused the neglect may be liable in a civil or criminal action.

Penalties for False Reporting

Any person who knowingly files a report of child abuse that is frivolous shall be punished by a fine of not more than $1000.

Penalties for Failure to Report

Any mandatory reporter who fails to report shall be punished by a fine of not more than $1000.
Any mandatory reporter who has reasonable cause to believe that a child has died as a result of abuse or neglect and who fails to report the death as required shall be punished by a fine of not more than $1000.

Relevant Internet Resources

*Web site for Statutes:*
http://www.mass.gov/legis/laws/mgl/index.htm

*Citations:*
Child Protection: Part I, Chapter 119, §§ 51A–51F
Child Welfare: Part I, Chapter 119, §§ 21–23, 26, 29C–33, and 36–39G

## MICHIGAN

Who Are Mandated Reporters?

Physicians, physician assistants, dentists, dental hygienists, medical examiners, nurses, persons licensed to provide emergency medical care, or audiologists; school administrators, counselors, or teachers; regulated child care providers; psychologists, marriage and family therapists, licensed professional counselors, social workers, or social work technicians; law enforcement officers; members of the clergy; department employees, including eligibility specialists, family independence managers, family independence specialists, social services specialists, social work specialists, social work specialist managers, or welfare; services specialists

*(continued)*

| | |
|---|---|
| When to Report | Mandated reporters must make a report when they have reasonable cause to suspect child abuse or neglect. |
| Confidentiality of Mandated Reporters | Although statute does not explicitly require the inclusion of the mandated reporter's name in the report, the identity of the reporter is protected by statute in any release of information to the subject of the report. |
| How Do Mandated Reporters Make a Report? | Mandated reporters would contact the Child Abuse State Hotline number @ (800) 942-4357 or (517) 373-3572. |
| Immunity Provisions | A person acting in good faith who makes a report, cooperates in an investigation, or assists in any other requirement pursuant to the reporting laws is immune from civil or criminal liability that might otherwise be incurred by that action. |
| | A person making a report or assisting in any other requirement of the reporting laws is presumed to have acted in good faith. |
| | This immunity from civil or criminal liability extends only to acts done according to the reporting of child abuse and neglect under Michigan law and does not extend to a negligent act that causes personal injury or death or to the malpractice of a physician that results in personal injury or death. |
| Penalties for False Reporting | Any person who intentionally makes a false report of child abuse or neglect knowing that the report is false is guilty of a crime as follows: |
| | ■ If the child abuse or neglect would not constitute a crime but would constitute a misdemeanor if the report were true, the person is guilty of a misdemeanor punishable by imprisonment for not more than 93 days or a fine of not more than $100, or both. |
| | ■ If the child abuse or neglect reported would constitute a felony if the report were true, the person is guilty of a felony punishable by the lesser of the following: (1) the penalty for the child abuse or neglect falsely reported; (2) imprisonment for not more than 4 years or a fine of not more than $2000, or both. |
| Penalties for Failure to Report | A mandatory reporter who fails to report as required is civilly liable for the damages proximately caused by the failure. |
| | A mandatory reporter who knowingly fails to report as required is guilty of a misdemeanor punishable by one or both of the following: |
| | ■ Imprisonment for not more than 93 days |
| | ■ A fine of not more than $500 |

| Relevant Internet Resources | *Web site for Statutes:* <br> http://www.legislature.mi.gov/ |
|---|---|
| | *Citations:* <br> Child Protection: §§ 722.621–722.638 <br> Child Welfare: §§ 712.1–712.20, 712A.19–712A.21, 722.131–722.140, 722.161–722.163, and 722.951–722.960 |
| | *Web site for Administrative Code:* <br> http://www.michigan.gov/dleg/0,1607,7-154-10576_35738_5698—,00.html <br> See Department of Human Services. |
| | *Web site for Agency Policies:* <br> http://www.michigan.gov/fia/ 0,1607,7-124-5458_7700—,00.html |
| | Department of Human Services <br> Mandated Reporter's Resource Guide <br> http://www.michigan.gov/documents/dhs/Pub-112_179456_7.pdf |
| | A Model Child Abuse Protocol <br> http://www.michigan.gov/documents/dhs/DHS-Pub-794_206830_7.pdf |

## MINNESOTA

| Who Are Mandated Reporters? | A professional or professional's delegate who is engaged in the practice of the healing arts, hospital administration, psychiatric treatment, child care, education, psychological treatment, social services, or law enforcement; a member of the clergy |
|---|---|
| When to Report | Mandated reporters must make a report when they know or have reason to believe that a child is being neglected or sexually or physically abused. |
| Confidentiality of Mandated Reporters | The report must include the name and address of the reporter. The name of the reporter shall be kept confidential while the report is under investigation. After the investigation is complete, the subject of the report may compel disclosure of the name only on the reporter's consent or a finding by the court that the report was false and made in bad faith. |
| How Do Mandated Reporters Make a Report? | Mandated reporters would contact the Child Abuse State Hotline number @ (651) 291-0211. |

*(continued)*

| | |
|---|---|
| Immunity Provisions | The following persons are immune from any civil or criminal liability that otherwise might result from their actions, if they are acting in good faith: |

- Any person making a voluntary or mandated report under the reporting laws or assisting in an assessment
- Any person with responsibility for performing duties under Minnesota's mandated reporting law or a supervisor employed by a local welfare agency or the commissioner of an agency responsible for operating or supervising a licensed or unlicensed day care facility, residential facility, agency, hospital, sanitarium, or other facility or institution required to be licensed, or a school, or a nonlicensed personal care provider organization
- Any public or private school or facility or the employee of any public or private school or facility who permits access by a local welfare agency, the Department of Education, or local law enforcement agency and assists in an investigation or assessment

A person who is a supervisor or person with responsibility for performing duties under Minnesota's mandated reporting law employed by a local welfare agency, the commissioner of human services, or the commissioner of education complying with the reporting laws or any related rule or provision of law is immune from any civil or criminal liability that might otherwise result from the person's actions, if the person is (1) acting in good faith and exercising due care or (2) acting in good faith and following the information collection procedures established by law.

This subdivision does not provide immunity to any person for failure to make a required report or for committing neglect, physical abuse, or sexual abuse of a child.

| | |
|---|---|
| Penalties for False Reporting | Any person who knowingly or recklessly makes a false report under the reporting laws shall be liable in a civil suit for any actual damages suffered by the person(s) so reported and for any punitive damages set by the court or jury, plus costs and reasonable attorney fees. |

| | |
|---|---|
| Penalties for Failure to Report | A mandatory reporter who knows or has reason to believe that a child is neglected or physically or sexually abused, or has been neglected or physically or sexually abused within the preceding 3 years, and fails to report the abuse is guilty of a misdemeanor. |

A mandatory reporter who knows or has reason to believe that two or more children not related to the perpetrator have been physically or sexually abused by the same perpetrator within the preceding 10 years and fails to report is guilty of a gross misdemeanor.

A parent, guardian, or caretaker who knows or reasonably should know that the child's health is in serious danger and who fails to report:

- Is guilty of a gross misdemeanor if the child suffers substantial or great bodily harm because of the lack of medical care
- Is guilty of a felony if the child dies because of the lack of medical care, and may be subject to one or both of the following: (1) imprisonment for not more than 2 years; a fine of not more than $4000

The law providing that a parent, guardian, or caretaker may, in good faith, select and depend on spiritual means or prayer for treatment or care of a child, does not exempt a parent, guardian, or caretaker from the duty to report under this provision.

| | |
|---|---|
| Relevant Internet Resources | *Web site for Statutes:*<br>http://www.revisor.leg.state.mn.us/stats/<br><br>*Citations:*<br>Child Protection: Chapter 260C, §§ 260C.001–260C.201<br>Child Welfare: Chapter 260C, §§ 260C.205–260C.317<br><br>*Web site for Administrative Code:*<br>https://www.revisor.leg.state.mn.us/rules/<br>See Human Services Department, Chapters 9543, 9545, 9550, and 9560.<br><br>Department of Human Services<br>Publications Index<br>http://www.dhs.state.mn.us/main/groups/publications/<br>　documents/pub/DHS_id_003699.hcsp<br><br>Social Services Manual<br>http://www.dhs.state.mn.us/main/groups/county_access/<br>　documents/pub/dhs_id_016961.hcsp |

## MISSISSIPPI

| | |
|---|---|
| Who Are Mandated Reporters? | Physicians, dentists, interns, residents, or nurses; public or private school employees or child care givers; psychologists, social workers, or child protection specialists; attorneys, ministers, or law enforcement officers; all other persons who have reasonable cause to suspect that a child is abused or neglected |
| When to Report | Mandated reporters must make a report when they have reasonable cause to suspect that a child is abused or neglected. |

*(continued)*

| | |
|---|---|
| Confidentiality of Mandated Reporters | The department's report shall include the name and address of the reporter, if known, and whether he or she is a material witness to the abuse. The identity of the reporting party shall not be disclosed to anyone other than law enforcement officers or prosecutors without an order from the appropriate youth court. |
| How Do Mandated Reporters Make a Report? | Mandated reporters would contact the Child Abuse State Hotline number @ (800) 222-8000 or (601) 359-4991. |
| Immunity Provisions | Any attorney, physician, dentist, intern, resident, nurse, psychologist, social worker, child protection specialist, child care giver, minister, law enforcement officer, school attendance officer, public school district employee, nonpublic school employee, or any other person participating in the making of a required report pursuant to the reporting laws or participating in a judicial proceeding resulting therefrom shall be presumed to be acting in good faith.<br><br>Any person or institution reporting in good faith shall be immune from any civil or criminal liability that might otherwise be incurred or imposed. |
| Penalties for False Reporting | It shall be unlawful for any person to report a crime or any element of a crime to any law enforcement or any officer of any court, by any means, knowing that such report is false. A violation of Mississippi mandated reporting law shall be punishable by one or both of the following:<br>■ Imprisonment in the county jail not to exceed 1 year<br>■ A fine not to exceed $1000 |
| Penalties for Failure to Report | Anyone who willfully violates any provision of this section shall be, on being found guilty, punished by a fine not to exceed $5000, by imprisonment in jail not to exceed 1 year, or both. |
| Relevant Internet Resources | *Web site for Statutes:*<br>http://www.mscode.com/free/statutes/toc.htm<br><br>*Citations:*<br>Child Protection: Title 43, Chapter 21<br>Child Welfare: Title 43, Chapters 15, 18, and 51; Title 93, Chapter 15 |

| MISSOURI | |
|---|---|
| Who Are Mandated Reporters? | Physicians, medical examiners, coroners, dentists, chiropractors, optometrists, podiatrists, residents, interns, nurses, hospital and clinic personnel, or other health practitioners; day care center workers or other child care workers, teachers, principals, or other school officials; psychologists, mental health professionals, social workers; ministers, which includes clergyperson, priest, rabbi, Christian Science practitioner, or other person serving in a similar capacity for any religious organization; juvenile officers, probation, parole officers, peace officers, law enforcement officials, jail or detention center personnel; other persons with responsibility for the care of children; commercial film and photographic print processors, computer providers, installers, repair persons; Internet service providers |
| When to Report | Mandated reporters must make a report when they have reasonable cause to suspect that a child has been subjected to abuse or neglect or when they observe a child being subjected to conditions or circumstances that would reasonably result in abuse or neglect. Commercial film and photographic print processors must make a report when they have knowledge of or observe any film, photograph, videotape, negative, slide, or computer-generated image or picture depicting a child engaged in an act of sexual conduct. |
| Confidentiality of Mandated Reporters | The report must include the name, address, occupation, and contact information for the person making the report. The names or other identifying information of reporters shall not be furnished to any child, parent, guardian, or alleged perpetrator named in the report. |
| How Do Mandated Reporters Make a Report? | Mandated reporters would contact the Child Abuse State Hotline number @ (800) 392-3738 or (573) 751-3448. |
| Immunity Provisions | Any person, official, or institution complying with the provisions of the reporting laws in the making of a report, the taking of color photographs, or the making of radiologic examinations, or both such taking of color |

(*continued*)

photographs and making of radiologic examinations, or the removal or retaining a child pursuant to statute, or in cooperating with the division or any other law enforcement agency, juvenile office, court, or child-protective service agency of this or any other state, in any of the activities pursuant to statute, or any other allegation of child abuse, neglect, or assault shall have immunity from any liability, civil or criminal, that otherwise might result by reason of such actions.

Provided, however, any person, official, or institution intentionally filing a false report, acting in bad faith or with ill intent, shall not have immunity from any liability, civil or criminal.

Any such person, official, or institution shall have the same immunity with respect to participation in any judicial proceeding resulting from the report.

| | |
|---|---|
| Penalties for False Reporting | Any person who intentionally files a false report of child abuse or neglect shall be guilty of a Class A misdemeanor.<br><br>Every person who has been previously convicted of making a false report to the Division of Family Services and who is subsequently convicted of making a false report is guilty of a Class D felony and shall be punished as provided by law. |
| Penalties for Failure to Report | Any person violating any provision of the reporting laws is guilty of a Class A misdemeanor. |
| Relevant Internet Resources | *Web site for Statutes:*<br>http://www.moga.mo.gov/statutesearch/<br><br>*Citations:*<br>Child Protection: Title XII, Chapter 210, §§ 210.109–210.167<br>Child Welfare: Title XII, Chapter 211, §§ 211.171, 211.177–211.183, and 211.442–211.477<br><br>*Regulation/Policy, Web site for Administrative Code:*<br>http://www.sos.mo.gov/adrules/csr/csr.asp<br>See Title 13, Divisions 35 and 40.<br><br>Department of Social Services, Children's Division<br>Child Welfare Manual<br>http://dss.missouri.gov/cd/info/cwmanual<br><br>Memorandums<br>http://www.dss.mo.gov/cd/info/memos/<br><br>Guidelines for Child Abuse and Neglect Reports<br>http://www.dss.mo.gov/cd/pdf/guidelines_can_reports.pdf |

| MONTANA | |
|---|---|
| Who Are Mandated Reporters? | Physicians, residents, interns, members of hospital staffs, nurses, osteopaths, chiropractors, podiatrists, medical examiners, coroners, dentists, optometrists, or any other health professionals; school teachers, other school officials, employees who work during regular school hours, operators or employees of any registered or licensed day care or substitute care facility, or any other operators or employees of child care facilities; mental health professionals or social workers; Christian Science practitioners or religious healers; foster care, residential, or institutional workers; members of clergy; guardians ad litem or court-appointed advocates authorized to investigate a report; peace officers or other law enforcement officials |
| When to Report | Mandated reporters must make a report when they know or have reasonable cause to suspect, as a result of information they receive in their professional or official capacity, that a child is abused or neglected. |
| Confidentiality of Mandated Reporters | The statutes reviewed did not prescribe whether the mandated reporter's name must be included in the report. However, the identity of the reporter shall not be disclosed in any release of information to the subject of the report. |
| How Do Mandated Reporters Make a Report? | Mandated reporters would contact the Child Abuse State Hotline number @ (866) 820-KIDS or (406) 444-5900. |
| Immunity Provisions | Anyone investigating or reporting any incident of child abuse or neglect, participating in resulting judicial proceedings, or furnishing hospital or medical records pursuant to the reporting laws is immune from any civil or criminal liability that might otherwise be incurred or imposed, unless the person was grossly negligent or acted in bad faith or with malicious purpose or provided information knowing the information to be false. |
| Penalties for False Reporting | Anyone reporting any incident of child abuse or neglect as required by law is immune from any liability, civil or criminal, that might otherwise be incurred or imposed unless the person was grossly negligent, acted in bad faith or with malicious purpose, or provided information knowing the information to be false. |

(*continued*)

| | |
|---|---|
| Penalties for Failure to Report | Any mandatory reporter who fails to report known or suspected child abuse or neglect or who prevents another person from reasonably doing so is civilly liable for the damages proximately caused by such failure or prevention.<br><br>Any mandatory reporter who purposely or knowingly fails to report when required or purposely or knowingly prevents another person from doing so is guilty of a misdemeanor. |
| Relevant Internet Resources | *Web site for Statutes:*<br>http://data.opi.state.mt.us/bills/mca_toc/index.htm<br><br>*Citations:*<br>Child Protection: Title 41, Chapter 3, Parts 1–4<br>Child Welfare: Title 41, Chapter 3, Parts 5 and 6; Title 41, Chapters 4 and 7; Title 52, Chapter 2<br><br>*Web site for Administrative Code:*<br>http://www.mtrules.org/<br>See Title 37, Chapters 47–52 and 97.<br><br>Department of Public Health and Human Services, Child and Family Services Division<br>What Happens Next? A Guide to the Child and Family Services Division<br>http://www.dphhs.mt.gov/aboutus/divisions/childfamilyservices/publications/whathappensnext.shtml<br><br>School Guidelines for Reporting Child Abuse and Neglect<br>http://www.dphhs.mt.gov/aboutus/divisions/childfamilyservices/publications/mtschoolguidelines.pdf |

## NEBRASKA

| | |
|---|---|
| Who Are Mandated Reporters? | Physicians, medical institutions, or nurses; school employees; social workers; all other persons who have reasonable cause to believe that a child has been subjected to abuse or neglect |
| When to Report | Mandated reporters must make a report when they have reasonable cause to believe that a child has been subjected to abuse or neglect or when they observe a child being subjected to conditions or circumstances that reasonably would result in abuse or neglect. |
| Confidentiality of Mandated Reporters | The initial oral report shall include the reporter's name and address. The name and address of the reporter shall not be included in any release of information. |
| How Do Mandated Reporters Make a Report? | Mandated reporters would contact the Child Abuse State Hotline number @ (800) 652-1999 or (402) 595-1324. |

| | |
|---|---|
| Immunity Provisions | Any person participating in an investigation or the making of a report of child abuse or neglect required by § 28-711 or participating in a judicial proceeding resulting therefrom shall be immune from any civil or criminal liability that might otherwise be incurred or imposed, except for maliciously false statements. |
| Penalties for False Reporting | Any person participating in an investigation, making a report of child abuse or neglect, or participating in a judicial proceeding resulting from a report shall be immune from any liability, civil or criminal, that might otherwise be incurred or imposed, except for maliciously false statements. |
| Penalties for Failure to Report | Any person who willfully fails to make any report of child abuse or neglect required by § 28.711 shall be guilty of a Class III misdemeanor. |
| Relevant Internet Resources | *Web site for Statutes:* http://uniweb.legislature.ne.gov/QS/laws.html *Citations:* Child Protection: Chapter 28, §§ 28-707 and 28-710 to 28-739 Child Welfare: Chapter 43, §§ 43-1301 to 43-1321 *Web site for Agency Policies:* http://www.hhs.state.ne.us/chs/chsrules.htm |

## NEVADA

| | |
|---|---|
| Who Are Mandated Reporters? | Physicians, dentists, dental hygienists, chiropractors, optometrists, podiatrists, medical examiners, residents, interns, nurses, or physician assistants; emergency medical technicians, other persons providing medical services, or hospital personnel; coroners; school administrators, teachers, counselors, or librarians; any persons who maintain or are employed by facilities or establishments that provide care for children, children's camps, or other facilities, institutions, or agencies furnishing care to children; psychiatrists, psychologists, marriage and family therapists, alcohol or drug abuse counselors, athletic trainers, or social workers; clergymen, practitioners of Christian Science, or religious healers, unless they have acquired the knowledge of the abuse or neglect from the offenders during confessions; persons licensed to conduct foster homes; officers or employees of law enforcement agencies or adult or juvenile probation officers; attorneys, unless they have acquired the knowledge of the abuse or neglect from clients who are, or may be, accused of the abuse or neglect; any person who is employed by or serves as a volunteer for an approved youth shelter; any adult person who is employed by an entity that provides organized activities for children; any person who maintains, is employed by, or serves as a volunteer for an agency or service that advises persons regarding abuse or neglect of a child and refers them to services |

*(continued)*

| | |
|---|---|
| When to Report | Mandated reporters must make a report when, in their professional capacity, they know or have reason to believe that a child is abused or neglected or when they have reasonable cause to believe that a child has died as a result of abuse or neglect. |
| Confidentiality of Mandated Reporters | Inclusion of the reporter's name in the report is not specifically required in statute; however, statute provides that the identity of the reporter shall be kept confidential. |
| How Do Mandated Reporters Make a Report? | Mandated reporters would contact the Child Abuse State Hotline number @ (800) 992-5757 or (775) 684-4400. |

Immunity Provisions

Except as otherwise provided below, immunity from civil or criminal liability extends to every person who in good faith:

- Makes a report pursuant to the reporting laws
- Conducts an interview or allows an interview to be taken
- Allows or takes photographs or x-rays
- Causes a medical test to be performed
- Provides a record, or a copy thereof, of a medical test to an agency that provides child welfare services to the child, a law enforcement agency that participated in the investigation of the report made pursuant to § 432B. 220, or the prosecuting attorney's office
- Holds a child pursuant to § 432B.400 (pertaining to the temporary detention of a child by a physician), takes possession of a child pursuant to § 432B.630 (pertaining to the delivery of a newborn child to a provider of emergency services), or places a child in protective custody
- Performs any act pursuant to § 432B.630(2)
- Refers a case or recommends the filing of a petition pursuant to § 432B.380 (pertaining to the referral of a case to a district attorney for criminal prosecution)
- Participates in a judicial proceeding resulting from a referral or recommendation

The provisions above do not confer any immunity from liability for the negligent performance of any act pursuant to § 432B.630.

In any proceeding to impose liability against a person for making a report pursuant to the reporting laws or performing any of the actions listed above, there is a presumption that a person acted in good faith.

Penalties for False Reporting

Any person who deliberately reports to any police officer, sheriff, district attorney, deputy sheriff, deputy district attorney, or member of the Department of Public Safety that a felony or misdemeanor has been committed, knowing such report to be false, is guilty of a misdemeanor.

| Penalties for Failure to Report | Any person who knowingly and willfully violates the provisions of the reporting laws is guilty of a misdemeanor. |
|---|---|
| Relevant Internet Resources | *Web site for Statutes:*<br>http://www.leg.state.nv.us/NRS/Index.cfm<br><br>*Citations:*<br>Child Protection: Chapter 432B<br>Child Welfare: Chapters 128 and 424<br><br>*Web site for Administrative Code:*<br>http://www.leg.state.nv.us/nac/chapters.html<br>See Chapters 127, 423, 424, 432, 432A, and 432B. |

## NEW HAMPSHIRE

| Who Are Mandated Reporters? | Physicians, surgeons, county medical examiners, psychiatrists, residents, interns, dentists, osteopaths, optometrists, chiropractors, nurses, hospital personnel, or Christian Science practitioners; teachers, school officials, nurses, or counselors; day care workers or any other child or foster care workers; social workers; psychologists or therapists; priests, ministers, or rabbis; law enforcement officials; all other persons who have reason to suspect that a child has been abused or neglected |
|---|---|
| When to Report | Mandated reporters must make a report when they have reason to suspect that a child has been abused or neglected. |
| Confidentiality of Mandated Reporters | Inclusion of the reporter's name in the report is not specifically required in statute. The disclosure of the reporter's identity is not addressed in statutes reviewed. |
| How Do Mandated Reporters Make a Report? | Mandated reporters would contact the Child Abuse State Hotline number @ (800) 894-5533, (603) 271-6556, or (800) 852-3388 (after hours). |
| Immunity Provisions | Anyone participating in good faith in the making of a report pursuant to the reporting laws is immune from any civil or criminal liability that might otherwise be incurred or imposed. Any such participant has the same immunity with respect to participation in any investigation by the Division for Children, Youth, and Families or judicial proceeding resulting from such report. |
| Penalties for False Reporting | A person is guilty of a misdemeanor if he or she knowingly gives or causes to be given false information to any law enforcement officer with the purpose of inducing such officer to believe that another has committed an offense. |

*(continued)*

| Penalties for Failure to Report | Anyone who knowingly violates any provision of the reporting laws shall be guilty of a misdemeanor. |
|---|---|
| Relevant Internet Resources | *Web site for Statutes:*<br>http://www.gencourt.state.nh.us/rsa/html/indexes/default.html<br><br>*Citations:*<br>Child Protection: Title XII, Chapter 169-C<br>Child Welfare: Title XII, Chapter 169-C, §§ 169-C:19 to 169-C:28, Chapters 170-A, 170-C, and 170-G<br><br>*Web site for Agency Policies:*<br>http://www.dhhs.state.nh.us/DHHS/DCYF/LAWS-RULES-POLICIES/default.htm |

## NEW JERSEY

| Who Are Mandated Reporters? | Any persons having reasonable cause to believe that a child has been subjected to child abuse or acts of child abuse |
|---|---|
| When to Report | Mandated reporters must make a report when they have reasonable cause to believe that a child has been subjected to abuse. |
| Confidentiality of Mandated Reporters | The identity of the reporter shall not be made public. Any information that could endanger any person shall not be released. |
| How Do Mandated Reporters Make a Report? | Mandated reporters would contact the Child Abuse State Hotline number @ (800) 792-8610. |
| Immunity Provisions | Anyone acting pursuant to the reporting laws in the making of a report under the reporting laws shall have immunity from any civil or criminal liability that might otherwise be incurred or imposed. Any such person shall have the same immunity with respect to testimony given in any judicial proceeding resulting from such report. |
| Penalties for False Reporting | A person who knowingly gives or causes to be given false information to any law enforcement officer to purposely implicate another commits a crime of the fourth degree.<br>A person commits a disorderly persons offense if he or she:<br>■ Reports or causes to be reported to law enforcement authorities an offense or other incident within his or her concern knowing that it did not occur.<br>Pretends to furnish or causes to be furnished information relating to an offense or incident when he or she knows he or she has no information relating to such offense or incident. |

| | |
|---|---|
| Penalties for Failure to Report | Any person knowingly violating the reporting laws, including the failure to report an act of child abuse having reasonable cause to believe that an act of child abuse has been committed, is a disorderly person. |
| Relevant Internet Resources | *Web site for Statutes:* http://www.njleg.state.nj.us |
| | *Citations:* Child Protection: Title 9, §§ 9:6-1 to 9:6-8.86 Child Welfare: Title 9, §§ 9:2-18 to 9:2-21, 9:6-8.8, and 9:6-8.45 to 9:6-8.70; Title 30, §§ 30:4C-11 to 30:4C-28 and 30:4C-50 to 30:4C-61.2 |
| | *Web site for Administrative Code:* http://law-library.rutgers.edu/ilg/njlaw.html#NJREGS |

## NEW MEXICO

| | |
|---|---|
| Who Are Mandated Reporters? | Physicians, residents, or interns; law enforcement officers or judges; nurses; teachers or school officials; social workers; members of the clergy; every person who knows or has a reasonable suspicion that a child is an abused or a neglected child |
| When to Report | Mandated reporters must make a report when they know or have a reasonable suspicion that a child is abused or neglected. |
| Confidentiality of Mandated Reporters | Inclusion of the reporter's name in the report is not specifically required in statute. However, any release of information to a parent, guardian, or legal custodian shall not include identifying information about the reporter. |
| How Do Mandated Reporters Make a Report? | Mandated reporters would contact the Child Abuse State Hotline number @ (800) 797-3260 or (505) 841-6100. |
| Immunity Provisions | Anyone reporting an instance of alleged child neglect or abuse or participating in a judicial proceeding brought as a result of a report required by the reporting laws is presumed to be acting in good faith and shall be immune from liability, civil or criminal, that might otherwise be incurred or imposed by the law, unless the person acted in bad faith or with malicious purpose. |
| Penalties for False Reporting | It is unlawful for any person to intentionally make a report to a law enforcement agency or official when he or she knows the report to be false at the time of making it, alleging a violation by another person of the provisions of the Criminal Code. Any person violating the provisions of New Mexico's law to make a false report is guilty of a misdemeanor. |

*(continued)*

| | |
|---|---|
| Penalties for Failure to Report | Any person who violates the provisions of New Mexico' law pertaining to the duty to report is guilty of a misdemeanor and shall be sentenced pursuant to law. |
| Relevant Internet Resources | *Web site for Statutes:* <br> http://www.conwaygreene.com/NewMexico.htm <br> *Citations:* <br> Child Protection: Chapter 32A, Article 4 <br> Child Welfare: Chapter 32A, Articles 3A, 3B, 11, and 17 <br> *Web site for Administrative Code:* <br> http://www.nmcpr.state.nm.us/nmac/_titles.htm <br> See Title 8, Chapters 8, 10, 26, and 27. |

## NEW YORK

| | |
|---|---|
| Who Are Mandated Reporters? | Physicians, physician assistants, surgeons, medical examiners, coroners, dentists, dental hygienists, osteopaths, optometrists, chiropractors, podiatrists, residents, interns, nurses, hospital personnel, emergency medical technicians, or Christian Science practitioners; school officials, social workers, social services workers, day care center workers, providers of family or group family day care, employees or volunteers in a residential care facility, or any other child care or foster care worker; psychologists, therapists, mental health professionals, substance abuse counselors, or alcoholism counselors; police officers, district attorneys or assistant district attorneys, investigators employed in the office of a district attorney, or other law enforcement officials |
| When to Report | Mandated reporters must make a report when they have reasonable cause to suspect that a child coming before them in their professional or official capacity is an abused or maltreated child. |
| Confidentiality of Mandated Reporters | The report shall include the name and contact information for the reporter. Any disclosure of information shall not identify the source of the report. |
| How Do Mandated Reporters Make a Report? | Mandated reporters would contact the Child Abuse State Hotline number @ (800) 342-3720 or (518) 474-8740. |
| Immunity Provisions | Any person, official, or institution participating in good faith in the making of a report or the taking of photographs, the removal or keeping of a child pursuant to Child Protection Law in New York State, or the disclosure of child protective services information in compliance with child reporting laws shall have immunity from any civil or criminal liability that might otherwise result by reason of such actions. |

For the purpose of any civil or criminal proceeding, the good faith of any such person, official, or institution required to report cases of child abuse or maltreatment or providing a reporting procedure service shall be presumed, provided such person, official, or institution was acting in the discharge of their duties and within the scope of their employment and that such liability did not result from the willful misconduct or gross negligence of such person, official, or institution.

**Penalties for False Reporting**

A person is guilty of falsely reporting an incident in the third degree when, knowing the information reported, conveyed, or circulated to be false or baseless, he reports, by word or action, to the statewide central register of child abuse and maltreatment, an alleged occurrence or condition of child abuse or maltreatment that did not in fact occur or exist.

Falsely reporting an incident in the third degree is a Class A misdemeanor.

**Penalties for Failure to Report**

Any mandatory reporter who willfully fails to report as required shall be guilty of a Class A misdemeanor.

Any mandatory reporter who knowingly and willfully fails to report as required shall be civilly liable for the damages proximately caused by such failure.

**Relevant Internet Resources**

*Web site for Statutes:*
http://public.leginfo.state.ny.us/menugetf.cgi?
    COMMONQUERY=LAWS

*Citations:*
Child Protection: Social Services Law, Article 6, Titles 1, 4, and 6
Child Welfare: Social Services Law, Article 6, Titles 1-A and 3

*Regulation/Policy, Web site for Agency Policies:*
http://www.ocfs.state.ny.us/main/policies/external/
    OCFS_2005/

Office of Children and Family Services
Summary Guide for Mandated Reporters in New York State
http://www.ocfs.state.ny.us/main/publications/
    Pub1159text.asp

## NORTH CAROLINA

**Who Are Mandated Reporters?**

Any institution an all persons who have cause to suspect that any juvenile is abused, neglected, or dependent, or has died as the result of maltreatment

**When to Report**

Mandated reporters must make a report when they have cause to suspect that any juvenile is abused, neglected, or dependent or has died as the result of maltreatment.

*(continued)*

| | |
|---|---|
| Confidentiality of Mandated Reporters | The report must include the name, address, and telephone number of the reporter. The department shall hold the identity of the reporter in strictest confidence. |
| How Do Mandated Reporters Make a Report? | Mandated reporters would contact the Child Abuse State Hotline number @ (800) 4-A-CHILD. |
| Immunity Provisions | Anyone who makes a report pursuant to the reporting laws, cooperates with the County Department of Social Services in a protective services assessment, testifies in any judicial proceeding resulting from a protective services report or assessment, or otherwise participates in the program authorized by law is immune from any civil or criminal liability that might otherwise be incurred or imposed for such action, provided that the person was acting in good faith. In any proceeding involving liability, good faith is presumed. |
| Penalties for False Reporting | Any person who willfully makes or causes to be made to a law enforcement agency or officer any false, misleading, or unfounded report, for the purpose of interfering with the operation of a law enforcement agency, or to hinder or obstruct any law enforcement officer in the performance of his duty, shall be guilty of a Class 2 misdemeanor. |
| Penalties for Failure to Report | No privilege shall be grounds for any person or institution failing to report that a juvenile may have been abused, neglected, or dependent, even if the knowledge or suspicion is acquired in an official professional capacity, except when the knowledge or suspicion is gained by an attorney from that attorney's client during representation only in the abuse, neglect, or dependency case. |
| Relevant Internet Resources | *Web site for Statutes:* http://www.ncga.state.nc.us/gascripts/Statutes/ StatutesTOC.pl |
| | *Citations:* Child Protection: Chapter 7B, Articles 1, 3, 4, 5, and 29 Child Welfare: Chapter 7B, Articles 6, 8, 9, 10, 11, and 38 |
| | *Web site for Administrative Code:* http://reports.oah.state.nc.us/ncac.asp See Title 10A, Chapter 70. |

| NORTH DAKOTA |
| --- |

| | |
| --- | --- |
| Who Are Mandated Reporters? | Physicians, nurses, dentists, optometrists, medical examiners or coroners, or any other medical or mental health professionals or religious practitioners of the healing arts; school teachers, administrators, or school counselors; addiction counselors or social workers; day care center or any other child care workers; police or law enforcement officers; members of the clergy |
| When to Report | Mandated reporters must make a report when they have knowledge of or reasonable cause to suspect that a child is abused or neglected if the knowledge or suspicion is derived from information received by them in their official or professional capacity. |
| Confidentiality of Mandated Reporters | Inclusion of the reporter's name is not specifically required in statute. However, statute provides that the identity of the reporter is protected. |
| How Do Mandated Reporters Make a Report? | Mandated reporters would contact the Child Abuse State Hotline number @ (800) 245-3736 or (701) 328-2316. |
| Immunity Provisions | Any person, other than the alleged violator, participating in good faith in the making of a report, assisting in an investigation or assessment, furnishing information, or in providing protective services or who is a member of the child fatality review panel is immune from any civil or criminal liability, except for criminal liability as provided for under penalties for failure to report and false reporting, that otherwise might result from reporting the alleged case of abuse, neglect, or death resulting from child abuse or neglect. For the purpose of any civil or criminal proceeding, the good faith of any person required to report cases of child abuse, neglect, or death must be presumed. |
| Penalties for False Reporting | Any person who willfully makes a false report, or provides false information that causes a report to be made, is guilty of a Class B misdemeanor unless the false report is made to a law enforcement official, in which case the person who causes the report to be made is guilty of a Class A misdemeanor. A person who willfully makes a false report, or willfully provides false information that causes a report to be made, is also liable in a civil action for all damages suffered by the person reported, including exemplary damages. |

*(continued)*

| Penalties for Failure to Report | Any person required by this chapter to report or to supply information concerning a case of known or suspected child abuse, neglect, or death resulting from abuse or neglect who willfully fails to do so is guilty of a Class B misdemeanor. |
|---|---|
| Relevant Internet Resources | *Web site for Statutes:*<br>http://www.legis.nd.gov/information/statutes/<br><br>*Citations:*<br>Child Protection: Title 50, Chapter 50-25.1<br>Child Welfare: Title 27, Chapter 27-20, §§ 27-20-02, 27-20-20.1, 27-20-30, 27-20-32.1, 27-20-32.2, and 27-20-44 to 27-20-48.1<br><br>*Web site for Administrative Code:*<br>http://www.legis.nd.gov/information/rules/admincode.html<br>See Title 75, Article 75-03.<br><br>*Web site for Agency Policies:*<br>http://www.state.nd.us/humanservices/policymanuals/home/ |

### OHIO

| Who Are Mandated Reporters? | Physicians, residents, interns, podiatrists, dentists, nurses, other health care professionals, speech pathologists, audiologists, coroners; licensed school psychologists; administrators or employees of child day care centers, residential camps, or child day camps; school teachers, employees, or authorities; licensed psychologists, marriage and family therapists, social workers, professional counselors, or agents of county humane societies; persons rendering spiritual treatment through prayer in accordance with the tenets of a well-recognized religion; superintendents, board members, or employees of a county board of mental retardation; investigative agents contracted by a county board of mental retardation or employees of the department of mental retardation and developmental disabilities; attorneys |
|---|---|
| When to Report | Mandated reporters must make a report when acting in an official or professional capacity and know or suspect that a child has suffered or faces a threat of suffering any physical or mental wound, injury, disability, or condition of a nature that reasonably indicates abuse or neglect of the child. |
| Confidentiality of Mandated Reporters | Inclusion of the reporter's name in the report is not specifically required in statute. However, the name of the person who made the report shall not be released. |

| How Do Mandated Reporters Make a Report? | Mandated reporters would contact the Child Abuse State Hotline number @ (800) 4-A-CHILD. |
|---|---|
| Immunity Provisions | Except as provided in the law regarding false reports, anyone or any hospital, institution, school, health department, or agency participating in the making of reports under § 2151.421(A), anyone or any hospital, institution, school, health department, or agency participating in good faith in the making of reports under § 2151.421(B), and anyone participating in good faith in a judicial proceeding resulting from the reports shall be immune from any civil or criminal liability for injury, death, or loss to person or property that otherwise might be incurred or imposed as a result of the making of the reports or the participation in the judicial proceeding. |
| Penalties for False Reporting | No person shall knowingly make or cause another person to make a false report alleging that any person has committed an act or omission that resulted in a child being abused or neglected.<br>Whoever makes or causes a false report of child abuse or child neglect, is guilty of a misdemeanor of the first degree. |
| Penalties for Failure to Report | Any person who fails to report suspected child abuse or neglect, as required by § 2151.421, is guilty of a misdemeanor of the fourth degree.<br>Any person, required to report by § 2151.421(A)(4) (requiring reports by clergy), who fails to report when knowing that a child has been abused or neglected and knowing that the person who committed the abuse or neglect was a cleric or another person other than a volunteer, designated by a church, religious society, or faith to act as a leader, official, or delegate on behalf of the church, religious society, or faith, is guilty of a misdemeanor of the first degree if the person who has failed to report and the person who committed the abuse or neglect belong to the same church, religious society, or faith.<br>The person who fails to report is guilty of a misdemeanor of the first degree if the child suffers or faces the threat of suffering the physical or mental wound, injury, disability, or condition that would be the basis of the required report when the child is under the direct care or supervision of the person who should have made the report. |

(*continued*)

| | |
|---|---|
| Relevant Internet Resources | *Web site for Statutes:*<br>http://codes.ohio.gov/orc<br>*Citations:*<br>Child Protection: Title XXI, Chapter 2151,<br>  §§ 2151.03–2151.05, 2151.141, 2151.28, 2151.33, 2151.331, 2151.35, 2151.353, 2151.3515–2151.3530, and 2151.421<br>Child Welfare: Title XXI, Chapter 2151,<br>  §§ 2151.3515–2151.39, 2151.412–2151.42, 2151.424, and 2151.55–2151.553<br>*Web site for Administrative Code:*<br>http://onlinedocs.andersonpublishing.com/oh/lpExt.dll?f=templates&fn=main-h.htm&cp=OAC<br>See Chapter 5101:2. |

## OKLAHOMA

| | |
|---|---|
| Who Are Mandated Reporters? | Physicians, surgeons, residents, interns, dentists, osteopaths, nurses, or other health care professionals; teachers; commercial film and photographic print processors; any person who has reason to believe that a child is a victim of abuse or neglect |
| When to Report | Mandated reporters must make a report when they have reason to believe that a child is a victim of abuse or neglect, or when a health care professional treats the victim of what appears to be criminally injurious conduct, including, but not limited to, child physical or sexual abuse; or when a health care professional attends the birth of a child who tests positive for alcohol or a controlled dangerous substance; or when any commercial film and photographic print processor has knowledge of or observes any film, photograph, video tape, negative, or slide, depicting a child engaged in an act of sexual conduct. |
| Confidentiality of Mandated Reporters | Reports may be made anonymously. The department shall not release the identity of the person who made the initial report unless a court orders the release of information for good cause shown. |
| How Do Mandated Reporters Make a Report? | Mandated reporters would contact the Child Abuse State Hotline number @ (800) 522-3511. |
| Immunity Provisions | Any person, in good faith and exercising due care, participating in the making of a report pursuant to reporting laws or allowing access to a child by persons authorized to investigate a report concerning the child shall have immunity from any civil or criminal liability that might otherwise be incurred or imposed. Any such participant shall have the same immunity with respect to participation in any judicial proceeding resulting from such report. |

The good faith of any physician, surgeon, osteopathic physician, resident, intern, physician's assistant, registered nurse, or any other health care professional in making a report pursuant to the reporting laws shall be presumed.

A child advocacy center that is accredited by the National Children's Alliance, and the employees thereof, who are acting in good faith and exercising due care shall have immunity from civil liability that be incurred or imposed through participation in the investigation process and any judicial proceeding resulting from the investigation process.

**Penalties for False Reporting**

Any person who knowingly and willfully makes a false report under the reporting laws or a report that the person knows lacks factual foundation may be reported by the Department of Human Services to local law enforcement for criminal investigation and, on conviction thereof, shall be guilty of a misdemeanor.

If a court determines that an accusation of child abuse or neglect made during a child custody proceeding is false and the person making the accusation knew it to be false at the time the accusation was made, the court may impose a fine, not to exceed $5000 and reasonable attorney fees incurred in recovering the sanctions, against the person making the accusation. This remedy is in addition to the paragraph above or to any other remedy provided by law.

**Penalties for Failure to Report**

Any person who knowingly and willfully fails to promptly report any incident of child abuse or neglect, may be reported by the Department of Human Services to local law enforcement for criminal investigation and, on conviction thereof, shall be guilty of a misdemeanor.

**Relevant Internet Resources**

*Web sites for Statutes:*
http://www.lsb.state.ok.us
http://www.oscn.net/applications/oscn/
  index.asp?ftdb=STOKST&level=1

*Citations:*
Child Protection: Title 10, Chapter 71
Child Welfare: Title 10, Chapters 25, 70, and 72

*Regulation/Policy, Web site for Administrative Code:*
http://www.sos.state.ok.us/oar/oar_welcome.htm
See Title 340—Department of Human Services

*(continued)*

| OREGON | |
|---|---|
| Who Are Mandated Reporters? | Physicians, interns, residents, optometrists, dentists, emergency medical technicians, naturopathic physicians, or nurses; employees of the Department of Human Resources, State Commission on Children and Families, Childcare Division of the Employment Department, the Oregon Youth Authority, a county health department, a community mental health and developmental disabilities program, a county juvenile department, a licensed child-caring agency, or an alcohol and drug treatment program; school employees, child care providers, psychologists, members of clergy, social workers, foster care; providers, counselors, or marriage and family therapists; peace officers, attorneys, firefighters, or court appointed special advocates; members of the legislative assembly |
| When to Report | Mandated reporters must make a report when any public or private officials have reasonable cause to believe that any child with whom the officials come in contact has suffered abuse. |
| Confidentiality of Mandated Reporters | Inclusion of the reporter's name is not specifically required in statute. However, the name, address, and other identifying information about the person who made the report may not be disclosed. |
| How Do Mandated Reporters Make a Report? | Mandated reporters would contact the Child Abuse State Hotline number @ (800) 854-3508, ext. 2402, or (503) 378-6704. |
| Immunity Provisions | Anyone participating in good faith in the making of a report of child abuse and who has reasonable grounds for the making thereof shall have immunity from any civil or criminal liability that might otherwise be incurred or imposed with respect to the making or content of such report. Any such participant shall have the same immunity with respect to participating in any judicial proceeding resulting from such report. |
| Penalties for False Reporting | This issue is not addressed in the statutes reviewed. |
| Penalties for Failure to Report | A person who violates the reporting laws commits a Class A violation. Prosecution under this law shall be commenced at any time within 18 months after the commission of the offense. |

Relevant Internet
Resources

*Web site for Statutes:*
http://www.leg.state.or.us/ors/

*Citations:*
Child Protection: Chapter 419B, §§ 419B.005–419B.050
Child Welfare: Chapter 419B, §§ 419B.192–419B.208,
    419B.340–419B.349, and 419B.470–419B.530

*Web site for Administrative Code:*
http://arcweb.sos.state.or.us/banners/rules.htm
See Chapter 413—Department of Human Services, Child
    Welfare Programs and Chapter 423—Oregon
    Commission on Children and Families.

*Web sites for Agency Policies:*
http://www.dhs.state.or.us/policy
http://www.dhs.state.or.us/policy/childwelfare/

Child Welfare Practices for Cases With Domestic Violence
http://dhsforms.hr.state.or.us/Forms/Served/CE9200.pdf

## PENNSYLVANIA

Who Are Mandated
Reporters?

Physicians, osteopaths, medical examiners, coroners,
funeral directors, dentists, optometrists, chiropractors,
nurses, hospital personnel, or Christian Science
practitioners; members of the clergy; school
administrators, teachers, or school nurses; social services
workers, day care center workers, or any other child care or
foster care workers or mental health professionals; peace
officers or law enforcement officials

When to Report

Mandated reporters must make a report when, in the
course of their employment, occupation, or practice of
their profession, they have reasonable cause to suspect,
on the basis of their medical, professional, or other
training and experience, that a child coming before them
is an abused child.

Confidentiality of
Mandated
Reporters

The mandated reporter must make a written report that
includes his or her name and contact information. The
release of the identity of the mandated reporter is
prohibited unless the secretary finds that the release will
not be detrimental to the safety of the reporter.

How Do Mandated
Reporters Make a
Report?

Mandated reporters would contact the Child Abuse State
Hotline number @ (800) 932-0313 or (717) 783-8744.

*(continued)*

| | |
|---|---|
| Immunity Provisions | A person, hospital, institution, school, facility, agency, or agency employee that participates in good faith in the making of a report, cooperating with an investigation, testifying in a proceeding arising out of an instance of suspected child abuse, taking of photographs, removal or keeping of a child pursuant to child custody law and any official or employee of a county agency who refers a report of suspected abuse to law enforcement authorities or provides services under this law shall have immunity from civil and criminal liability that might otherwise result by reason of those actions.<br><br>For the purpose of any civil or criminal proceeding, the good faith of a person required to report pursuant to child abuse reporting law and of any person required to make a referral to law enforcement officers under this law shall be presumed. |
| Penalties for False Reporting | A person who knowingly gives false information to any law enforcement officer with intent to implicate another commits a misdemeanor of the second degree.<br><br>A person commits a misdemeanor of the third degree if he or she:<br>■ Reports to law enforcement authorities an offense or other incident knowing that it did not occur<br>■ Pretends to furnish such authorities with information relating to an offense or incident when he or she knows he or she has no information relating to such offense or incident |
| Penalties for Failure to Report | A mandatory reporter who willfully fails to report as required commits a misdemeanor of the third degree for the first violation and a misdemeanor of the second degree for a second or subsequent violation. |
| Relevant Internet Resources | *Web site for Statutes:*<br>http://members.aol.com/StatutesPA/Index.html<br><br>*Citations:*<br>Child Protection: Title 23, Chapters 61 and 63<br>Child Welfare: Title 23, Chapter 25, §§ 2511–2513; Title 23, Chapter 56; Title 42, Chapter 63, §§ 6301–6303 and 6351<br><br>*Web site for Administrative Code:*<br>http://www.pacode.com/secure/browse.asp<br>See Title 55, Part V—Children, Youth, and Families Manual |

| RHODE ISLAND | |
| --- | --- |
| Who Are Mandated Reporters? | Physicians or duly certified registered nurse practitioners; any person who has reasonable cause to know or suspect that a child has been abused or neglected |
| When to Report | Mandated reporters must make a report when they have reasonable cause to know or suspect that a child has been abused or neglected; when any physicians or nurse practitioners have cause to suspect that a child brought to them for treatment is an abused or neglected child, or when they determine that a child under the age of 12 years is suffering from any sexually transmitted disease |
| Confidentiality of Mandated Reporters | Inclusion of the reporter's name is not specifically required in statute. Disclosure of the reporter's identity is not addressed in statutes reviewed. |
| How Do Mandated Reporters Make a Report? | Mandated reporters would contact the Child Abuse State Hotline number @ (800) RI-CHILD. |
| Immunity Provisions | Any person participating in good faith in making a report pursuant to the reporting laws shall have immunity from any civil or criminal liability that might otherwise be incurred or imposed. Any such participant shall have the same immunity with respect to participation in any judicial proceeding resulting from the report. |
| Penalties for False Reporting | Any person who knowingly and willingly makes or causes to be made to the department a false report of child abuse or neglect shall be guilty of a misdemeanor and, on conviction thereof, shall be fined not more than $1000 or imprisoned not more than 1 year, or both. |
| Penalties for Failure to Report | Any mandatory reporter who knowingly fails to report as required or who knowingly prevents any person acting reasonably from doing so, shall be guilty of a misdemeanor and on conviction shall be subject to a fine of not more than $500, imprisonment for not more than 1 year, or both.<br>In addition, any mandatory reporter who knowingly fails to perform any act required by the reporting laws or who knowingly prevents another person from performing a required act shall be civilly liable for the damages proximately caused by that failure. |

*(continued)*

| Relevant Internet Resources | *Web site for Statutes:* <br> http://www.rilin.state.ri.us/statutes/statutes.html <br><br> *Citations:* <br> Child Protection: Title 40, Chapter 11; Title 42, Chapter 72, §§ 42-72-7 to 42-72-11 <br> Child Welfare: Title 15, Chapter 7, §§ 15-7-7 and 15-7-7.2; Title 40, Chapter 11, §§ 40-11-12 to 40-11-12.2; Title 40, Chapter 15 <br><br> *Web site for Administrative Code:* <br> http://www.rules.state.ri.us/rules/ <br> Select "Children, Youth, and Families, Dept. of" as agency. <br><br> *Web site for Agency Policies:* <br> http://www.ridhscode.org/ <br> See Social Services, Section 0520. |
|---|---|

## SOUTH CAROLINA

| Who Are Mandated Reporters? | Physicians, nurses, dentists, optometrists, medical examiners, or coroners; any other medical, emergency medical services, or allied health professionals; school teachers or counselors, principals, or assistant principals; child care workers in any child care centers or foster care facilities; mental health professionals, social or public assistance workers, or substance abuse treatment staff; members of the clergy, including Christian Science practitioners or religious healers; police or law enforcement officers, judges, funeral home directors or employees; persons responsible for processing films or computer technicians |
|---|---|
| When to Report | Mandated reporters must make a report when in their professional capacity they have received information that gives them reason to believe that a child has been or may be abused or neglected. |
| Confidentiality of Mandated Reporters | Inclusion of the reporter's name is not specifically required in statute. However, the identity of the person making a report pursuant to South Carolina law must be kept confidential by the agency or department receiving the report and must not be disclosed. |
| How Do Mandated Reporters Make a Report? | Mandated reporters would contact the Child Abuse State Hotline number @ (803) 898-7318. |

| | |
|---|---|
| Immunity Provisions | A person required or permitted to report pursuant to the reporting laws or who participates in an investigation or judicial proceedings resulting from the report, acting in good faith, is immune from civil and criminal liability that might otherwise result by reason of these actions. In all such civil or criminal proceedings, good faith is rebuttably presumed. Immunity extends to full disclosure by the person of facts that gave the person reason to believe that the child's physical or mental health or welfare had been or might be adversely affected by abuse or neglect. |
| Penalties for False Reporting | It is unlawful to knowingly make a false report of abuse or neglect. A person who violates this statute is guilty of a misdemeanor and, on conviction, must be fined not more than $5000, imprisoned not more than 90 days, or both. |
| Penalties for Failure to Report | Any mandatory reporter or any person required to perform any other function under the reporting laws, who knowingly fails to do so, or a person who threatens or attempts to intimidate a witness, is guilty of a misdemeanor and, on conviction, must be fined not more than $500, be imprisoned for not more than 6 months, or both. |
| Relevant Internet Resources | *Web site for Statutes:* http://www.scstatehouse.net/code/statmast.htm *Citations:* Child Protection: Title 20, Chapter 7, §§ 20-7-490, 20-7-510 to 20-7-570, and 20-7-635 to 20-7-695 Child Welfare: Title 20, Chapter 7, §§ 20-7-762 to 20-7-775, 20-7-1560 to 20-7-1582, 20-7-1630 to 20-7-1645, and 20-7-1980 to 20-7-2070 *Web site for Administrative Code:* http://www.scstatehouse.net/coderegs/statmast.htm See Chapter 24—Office of the Governor, Division for Review of the Foster Care of Children, and Chapter 114—Department of Social Services |

## SOUTH DAKOTA

| | |
|---|---|
| Who Are Mandated Reporters? | Physicians, dentists, osteopaths, chiropractors, optometrists, nurses, coroners; teachers, school counselors or officials, child welfare providers; mental health professionals or counselors, psychologists, social workers, chemical dependency counselors, employees or volunteers of domestic abuse shelters, or religious healing practitioners; parole or court services officers or law enforcement officers; any safety-sensitive position, as defined in § 23-3-64 |

(*continued*)

| | |
|---|---|
| When to Report | Mandated reporters must make a report when they have reasonable cause to suspect that a child has been abused or neglected. |
| Confidentiality of Mandated Reporters | Inclusion of the reporter's name in the report is not specifically required in statute. However, the name of the reporter is not disclosed unless:<br>■ The report is determined to be unsubstantiated<br>■ Within 30 days, the subject of the report requests disclosure of the reporter's identity<br>■ A hearing is held to determine whether the report was made with malice and without reasonable foundation and that release of the name will not endanger the life or safety of the reporter |
| How Do Mandated Reporters Make a Report? | Mandated reporters would contact the Child Abuse State Hotline number @ (605) 773-3227. |
| Immunity Provisions | Any person or party participating in good faith in making a report or submitting copies of medical examination, treatment, or hospitalization records pursuant to the reporting laws is immune from any liability, civil or criminal that might otherwise be incurred or imposed and has the same immunity for participation in any judicial proceeding resulting from the report.<br>Immunity also extends in the same manner to persons requesting the taking of photographs and x-rays pursuant to the reporting laws, to persons taking the photographs and x-rays, to child protection teams established by the Secretary of Social Services, to public officials or employees involved in the investigation and treatment of child abuse or neglect or making a temporary placement of the child pursuant to this chapter, or to any person who in good faith cooperates with a child protection team or the Department of Social Services in investigation, placement, or a treatment plan.<br>The provisions of South Dakota law granting or allowing the grant of immunity do not extend to any person alleged to have committed an act or acts of child abuse or neglect. |
| Penalties for False Reporting | A person commits false reporting to authorities when he or she:<br>■ Makes a report or intentionally causes the transmission of a report to law enforcement authorities of a crime or other incident within his or her official concern, knowing that it did not occur<br>■ Makes a report or intentionally causes the transmission of a report to law enforcement authorities that furnishes information relating to an offense or other incident within his or her official concern, knowing that such information is false<br>False reporting to authorities is a Class 1 misdemeanor. |

| Penalties for Failure to Report | Any mandatory reporter who knowingly and intentionally fails to make the required report is guilty of a Class 1 misdemeanor. This provision includes: |
| | ■ Reports that must be made to the coroner when the reporter suspects that a child has died as a result of abuse or neglect |
| | ■ Reports required of hospital staff |
| | ■ Reports that are required of staff of public or private schools |
| Relevant Internet Resources | *Web site for Statutes:* |
| | http://legis.state.sd.us/statutes/index.aspx |
| | *Citations:* |
| | Child Protection: Title 26, Chapter 8A, §§ 26-8A-1 to 26-8A-20 |
| | Child Welfare: Title 26, Chapter 8A, §§ 26-8A-21 to 26-8A-33; Title 26, Chapter 13 |
| | *Web site for Administrative Code:* |
| | http://legis.state.sd.us/rules/RulesList.aspx |
| | See Rule 67:14—Social Services: Office of Children, Youth and Family Services |

## TENNESSEE

| Who Are Mandated Reporters? | Physicians, osteopaths, medical examiners, chiropractors, nurses, hospital personnel, or other health or mental health professionals; school teachers, other school officials or personnel, day care center workers, or other professional child care, foster care, residential, or institutional workers; social workers; practitioners who rely solely on spiritual means for healing; judges or law enforcement officers; neighbors, relatives, or friends; any person who has knowledge that a child has been harmed by abuse or neglect |
| When to Report | A mandated reporter must make a report when: |
| | ■ He or she has knowledge that a child has been harmed by abuse or neglect |
| | ■ He or she is called on to render aid to any child who is suffering from an injury that reasonably appears to have been caused by abuse |
| | ■ He or she knows or has reasonable cause to suspect that a child has been sexually abused. |
| Confidentiality of Mandated Reporters | Inclusion of the reporter's name is not specifically required in statute. However, the name of the reporter shall not be released, except as may be ordered by the court. |
| How Do Mandated Reporters Make a Report? | Mandated reporters would contact the Child Abuse State Hotline number @ (877) 237-0004. |

*(continued)*

Immunity
Provisions

If a health care provider makes a report of harm, as required
by the reporting laws, and if the report arises from an
examination of the child performed by the health care
provider in the course of rendering professional care or
treatment of the child, then the health care provider shall
not be liable in any civil or criminal action that is based
solely on:
- The health care provider's decision to report what he or
  she believed to be harm
- The health care provider's belief that reporting such
  harm was required by law
- The fact that a report of harm was made

"Health care provider" means any physician, osteopathic
physician, medical examiner, chiropractor, nurse, hospital
personnel, mental health professional, or other health
care professional.

Nothing in this subsection shall be construed to confer any
immunity on a health care provider for a criminal or civil
action arising out of the treatment of the child about
whom the report was made.

If absolute immunity is not conferred on a person pursuant
to the subdivision above, and, if acting in good faith, the
person makes a report of harm, as required by the
reporting laws, then the person shall not be liable in any
civil or criminal action that is based solely on:
- The person's decision to report what the person
  believed to be harm
- The person's belief that reporting such harm was
  required by law
- The fact that a report of harm was made

Because of the overriding public policy to encourage all
persons to report the neglect of or harm or abuse to
children, any person on whom good faith immunity is
conferred pursuant to this subdivision shall be presumed
to have acted in good faith in making a report of harm.

No immunity conferred shall attach if the person reporting
the harm perpetrated or inflicted the abuse or caused the
neglect.

Penalties for
False Reporting

Any person who either verbally or by written or printed
communication knowingly and maliciously reports or
causes, encourages, aids, counsels, or procures another to
report a false accusation of child sexual abuse commits a
Class E felony.

Penalties for
Failure to Report

Any person who knowingly fails to make a report required by
§ 37.1.403 commits a Class A misdemeanor.

A person believed to have violated this section shall be
brought before the court. If the defendant pleads not
guilty, the juvenile court judge shall bind the defendant
over to the grand jury. If the defendant pleads guilty, the
juvenile court judge shall sentence the defendant under
this section with a fine not to exceed $2500.

| Relevant Internet Resources | *Web site for Statutes:*<br>http://www.michie.com/tennessee/lpext.dll?f=<br>    templates&fn=main-h.htm&cp=tncode |
|---|---|
| | *Citations:*<br>Child Protection: Title 37, Chapter 1, Parts 1, 4, and 6<br>Child Welfare: Title 37, Chapter 1, Part 1; Chapter 2,<br>    Parts 2–4; Chapter 3, Part 6; and Chapter 4, Part 2 |
| | *Web site for Administrative Code:*<br>http://www.state.tn.us/sos/rules/rules2.htm<br>See Chapters 0250 and 1240. |
| | *Web site for Agency Policies:*<br>http://www.tennessee.gov/youth/dcsguide/policies.htm |
| | Department of Children's Services<br>The Tennessee Handbook for Parents and Guardians in<br>    Child Abuse and Neglect Cases<br>http://www.tsc.state.tn.us/geninfo/Programs/Parenting/<br>    Parents%20handbook3.pdf |

## TEXAS

| Who Are Mandated Reporters? | A professional, for purposes of the reporting laws, is an individual who is licensed or certified by the state or who is an employee of a facility licensed, certified, or operated by the state and who, in the normal course of official duties or duties for which a license or certification is required, has direct contact with children. Professionals include teachers or day care employees; nurses, doctors, or employees of a clinic or health care facility that provides reproductive services; juvenile probation officers or juvenile detention or correctional officers; a person who has cause to believe that a child has been adversely affected by abuse or neglect |
|---|---|
| When to Report | Mandated reporters must make a report when they have cause to believe that a child has been adversely affected by abuse or neglect. |
| Confidentiality of Mandated Reporters | Inclusion of the reporter's name in the report is not specifically required in statute. However, the identity of the reporter is confidential and may not be disclosed to the subject of the report. |
| How Do Mandated Reporters Make a Report? | Mandated reporters would contact the Child Abuse State Hotline number @ (800) 252-5400. |

(*continued*)

| | |
|---|---|
| Immunity Provisions | A person acting in good faith who reports or assists in the investigation of a report of alleged child abuse or neglect or who testifies or otherwise participates in a judicial proceeding arising from a report, petition, or investigation of alleged child abuse or neglect is immune from civil or criminal liability that might otherwise be incurred or imposed. |
| | Immunity from civil and criminal liability extends to an authorized volunteer of the Department of Human Services or a law enforcement officer who participates at the request of the department in an investigation of alleged or suspected abuse or neglect or in an action arising from an investigation if the person was acting in good faith and in the scope of the person's responsibilities. |
| | A person who reports the person's own abuse or neglect of a child or who acts in bad faith or with malicious purpose in reporting alleged child abuse or neglect is not immune from civil or criminal liability. |
| Penalties for False Reporting | A person commits an offense if, with the intent to deceive, he or she knowingly makes a report of child abuse or neglect that is false. An offense under this subsection is: |
| | ■ A state jail felony |
| | ■ A felony of the third degree if the person has previously been convicted of false reporting. |
| | A person who is convicted of false reporting in Texas shall: |
| | ■ Pay any reasonable attorney's fees incurred by the person who was falsely accused of abuse or neglect |
| | ■ Be liable to the state for a civil penalty of $1000 |
| Penalties for Failure to Report | A person commits an offense if the person has cause to believe that a child's physical or mental health or welfare has been or may be adversely affected by abuse or neglect and knowingly fails to report in accordance with the reporting laws. Failure to Report in Texas is a Class B misdemeanor. |
| Relevant Internet Resources | *Web site for Statutes:* http://www.capitol.state.tx.us |
| | *Citations:* Child Protection: Family Code, Title 5, Chapter 261 Child Welfare: Family Code, Title 5, Chapters 161, 262, 263, and 264 |
| | *Web site for Administrative Code:* http://info.sos.state.tx.us/pls/pub/readtac$ext.ViewTAC See Title 40, Part 19. |

| UTAH | |
|---|---|
| Who Are Mandated Reporters? | Any person licensed under the Medical Practice Act or the Nurse Practice Act; any person who has reason to believe that a child has been subjected to abuse or neglect |
| When to Report | Mandated reporters must make a report when they have reason to believe that a child has been subjected to abuse or neglect or when they observe a child being subjected to conditions or circumstances that would reasonably result in sexual abuse, physical abuse, or neglect. |
| Confidentiality of Mandated Reporters | Inclusion of the reporter's name in the report is not specifically required in statute. However, the name and contact information of the reporter shall be deleted prior to any release of records to the subject of the report. |
| How Do Mandated Reporters Make a Report? | Mandated reporters would contact the Child Abuse State Hotline number @ (800) 678-9399. |
| Immunity Provisions | Any person, official, or institution participating in good faith in making a report, taking photographs or x-rays, assisting an investigator from the division, serving as a member of a child protection team, or taking a child into protective custody pursuant to the reporting laws is immune from any liability, civil or criminal, that otherwise might result by reason of those actions. Utah law does not provide immunity with respect to acts or omissions of a governmental employee except as provided by Title 63, Chapter 30d, Utah Governmental Immunity Act of Utah. |
| Penalties for False Reporting | A person is guilty of a class B misdemeanor if he or she: <ul><li>Knowingly gives or causes to be given false information to any peace officer or any state or local government agency or personnel with a purpose of inducing the recipient of the information to believe that another has committed an offense</li><li>Knowingly gives or causes to be given to any peace officer, any state or local government agency or personnel, or to any licensed social worker, psychologist, or marriage and family therapist information concerning the commission of an offense, knowing that the offense did not occur or knowing that he or she has no information relating to the offense or danger</li><li>Knowingly gives or causes to be given false information to any state or local government agency or personnel with a purpose of inducing a change in the person's licensing or certification status or the licensing or certification status of another</li></ul> |

(*continued*)

| | |
|---|---|
| Penalties for Failure to Report | Any person, official, or institution required to report a case of suspected child abuse, child sexual abuse, neglect, fetal alcohol syndrome, or fetal drug dependency who willfully fails to do so is guilty of a Class B misdemeanor. Action for failure to report must be commenced within 4 years from the date of knowledge of the offense and the willful failure to report. |
| Relevant Internet Resources | *Web sites for Statutes:*<br>http://www.le.state.ut.us/<br>http://www.le.state.ut.us/%7Ecode/code.htm<br><br>*Citations:*<br>Child Protection: Title 62A, Chapter 4a, §§ 62A-4a-401 to 62A-4a-414<br>Child Welfare: Title 62A, Chapter 4a, §§ 62A-4a-201 to 62A-4a-209, 62A-4a-701 to 62A-4a-709, 62A-4a-801, and 62A-4a-802; Title 78, Chapter 3a, §§ 78-3a-301 to 78-3a-414<br><br>*Web site for Administrative Code:*<br>http://www.rules.utah.gov/publicat/code.htm<br>See Human Services, Titles R501-7, R501-12, R501-18, and R512. |

## VERMONT

| | |
|---|---|
| Who Are Mandated Reporters? | Physicians, surgeons, osteopaths, chiropractors, physician's assistants, hospital administrators, nurses, medical examiners, dentists, psychologists, or other health care providers; school superintendents, school teachers, school librarians, day care workers, school principals, school guidance counselors, mental health professionals, or social workers; probation officers, police officers, camp owners, camp administrators or counselors; members of the clergy |
| When to Report | Mandated reporters must make a report when they have reasonable cause to believe that a child has been abused or neglected. |
| Confidentiality of Mandated Reporters | Reports shall contain the name and address of the reporter. The name of the person making the report shall be confidential unless:<br>■ The person making the report requests disclosure.<br>■ A court determines that the report was not made in good faith. |
| How Do Mandated Reporters Make a Report? | Mandated reporters would contact the Child Abuse State Hotline number @ (800) 649-5285 or (802) 863-7533 (after hours). |

| | |
|---|---|
| Immunity Provisions | Any person enumerated Vermont's mandated reporting law, other than a person suspected of child abuse, who in good faith makes a report to the department of social and rehabilitation services shall be immune from any civil or criminal liability that might otherwise be incurred or imposed as a result of making a report. |
| Penalties for False Reporting | This issue is not addressed in the statutes reviewed. |
| Penalties for Failure to Report | A person who violates the law requiring mandated reporters to report suspected child abuse or neglect shall be fined not more than $500.<br>A person who violates the reporting laws with the intent to conceal abuse or neglect of a child shall be imprisoned not more than 6 months, fined not more than $1000, or both. |
| Relevant Internet Resources | *Web site for Statutes:*<br>http://www.leg.state.vt.us/statutes/statutes2.htm<br>*Citations:*<br>Child Protection: Title 33, Chapter 49<br>Child Welfare: Title 15A, Article 3, §§ 3-504 to 3-506;<br>    Title 33, Chapter 55, §§ 5528, 5531, and 5540;<br>    Title 33, Chapter 59 |

## VIRGINIA

| | |
|---|---|
| Who Are Mandated Reporters? | Persons licensed to practice medicine or any of the healing arts, hospital residents or interns, nurses, or duly accredited Christian Science practitioners; teachers or other persons employed in public or private schools, kindergartens, or nursery schools; persons providing child care full-time or part-time for pay on a regularly planned basis; social workers, mental health professionals, or any person responsible for the care, custody, and control of children; probation officers, law enforcement officers, mediators, or court appointed special advocates |
| When to Report | Mandated reporters must make a report when, in their professional or official capacity, they have reason to suspect that a child is abused or neglected. |
| Confidentiality of Mandated Reporters | Inclusion of the reporter's name in the report is not specifically required in statute. Disclosure of the identity of the reporter is not addressed in statutes reviewed. |
| How Do Mandated Reporters Make a Report? | Mandated reporters would contact the Child Abuse State Hotline number @ (800) 552-7096 or (804) 786-8536. |

*(continued)*

| | |
|---|---|
| Immunity Provisions | Any person who makes a report or complaint pursuant to the reporting laws, takes a child into custody pursuant to law, or participates in a judicial proceeding resulting therefrom shall be immune from any civil or criminal liability in connection therewith, unless it is proven that such person acted in bad faith or with malicious intent. |
| Penalties for False Reporting | Any person 14 years of age or older who makes or causes to be made a report of child abuse or neglect that he or she knows to be false shall be guilty of a Class 1 misdemeanor.<br><br>Any person 14 years of age or older who has been previously convicted under of False reporting in Virginia and who is subsequently convicted of making a false report of child abuse or neglect shall be guilty of a Class 6 felony. |
| Penalties for Failure to Report | Any person required to report pursuant to Virginia's law who fails to do so within 72 hours of his or her first suspicion of child abuse or neglect shall be fined:<br>■  Not more than $500 for the first failure<br>■  Not less than $100 nor more than $1000 for any subsequent failures |
| Relevant Internet Resources | *Web sites for Statutes:*<br>http://legis.state.va.us<br>http://legis.state.va.us/Laws/CodeofVa.htm<br><br>*Citations:*<br>Child Protection: Title 63.2, Chapter 15<br>Child Welfare: Title 63.2, Chapters 9–11; Title 16.1, Chapter 11, §§ 16.1-281 to 16.1-283<br><br>*Web site for Administrative Code:*<br>http://leg1.state.va.us/000/reg/TOC.HTM<br>See Title 22, Agency 40.<br><br>Department of Social Services<br>CPS Policy Manual<br>http://www.dss.virginia.gov/family/cps/policy.html |

## WASHINGTON

| | |
|---|---|
| Who Are Mandated Reporters? | Practitioners, county coroners or medical examiners, pharmacists, or nurses; professional school personnel or child care providers; social service counselors or psychologists; employees of the State Department of Social and Health Services; juvenile probation officers, law enforcement officers, personnel of the Department of Corrections, or placement and liaison specialists; responsible living skills program staff, HOPE center staff, state family and children's ombudsman, or any volunteer in the ombudsman's office; any adult with whom a child resides |

| When to Report | Mandated reporters must make a report when they have reasonable cause to believe that a child has suffered abuse or neglect. |
|---|---|
| Confidentiality of Mandated Reporters | The department shall make reasonable efforts to learn the name, address, and telephone number of the reporter. The department shall provide assurances of appropriate confidentiality of information in the report. |
| How Do Mandated Reporters Make a Report? | Mandated reporters would contact the Child Abuse State Hotline number @ (866) END-HARM. |
| Immunity Provisions | Any person participating in good faith in the making of a report pursuant to the reporting laws or testifying as to alleged child abuse or neglect in a judicial proceeding shall be immune from any liability arising out of such reporting or testifying.<br>A person convicted of knowingly making a false report shall not be immune from liability under Washington law.<br>An administrator of a hospital or similar institution or any licensed physician taking a child into custody pursuant to § 26.44.056 shall not be subject to criminal or civil liability for such taking into custody.<br>A person who, in good faith and without gross negligence, cooperates in an investigation arising as a result of a report made pursuant to Washington law shall not be subject to civil liability arising out of his or her cooperation. Immunity for cooperating with the investigation does not apply to a person who caused or allowed the child abuse or neglect to occur. |
| Penalties for False Reporting | A person who intentionally and in bad faith knowingly makes a false report of alleged abuse or neglect shall be guilty of a misdemeanor.<br>Every person convicted of a misdemeanor shall be punished by one or both of the following:<br>■ Imprisonment in the county jail for not more than 90 days<br>■ A fine of not more than $1000 |
| Penalties for Failure to Report | Every person who is required to make a report pursuant to the reporting laws and who knowingly fails to make such a report shall be guilty of a gross misdemeanor.<br>Every person convicted of a gross misdemeanor shall be punished by one or both of the following:<br>■ Imprisonment in the county jail for not more than 1 year<br>■ A fine of not more than $5000 |

*(continued)*

| Relevant Internet Resources | *Web site for Statutes:*<br>http://apps.leg.wa.gov/rcw/ |
|---|---|
| | *Citations:*<br>Child Protection: Title 26, Chapter 26.44<br>Child Welfare: Title 13, Chapter 13.34; Title 26, Chapter 26.34 |
| | *Web site for Administrative Code:*<br>http://apps.leg.wa.gov/wac/<br>See Titles 112, 275, 388, and 440. |
| | *Web site for Agency Policies:*<br>http://www1.dshs.wa.gov/CA/pubs/manuals_pp.asp |
| | Department of Social and Health Services, Children's Administration<br>Publications/Program Information Index<br>http://www1.dshs.wa.gov/ca/pubs/programs.asp |

## WEST VIRGINIA

| Who Are Mandated Reporters? | Medical, dental, or mental health professionals; emergency medical services personnel; school teachers or other school personnel; child care workers or foster care workers; Christian Science practitioners or religious healers; social service workers; peace officers or law enforcement officials, circuit court judges, family law masters, employees of the division of juvenile services, or magistrates; members of the clergy. |
|---|---|
| When to Report | Mandated reporters must make a report when they have reasonable cause to suspect that a child is abused or neglected, when they observe the child being subjected to conditions that are likely to result in abuse or neglect, or when they believe that a child has suffered serious physical abuse or sexual abuse or sexual assault. |
| Confidentiality of Mandated Reporters | Inclusion of the reporter's name in the report is not specifically required in statute.<br>Disclosure of the reporter's identity is no addressed in statutes reviewed. |
| How Do Mandated Reporters Make a Report? | Mandated reporters would contact the Child Abuse State Hotline number @ (800) 352-6513. |
| Immunity Provisions | Any person, official, or institution participating in good faith in any act permitted or required by the reporting laws shall be immune from any civil or criminal liability that otherwise might result by reason of such actions. |
| Penalties for False Reporting | This issue is not addressed in the statutes reviewed. |

| | |
|---|---|
| Penalties for Failure to Report | Any mandated reporter who knowingly fails to report as required, or knowingly prevents another person acting reasonably from doing so, shall be guilty of a misdemeanor, and on conviction shall be subject to one or both of the following:<br>■  Confinement in the county jail not more than 10 days<br>■  A fine of not more than $100 |
| Relevant Internet Resources | *Web site for Statutes:*<br>http://www.legis.state.wv.us/WVCODE/Code.cfm<br><br>*Citations:*<br>Child Protection: Chapter 49, §§ 49-6A-1 to 49-6A-10<br>Child Welfare: Chapter 49, §§ 49-2-1 to 49-2-17, 49-2A-1 to 49-2A-2, 49-2D-1 to 49-2D-9, 49-6-1 to 39-6-12, and 49-6D-1 to 49-6D-3<br><br>*Web site for Administrative Code:*<br>http://www.wvsos.com/csr/<br>See Social and Human Services, Children & Youth Commission and Human Services sections.<br><br>*Web site for Agency Policies:*<br>http://www.wvdhhr.org/bcf/policy/ |

## WISCONSIN

| | |
|---|---|
| Who Are Mandated Reporters? | Physicians, coroners, medical examiners, nurses, dentists, chiropractors, optometrists, acupuncturists, other medical or mental health professionals, physical therapists, dietitians, occupational therapists, speech/language pathologists, audiologists, or emergency medical technicians; school teachers, administrators or counselors, child care workers in day care centers, group homes, or residential care centers, or day care providers; alcohol or other drug abuse counselors, marriage and family therapists, or professional counselors; social workers, public assistance workers, first responders, police or law enforcement officers, mediators, or court appointed special advocates; members of the clergy or a religious order, including brothers, ministers, monks, nuns, priests, rabbis, or sisters |
| When to Report | Mandated reporters must make a report when, in the course of their professional duties, they have reasonable cause to suspect that a child has been abused or neglected or when, in the course of their professional duties, they have reason to believe that a child has been threatened with abuse or neglect or that abuse or neglect will occur. |

*(continued)*

| | |
|---|---|
| Confidentiality of Mandated Reporters | Inclusion of the reporter's name in the report is not specifically required in statute. However, statute provides that the identity of the reporter shall not be disclosed to the subject of the report. |
| How Do Mandated Reporters Make a Report? | Mandated reporters would contact the Child Abuse State Hotline number @ (608) 266-3036. |
| Immunity Provisions | Any person or institution participating in good faith in making a report, conducting an investigation, ordering or taking photographs, or ordering or performing medical examinations of a child or an expectant mother pursuant to the reporting laws shall have immunity from any liability, civil or criminal, that results by reason of the action.<br>For the purpose of any civil or criminal proceeding, the good faith of any person reporting under this reporting law shall be presumed.<br>The immunity provided herein does not apply to liability for abusing or neglecting a child or for abusing an unborn child. |
| Penalties for False Reporting | This issue is not addressed in the statutes reviewed. |
| Penalties for Failure to Report | Whoever intentionally violates the reporting laws by failure to report as required may be fined not more than $1000, imprisoned not more than 6 months, or both. |
| Relevant Internet Resources | *Web sites for Statutes:*<br>http://www.legis.state.wi.us/../rsb/stats.html<br>http://folio.legis.state.wi.us/cgi-bin/om_isapi.dll?clientID=43827797&infobase=stats.nfo&jump=ch.%2048<br><br>*Citations:*<br>Child Protection: Chapter 48, §§ 48.02 and 48.981<br>Child Welfare: Chapter 48, §§ 48.01, 48.02, and 48.98; Subchapters VI, VII, VIII, X, XI, XI, XII, XIII, XIV, XVI, and XVII<br><br>*Web site for Administrative Code:*<br>http://www.legis.state.wi.us/rsb/code/codtoc.html<br>See Health and Family Services.<br><br>*Index of Codes Related to Child Protective Services:*<br>http://dhfs.wisconsin.gov/Children/CPS/statsadmin/statsINDX.htm |

## WYOMING

| | |
|---|---|
| Who Are Mandated Reporters? | All persons must report. |

| | |
|---|---|
| When to Report | Mandated reporters must make a report when they know or have reasonable cause to believe or suspect that a child has been abused or neglected or when they observe any child being subjected to conditions or circumstances that would reasonably result in abuse or neglect. |
| Confidentiality of Mandated Reporters | The reporter is not specifically required to provide his or her name in the written report.<br>If photographs or x-rays of the child are taken, the person taking them must be identified.<br>Disclosure of the reporter's identity is not addressed in statutes reviewed. |
| How Do Mandated Reporters Make a Report? | Mandated reporters would contact the Child Abuse State Hotline number @ (800) 457-3659. |
| Immunity Provisions | Any person, official, institution, or agency participating in good faith in any act required or permitted by the reporting laws is immune from any civil or criminal liability that might otherwise result by reason of the action.<br>For the purpose of any civil or criminal proceeding, the good faith of any person, official, or institution participating in any act permitted or required by the reporting laws shall be presumed. |
| Penalties for False Reporting | Any person who knowingly and intentionally makes a false report of child abuse or neglect, or who encourages or coerces another person to make a false report, is guilty of a misdemeanor that is punishable by one of both of the following:<br>■ Imprisonment for not more than 6 months<br>■ A fine of not more than $750 |
| Penalties for Failure to Report | This issue is not addressed in the statutes reviewed. |
| Relevant Internet Resources | *Web sites for Statutes:*<br>http://legisweb.state.wy.us/titles/statutes.htm<br>Note: See Family Support and Child Welfare<br><br>*Citations:*<br>Child Protection: Title 14, Chapter 3, Article 2<br>Child Welfare: Title 14, Chapter 2, Article 3; Title 14, Chapter 3, Article 4; Title 14, Chapter 5<br><br>*Web site for Administrative Code:*<br>http://soswy.state.wy.us/Rule_Search_Main.asp<br>Select "Department of Family Services" as the agency. |

# List of Relevant Internet Resources

The following organizations provide general and topical information on child abuse and the child welfare system in the United States. For relevant Internet resources for state policy, see appendix A.

**American Professional Society on the Abuse of Children (APSAC)**
**350 Poplar Avenue**
**Elmhurst, IL 60126**
**(630) 941-1235**
**http://www.apsac.org**
This national organization provides education and other information sources to professionals who work in child welfare and related fields.

**Annie E. Casey Foundation**
**701 St. Paul Street**
**Baltimore, MD 21202**
**(410) 547-6600**
**http://www.aecf.org**
This foundation provides grants to states, cities, and neighborhoods to meet the needs of vulnerable children through innovative programs.

**Casey Family Services**
**127 Church Street**
**New Haven, CT 06510**
**(203) 401-6900**
**http://www.caseyfamilyservices.org**
This organization is the direct services arm of the Annie E. Casey Foundation, providing foster care services in seven states and developing and implementing model programs for child welfare program administration and development nationwide.

**Childhelp**
**15757 N. 78th Street**
**Scottsdale, AZ 85260**
**(480) 922-8212**
**http://www.childhelp.org**
**National Hotline for Counseling and Information**
    **(800) 4-A-CHILD**
This organization serves many purposes including education and training. Most notably, it runs a 24-hour nationwide hotline to provide crisis counseling and referral to prevent child abuse.

**Child Welfare Information Gateway**
**Children's Bureau**
**Administration for Children and Families**
**U.S. Department of Health and Human Services**
**http://www.childwelfare.gov**
The services of this federal resource were formerly found in the National Clearinghouse on Child Abuse and Neglect Information and the National Adoption Information Clearinghouse. The Web site provides extensive information on all aspects of the American child welfare system, including links to relevant federal legislation and online libraries of national and state-specific information.

**Child Welfare League of America**
**2345 Crystal Drive, Suite 250**
**Arlington, VA 22202**
**(703) 412-2400**
**http://www.cwla.org**
An association whose members include over 800 public and private child welfare organizations. The mission is to improve the safety and well-being

of American children and families. This mission is accomplished through research, training, consultation, and publications.

**Kempe Center for the Prevention and Treatment of Child Abuse
     and Neglect**
**1825 Marion Street**
**Denver, CO 80218**
**(303) 864-5300**
**http://www.kempe.org**
This organization develops and provides innovative programs in the service of prevention and treatment of child abuse and neglect.

**Prevent Child Abuse America**
**500 North Michigan Avenue**
**Suite 200**
**Chicago, IL 60611**
**(312) 663-3520**
**http://www.preventchildabuse.org**
Through the national organization and its local affiliated chapters, efforts are made to build awareness to prevent and respond to child abuse and neglect.

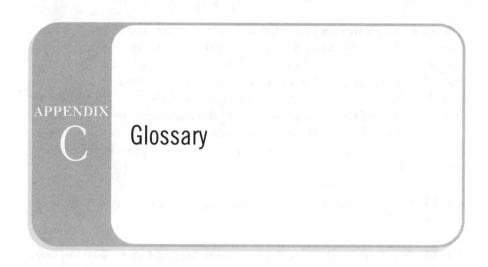

# Glossary

**Abuse:** A term (abbreviated "AB") used in state child abuse forms and regulations to denote a category of child mistreatment. Abuse has a specific definition in law, referring to mistreatment of a child that is so severe that it presents actual serious physical damage to a child that is permanent or protracted; causes death, disablement, or disfigurement; or a risk thereof. It also includes sexual offenses as defined in the penal code.

**Alleged Perpetrator:** An individual who is suspected to have caused or knowingly allowed the maltreatment of a child as stated in an incident of child abuse or neglect.

**Alleged Victim:** Child about whom a report regarding maltreatment has been made to a child protective services (CPS) agency.

**Assessment:** A process by which the CPS agency determines whether the child or other persons involved in the report of alleged maltreatment is in need of services.

**Biologic Parent:** The birth mother or father of the child.

**CAPTA:** See *Child Abuse Prevention and Treatment Act*.

**Chain of Evidence:** A term that refers to the fact that to be in proper forensic form (usable as evidence in a court), an item must be accounted for from the time it played a role in the event to the time it is brought to the court. For example, if someone observes a parent striking a child with a stick and intervenes, taking the stick from the father and then keeping it for a period of time before informing the authorities of its existence, the stick would be considered to have less value as a piece of evidence because its whereabouts for a period of time could not be absolutely accounted for.

**Child:** A person younger than 18 years of age or considered to be a minor under state law.

**Child Abuse Prevention and Treatment Act, 42 U.S.C. 5101 *et seq.* (CAPTA):** Federal legislation amended and reauthorized in 1996 that provides the foundation for federal involvement in child protection and child welfare services. The 1996 amendments provide for, among other things, annual state data reports on child maltreatment to the secretary of Health and Human Services. The most recent reauthorization of CAPTA, the Keeping Children and Families Safe Act of 2003, 42 U.S.C. 5106, retained these provisions.

**Child Advocacy Center:** A physical location that is purposely designed as a "child-friendly" environment, which serves as a warm, quiet, and nonstressful place where victimized (often sexually abused) children can be interviewed, medically examined, and psychologically counseled or assessed. Professionals who typically staff a child advocacy center (often not full-time) include pediatricians, CPS caseworkers, social workers, police, prosecutors, and psychologists. The typical child advocacy center contains interviewing rooms, examinations rooms, meeting and conference rooms. The environment includes a homelike setting with smaller than normal furniture, lots of toys and stuffed animals, and subdued lighting.

**Child Death Review Team:** A state or local team of professionals who review all or a sample of cases of children who are alleged to have died due to maltreatment or other causes.

**Child Maltreatment:** An act or failure to act by a parent, caregiver, or other person as defined under state law that results in physical abuse, neglect, medical neglect, sexual abuse, emotional abuse, or an act or failure to act that presents an imminent risk of serious harm to a child.

**Child Protective Services Agency (CPS):** An official agency of a state having the responsibility of protective services and activities for children.

**Child Protective Services Supervisor:** The manager of the caseworker assigned to a report of child maltreatment at the time of the report disposition.

**Child Protective Services Worker:** The person assigned to a report of child maltreatment at the time of the report disposition.

**Child Risk Factor:** A child's characteristic, disability, problem, or environment that would tend to increase the risk of him or her becoming a maltreatment victim.

**Child Victim:** A child for whom an incident of abuse or neglect has been substantiated or indicated by an investigation or assessment. A state may include some children with alternative dispositions as victims.

**Children's Bureau:** A federal agency within the Administration on Children, Youth and Families, Administration for Children and Families, U.S. Department of Health and Human Services that is responsible for the collection and analysis of data from the National Child Abuse and Neglect Data System (NCANDS) data.

**Code of Ethics of the National Association of Social Workers (NASW Code):** A document prescribed by the NASW that outlines the goals of the social work profession as well as provides guidance for the ethical behavior of social workers.

**Confidentiality:** Information will not be shared beyond the relationship, with exceptions. Confidentiality in the social worker–client relationship means that what the client tells the social worker, the social worker will not reveal to others.

**Counseling Services:** Activities that apply the therapeutic processes to personal, family, situational, or occupational problems in order to bring about a positive resolution of the problems or improved individual or family functioning or circumstances.

**CPS:** See *Child Protective Services Agency*.

**Custodian:** Refers to an adult who takes day-to-day responsibility for caring for a child, meeting the child's needs, and protecting the child from harm. Most often, a child's parent is the child's custodian *and* guardian, but the two are not necessarily the same. For example, when a child is in foster care or in the care of relatives, the foster parents (or the Commissioner of Social Services) or the relative will be the child's custodian. However, unless guardianship has been relieved by a court or signed away, the parent continues to be the child's guardian and must be consulted in any significant activities involving the child (such as most medical procedures or an airplane trip, etc.).

**Determination:** A term that refers to the local department of social services' ultimate finding concluding the investigation that begins with the CPS report accepted by the state central register. The law stipulates that a determination must be completed by the 60th day of the investigation, although it provides no penalties if this requirement is not met. The finding will be either "indicated" (the investigation found some credible evidence of child abuse or neglect) or "unfounded" (the investigation found insufficient credible evidence of child abuse or neglect).

**Domestic Violence:** Incidents of physical or emotional abuse perpetrated by one of the spouses or parent figures on the other spouse or parent figure in the home environment.

**Emotionally Disturbed:** A clinically diagnosed condition exhibiting one or more of the following characteristics over a long period of time and to a marked degree: an inability to build or maintain satisfactory interpersonal relationships, inappropriate types of behavior or feelings under normal circumstances, a general pervasive mood of unhappiness or depression, or a tendency to develop physical symptoms or fears associated with personal problems. The diagnosis is based on the American Psychiatric Association's *Diagnostic and Statistical Manual of Mental Disorders-Fourth Edition* (2000) text revision (*DSM-IV-TR*). The term includes schizophrenia and autism.

**Expunge:** The dictionary definition of this word is to "efface completely or destroy." In New York State, prior to Elissa's law, which took effect in February 1996, the law required that all records and references to records of unfounded CPS investigations were to be expunged.

**False Report:** A report of alleged child abuse or neglect made to CPS by a reporter who knew, or should have known, that the allegation was untrue.

**Family:** A group of two or more persons related by birth, marriage, adoption, or emotional ties.

**Family Preservation Services:** Activities designed to help families alleviate crises that might lead to out-of-home placement of children, maintain the safety of children in their own homes, support families preparing to reunify or adopt, and assist families in obtaining services and other supports necessary to address their multiple needs in a culturally sensitive manner.

**Family Support Services:** Community-based preventive activities designed to alleviate stress and promote parental competencies and behaviors that will increase the ability of families to nurture their children successfully, enable families to use other resources and opportunities available in the community, and create supportive networks to enhance child-rearing abilities of parents.

**Fatality:** Death of a child as a result of abuse or neglect because either an injury resulting from the abuse or neglect was the cause of death or abuse or neglect were contributing factors to the cause of death.

**Forensic:** Refers to documents, accounts, or materials that may be utilized in a court of law as evidence.

**Forensic Interview:** Refers to interviews of alleged victims conducted by investigators in cases of severe physical and sexual abuse.

**Forensic Interview (Extended):** A more in-depth forensic interview that sometimes occurs after the initial stages of an abuse investigation. This type of interview usually is conducted by specially trained professionals with graduate-level education in the areas relevant to this type of interviewing. The interview usually takes place at centers that facilitate the interview process, such as therapist and doctor offices.

**Foster Care:** Twenty-four-hour substitute care for children placed away from their parents or guardians and for whom the state agency has placement and care responsibility. This includes family foster homes, foster homes of relatives, group homes, emergency shelters, residential facilities, child care institutions, and preadoptive homes.

**"Good Faith" Report:** A report made when the reporter has reason to believe that the allegation made was true to the best of his or her knowledge. The reporter does not have to be sure that the allegations are true for the report to be in good faith.

**Guardian:** An adult who has a formal obligation to assure that a child's rights, safety, and needs are adequately met has the right and the responsibility to make certain decisions on behalf of the child's best interests. Ordinarily and automatically, a parent is the guardian for his or her child. However, a court may remove the parent from that status or may appoint another person to fill this role. Guardianship is not the same as, or automatically concurrent with, custody.

**Guardian Ad Litem:** A formal legal term used to describe an attorney who is assigned by a judge to protect a child's legal rights and to provide the child with legal representation in court actions that involve the child's parents (e.g., abuse or neglect hearing, matrimonial action, termination of parental rights).

**Health Insurance Portability and Accountability Act of 1996 (HIPAA):** A federal statute passed by Congress and signed into law by President Bill Clinton in an attempt to safeguard patient/client information.

**Immunity:** Protection from retaliatory legal action.

**Inadequate Housing:** A risk factor related to substandard, overcrowded, or unsafe housing conditions, including homelessness.

**Indicated or Reason to Suspect:** An investigation disposition that concludes that maltreatment cannot be substantiated under state law or policy, but there is reason to suspect that the child may have been maltreated or was at risk of maltreatment. This is applicable only to states that distinguish between substantiated and indicated dispositions.

**Informed Consent:** The process through which a social worker informs the client, in understandable language, the purpose of their working relationship and limitations of confidentiality protections.

**Initial Investigation:** The CPS initial contact or attempt to have face-to-face contact with the alleged victim. If face-to-face contact is not possible with the alleged victim, initial investigation would start when CPS first contacts any party who could provide information essential to the investigation or assessment.

**Investigation:** The gathering and assessment of objective information to determine if a child has been or is at risk of being maltreated. Generally includes face-to-face contact with the victim and results in a disposition as to whether or not the alleged report is substantiated.

**Legal, Law Enforcement, or Criminal Justice Personnel:** People employed by a local, state, tribal, or federal justice agency. This includes law enforcement, courts, the district attorney's office, probation or other community corrections agencies, and correctional facilities.

**Mandated Reporter:** A person required to report suspected child abuse and maltreatment.

**MDT:** See *Multidisciplinary Team*.

**Medical Neglect:** A type of maltreatment caused by failure of the caregiver to provide for the appropriate health care of the child although financially able to do so or offered financial or other means to do so.

**Mental Health Services:** Activities that aim to overcome issues involving emotional disturbance or maladaptive behavior adversely affecting socialization, learning, or development. Usually provided by public or private mental health agencies and includes both residential and nonresidential activities.

**Multidisciplinary Team (MDT):** A term that refers to a team of police officers and caseworkers who perform joint investigations in situations involving child abuse that rise to the level of a criminal act, especially sexual abuse. In child abuse literature, the term more often refers to teams and/or panels involving several professional disciplines that are typically related to child abuse matters, such as CPS caseworkers, police, prosecutors, physicians, social workers, therapists, domestic violence professionals, and community activists. Multidisciplinary teams are increasingly more likely to be housed in child advocacy centers.

**National Association of Social Workers (NASW):** The premier professional organization for social workers in the United States.

**Neglect:** A particular form of child maltreatment that generally includes deprivation of necessities, medical neglect, psychological or emotional maltreatment, and other forms included in state law. Neglect often refers to mistreatment of a child wherein a person responsible for a child has failed to provide a wide array of ordinary needs, including food, clothing, shelter, supervision, medical care, education, guardianship, emotional comfort, protection, and such. It also includes the use of corporal punishment that is excessive. It may also include use of intoxicating substances by the caretaker to the extent that the caretaker is unable to provide adequate care or is emotionally neglectful. Neglect may also include child abandonment.

**Perpetrator:** The person who has been determined to have caused or knowingly allowed the maltreatment of a child.

**Physical Abuse:** A type of maltreatment that refers to physical acts that caused or could have caused physical injury to a child.

**Preventive Services:** Activities aimed at preventing child abuse and neglect. Such activities may be directed at specific populations identified as being at increased risk of becoming abusive and may be designed to increase the strength and stability of families, to increase parental confidence and competence in their parenting abilities, and to afford children a stable and supportive environment. They include child abuse and neglect preventive services provided through such federal funds as the Child Abuse and Neglect Basic State Grant, Community-Based Family

Resource and Support Grant, Promoting Safe and Stable Families Program (title IV-B, subpart 2), Maternal and Child Health Block Grant, Social Services Block Grant (title XX), and state and local funds. Such activities do not include public awareness campaigns.

**Privilege:** Evidentiary rule that protects confidential information from being brought to light in a legal proceeding.

**Protective Custody:** A term that refers to the summary removal of a child who has been reported to a child abuse hotline from his or her environment in order to be protected from immediate harm. This is a serious action that can only be undertaken by persons designated in state law. For example, in New York State, police officers, CPS personnel, a physician with a child in her or her presence (but only until CPS or the police arrive), or a hospital administrator with a child in his or her facility (for up to 24 hours). Can take a child into protective custody. A child who is taken into protective custody must be taken to a place so designated by the commissioner, usually a foster home. No matter who has invoked protective custody, CPS must defend the action in family court, usually within 24 hours. The parent or guardian has a right to an immediate hearing before a family court judge to determine if the child will be retained in custody or returned to the parent pending the first court hearing. Persons without legal authority may be subject to severe legal difficulties if they take protective custody of a child (custodial interference, obstruction of governmental administration, kidnapping, to list a few possibilities).

**Psychological or Emotional Maltreatment:** A type of maltreatment that refers to acts or omissions, other than physical abuse or sexual abuse, that caused or could have caused conduct, cognitive, affective, or other mental disorders and includes emotional neglect, psychological abuse, and mental injury. Frequently occurs as verbal abuse or excessive demands on a child's performance.

**Report Disposition:** The conclusion reached by the responsible agency regarding the report of maltreatment pertaining to the child.

**Risk Factor:** A characteristic, disability, problem, or environment that would tend to decrease the ability to provide adequate care for a child.

**Screened-in Reports:** Referrals of child maltreatment that meet the state's standards for acceptance.

**Screened-out Referrals:** Allegations of child maltreatment that do not meet the state's standards for acceptance.

**Screening:** The process of making a decision about whether or not to accept a referral of child maltreatment.

**Sexual Abuse:** A type of maltreatment that refers to the involvement of the child in sexual activity to provide sexual gratification or financial benefit to the perpetrator, including contacts for sexual purposes, molestation, statutory rape, prostitution, pornography, exposure, incest, or other sexually exploitative activities. A term used to refer to actions by a child's caretaker that involve the child in either a sexual action that would be considered a violation of the criminal code or that was undertaken for the caretaker's sexual gratification.

**Social Work:** Professional practice aimed at advancing the social condition of individuals, groups, and communities, especially the underprivileged.

**Standards of Proof:** The level of proof required in a legal action to discharge the burden of proof used to convince the court that a given allegation is true. The degree of proof required depends on the circumstances of the allegation.

**Subject of the Report:** The person who is identified as the alleged perpetrator in a report of suspected child abuse or neglect.

**Substance Abuse Services:** Activities designed to deter, reduce, or eliminate substance abuse or chemical dependency.

**Substantiated:** A type of investigation disposition concluding that the allegation of maltreatment or risk of maltreatment was supported or founded by state law or policy. This is the highest level of finding by a state agency.

**Unsubstantiated:** A type of investigation disposition determining that there is not sufficient evidence under state law to conclude or suspect that a child has been maltreated or is at risk of being maltreated.

**Victim:** A child having a substantiated or indicated maltreatment disposition.

# Index

Note:
An *f* following a page number indicates a figure.